54-8416 reviewed 4/8/15

EACH COPY OF THIS SPECIAL EDITION

IS AUTOGRAPHED BY THE EDITOR

Edward Younger

Inside The Confederate Government

Robert Garlick Hill Kean

INSIDE THE
CONFEDERATE GOVERNMENT

The Diary of

ROBERT GARLICK HILL KEAN

HEAD OF THE BUREAU OF WAR

Edited by Edward Younger

New York

OXFORD UNIVERSITY PRESS

1957

Printed in the United States of America

To Dr. and Mrs. Robert H. Kean

Contents

ACKNOWLEDGMENTS

With their time, energy, and wisdom several of my friends have been of great help to me in preparing this book for publication. To acknowledge their services here is to give only an inadequate expression of my sincere thanks and deep appreciation.

Allan Nevins of Columbia University and Harry Clemons of the University of Virginia gave me encouragement and wise counsel. Cary Johnson of the University of Virginia History Department and Frank Berkeley and John Wyllie of the University of Virginia Library read and criticized the Introduction. Richard Harwell and Robert Scribner of the Virginia State Library and Gleason Bean of the Washington and Lee University History Department read and criticized the entire manuscript and helped me identify several of the personalities in the Diary. Mrs. Lawrence Greaver of the University of Virginia Library saved me endless time and energy by typing the manuscript from the original Diary.

Archer Jones and Bill Runge, University of Virginia graduate students in history, gave me valuable research assistance. Jean Hackle, another University of Virginia graduate student in history, produced an excellent study of the life of the diarist and gave me invaluable editorial assistance. To her more than to any other person I am indebted. Ruth Ritchie went far beyond her duties as secretary of the University of Virginia Institute for Social Science Research by preparing the index and calling my attention to many potential errors.

Dr. and Mrs. Robert H. Kean, owners of the Diary, have been as free of their time and energy in helping me prepare the manuscript as they have been in giving me unlimited use of their Kean materials. At the Oxford University Press, Lee E. Grove, Margaret J. Talbott, and Carroll G. Bowen, have been uniformly co-operative and helpful.

The University of Virginia Institute for Social Science Research, with a summer grant, and the Richmond Area University Center, with a grant for research assistance, have given me the uninterrupted time and competent aid necessary to finish the project.

Finally, all the while, my wife and daughter, Barbara and Ellen Younger, have been patient and understanding.

EDWARD YOUNGER

4 Dawson's Row
University of Virginia
March, 1957

THE DIARIST AND THE DIARY

I

Robert Garlick Hill Kean,* Head of the Confederate Bureau of War, trudged wearily to the War Office that fateful Sunday morning of April 2, 1865. Disaster was written on the horizon and fatigue on the faces of the men at the War Office. Postmaster General Reagan and several others were merely sitting around, hopelessly dreading to start work, awaiting news that could be only bad news. At nine-thirty a messenger hurried in from the telegraph office. The message he carried could not have been a surprise to R. G. H. Kean. General Lee's thin lines at last had been broken. Preparations must commence at once to evacuate Richmond.

Several times recently Kean and his immediate superior, John A. Campbell, the assistant secretary of war, had discussed this eventuality. From inside the Confederate government they had early perceived the gradual decay of the very foundations of their new nation, as the enemy's power ever mounted. And, while perceiving defeat, they had been unable to perceive much hope for the South and its weary people. An unfathomable

---

* Pronounced 'cane.'

future promised, for certain, only humiliation, despair, and gloom.

This was no time for speculation. Immediate tasks lay at hand. Dutiful and with keen appreciation for historical materials, Kean started packing valuable papers of the War Office. The Office became a beehive of activity. At eleven, a second telegram arrived from General Lee; Richmond would have to be evacuated that night. Kean worked hard and at three that afternoon went to his house where his wife was making frantic preparations to leave for Albemarle County on a James River and Kanawha Canal boat. The canal was rapidly clogging up with boatloads of people seeking safety somewhere to the west. By six o'clock Kean had his records packed and at the Danville Depot. With them he boarded the same train which at eleven carried away the President and the Cabinet. The next afternoon they arrived at Danville where hospitable citizens, relatively unhurt by the war, enthusiastically took them in.

The secretary of war, General John C. Breckinridge, did not accompany the fleeing government; nor did the assistant secretary, John A. Campbell. Kean himself had to open up the War Office. For a week, no news from Lee, and then the crushing report of his surrender at Appomattox. That night, Monday, April 10, the President and his Cabinet hastily departed for Charlotte, North Carolina. From the west Stoneman's 6000 veteran raiders were closing in. From the east Sherman's dreaded legions were relentlessly pushing back General Joseph E. Johnston's small Confederate force. The route to safety was fraught with danger.

In Danville confusion prevailed in the bureau offices where no clear orders from above had been given. With the Army of Northern Virginia gone, the rush from the town turned into a stampede. The next day Kean got his cases on a troop train and caught up with the Presidential party at Greensboro on Thursday night. General Breckinridge was there; so were Generals Johnston and Beauregard, two of the President's bitterest enemies. On Saturday the Presidential party slipped away as quietly as their ambulance, carriage, and wagon train would permit. Stoneman's raiders were all around, and to the south ahead of the fleeing government, they were destroying railroad bridges and tracks.

Kean with his records followed in wagons on Sunday, not knowing that Davis had reluctantly and sorrowfully consented to let Johnston negotiate with Sherman. While camping at High Point four days later, Kean learned that Sherman had offered Johnston peace terms. The terms were extremely lenient and must have relieved Kean of much foreboding. When the Confederacy laid down her arms, the Southern states were to reenter the Union with their state governments unimpaired and their constitutional rights recognized. The protection of Southern persons and property was guaranteed. But Kean's spiraling hope must have crumpled when word fast followed that President Lincoln had been assassinated. Would Andrew Johnson and the Radicals approve Sherman's terms? Would Southern leaders be held responsible for Lincoln's death? Apprehensively, Kean moved on and caught up with the fleeing government at Charlotte.

Davis and his Cabinet had approved Sherman's peace terms only to learn two days later that they had been rejected by Johnson and Stanton. The high Confederate officials were now fugitives with rewards on their heads and zealously pursued by Federal cavalry units. Flight again was imperative.

To expedite their flight, some suggested destroying the Confederate records. Kean vigorously protested, insisting that they contained matters of history which would be invaluable in vindicating the South against any malignant or untruthful charge which might be trumped up against her. Breckinridge instructed Kean to store his war records in Charlotte, guard against their destruction, and surrender them, if they were found, to the Federal officer who would perhaps soon occupy Charlotte.

Meanwhile a group of 52 Virginia officers held a meeting and appointed a committee to learn from the secretary of war what was expected of them. In reality, they thought the end had come and that it was fruitless to follow the fugitive government without means and transportation. Accordingly, Breckinridge authorized them to return home.

Kean, learning that Johnston was surrendering his army to Sherman, decided to return home too. And he turned over the custody of his papers to the assistant secretary of the Confederate Senate, whose Senate Journals were stored in the same place with Kean's records.

So, on the day that the remnant of the Confederate government fled on south into history, Kean and his party of Virginians headed north for home. Keeping well to the west of the wreckage of Lee's and Johnston's armies, he reached Edgehill, his wife's home in Albemarle County. He had been en route 14 days; his wife, weeks before, had arrived safely from Richmond. Virginia was quietly submitting to military government. Military garrisons were operating in all the country towns, Negroes were flocking to the towns and cities, and times were desperately hard. There was serious doubt that the summer crops could be saved so as to ward off starvation. In Lynchburg a Yankee commissary captain had established himself in Kean's home. Peace had come, but only humiliation and uncertainty lay ahead.

One record Kean did not leave in Charlotte was his Diary. In it he had not written a single word since March 23. Now, June 1, he would write from memory a brief account of the high tragedy of those eventful days. And for the next seven months, before concluding his Diary in December 1865, he would record the events and his impressions of the early stages of reconstruction.

The Diary had been begun four years before when the future seemed bright for the new nation. Kean was then 33 years old, and as a private in the Southern Army of the Potomac, had participated in the grand victory of Bull Run. A few months later he was promoted to captain and appointed Head of the Bureau of War in Richmond where he remained until the end. From this vantage point inside the Confederate government, he kept adding to his Diary, and it grew to be a history of the inside doings and of the declining fortunes of the Confederacy and her leaders. It is a history that can better be understood and evaluated if the author and the circumstances under which he worked are better known.

2

R. G. H. Kean was born in 1828 in Caroline County, Virginia, at Mount Airy, his mother's ancestral home. His forbears on both sides were substantial citizens but not great planters. The first American Kean immigrated from northern Ireland during the era of the American Revolution. One of his sons, Andrew, an accomplished Latin scholar, studied medicine and eventually settled in Goochland county. As a doctor he served the sick from Richmond to Charlottesville and on both sides of the James river. So great was his reputation that Thomas Jefferson invited him to hold the first chair of medicine at the University of Virginia. But Dr. Kean did not consider himself adequately prepared in formal medicine. He stuck to the work he knew best— his private practice.

Although Andrew Kean formed no official connection with the University of Virginia, his son, grandson, great-grandson, and great-great-grandson attended the University. His second son, John Vaughan Kean, enrolled at the new University at its very first session and was appointed by Jefferson as the first Librarian. Thus from its beginning, the Keans have been among the University's most distinguished alumni, serving as Librarian, Visitor, Rector, and donor. None gave more time than R. G. H. Kean, the Diarist and the son of John Vaughan Kean.

John Vaughan Kean married Caroline Hill, established his own private school at Olney in Caroline County, and was called 'Schoolmaster Napoleon Kean with the little head of all knowledge.' Two sons were born of this union and the second, named Robert Garlick Hill, was called Garlick. When he was three, his mother died, and the two boys for a time were mothered and taught by their Aunt Elizabeth Hill, who also ran a private school.

In his early years young Garlick Kean was diligently instructed by his father and aunt, both teachers by profession. Showing promise as a student, he was sent to the newly established Episcopal High School in Alexandria near Washington, not far from where a few years later Kean would be encamped as a Confederate soldier. This school specialized in preparing boys for college and for the adjoining Episcopal Theological Seminary. Under its first headmaster, William Nelson Pendleton, later General Robert E. Lee's chief of artillery, it was becoming famous for its thorough and advanced work. But unfortunately in 1844 it was temporarily closed from financial stress and Kean had to return home. For a short time he attended Rappahannock Academy at Port Royal and then settled down at Frederick Coleman's famous Concord Academy. This was a classical school located at Guiney's, a railroad station between Richmond and Fredericksburg that later would become a familiar name to the boys in gray and blue. At Concord, Coleman's teaching was said to be like the man himself—massive, forceful, dominating. The curriculum was broad including classical and modern languages, natural and moral philosophy, and mathematics ranging from arithmetic to calculus. With an M. A. degree from the University of Virginia, Coleman concentrated on preparing his students for the University. While driving them hard in their studies, he put them strictly on their honor in their personal conduct. His students are said to have contributed much to the success of the honor system which had been recently adopted at Jefferson's University.

At the age of 20 in 1848, Kean completed his work at Concord Academy, for a while tutored in the home of a private family, and then enrolled at the University of Virginia. The University after twenty-three years of existence was undergoing significant changes. It was fast becoming the leading university in the South and the magnet for students throughout the region. The mushrooming enrollment was kept in bounds only by persisting high scholastic standards, which in Kean's day allowed one in sixteen to pass math, one in eleven to pass classical languages, and one in eighteen to pass law. Degrees were hard to earn.

Student turbulence of the earlier decades was waning under the influence of the honor system and a strong, understanding faculty. Objectionable rules had been relaxed and the student uniform had yielded to frock coats and swallowtails. Student-professor relations had improved. Professors entertained their classes at dinners and evening receptions. While gaiety and social activity abounded, there was also a pervasive spirit of sobriety and responsibility among the students. Under the influence of such faculty members as William Holmes McGuffey, James Lawrence Cabell, and young John B. Minor, religious activities were making headway in this secular school.

Young Garlick Kean shone at social events. But he had little use for ribaldry and pranks. Scholarly and introspective, he preferred to associate with the more serious element of student body and faculty. For two years he lived in the home of one of his professors. His main interest lay in his studies, the literary societies, and religious activities. He attended services conducted by a University-employed chaplain, became an active member of the Sons of Temperance, raised funds to construct a Temperance Hall, joined the Society of Missionary Inquiry, and taught Sunday School classes. He also joined the Jefferson Literary Society, and in his second year was one of its two final orators.

Kean fell under the influence of an outstanding faculty and a strong, broad curriculum. The University was a group of schools, each under the supervision of a professor. Degrees were conferred in any single school or in several of them collectively. In his first year Kean took ancient and modern languages and mathematics. He excelled in Greek and received the degree of graduate not only in Greek and Latin but also in French and Spanish. In his second year he continued ancient languages and added natural and moral philosophy and chemistry. At the end of two years he qualified for the intermediate degree of Bachelor of Arts. Studious and with a strong scholarly background, Kean was excelled by few if any students. Each year he made an impressive record in his intermediate and final examinations, and at the end of his third year he was one of the four students whose essays were chosen to be read on the public days.

Having demonstrated proficiency in both the classical and scientific classes, he began the study of law under Professor John B. Minor, who was at thirty-two beginning an illustrious career which would extend almost to the twentieth century. A year before, an additional law professor had been added to help handle the increasing enrollment. This was James P. Holcombe whose family had left Virginia because they opposed slavery.

Professor Holcombe was ardently pro-slavery and in time would become a Confederate Congressman and a famous spy. The first year in the Law School Kean devoted to general legal studies, the second to the theory and practice of law, and the third to broad cultural subjects. Following his graduation in 1853, Professor Minor wrote that no one within his experience had left the University so well grounded in legal knowledge.

While Kean pursued his University studies he also pursued a young lady named Jane Nicholas Randolph who lived at nearby Edgehill, the family home. Jane Randolph was the daughter of Thomas Jefferson Randolph, favorite grandson of Thomas Jefferson. Her uncle, George Wythe Randolph, was then a prominent lawyer in Richmond. Connected by blood with the Jefferson, Randolph, Nicholas, Bolling, Page, and Cary families of Virginia and the Smith family of Baltimore, she presented an illustrious lineage as well as personal charm and strong character. The courtship developed slowly, for Jane Randolph was frequently ill and her family feared she might develop tuberculosis. But eventually the young couple were engaged, and with his law studies completed in 1853, Kean moved to the bustling town of Lynchburg to begin his practice and to prepare a home for his future bride. The next year they were married.

Lynchburg was a prosperous trading center and tobacco market, lying at the foothills of the Blue Ridge mountains. It was on its way toward becoming a center of railroads and manufactures. In this environment, young Kean's scholarship and fine legal knowledge gained immediate attention. As a lawyer he enjoyed a growing practice. As a talented citizen of the community, he participated in civic and religious activities, becoming the corresponding secretary of the town's first Y. M. C. A. and a vestryman of St. Paul's Episcopal church. Although urged to run for the Virginia Assembly, he eschewed politics. His wife, whom he feared could not adjust herself to the meager income of a beginner lawyer, turned out to be the 'most accomplished economist and the best poor man's wife in the world.' As the prosperous 'fifties sped along, three children arrived to grace the Kean household.

Only those events beyond Kean's control seemed to stand in the way of a bright future. With some anxiety, he watched the bitter sectional crisis swell up. Suddenly in October 1859 the storm broke with John Brown's raid at Harper's Ferry. In the martial South everywhere, volunteer military companies sprang up. At least a dozen such companies were formed in Lynchburg, and Kean at once joined the later famous Home Guard, which from Bull Run to Appomattox was to participate in 11 major battles and 13 skirmishes. While these companies drilled the next year, adding to the atmosphere of gaiety in the town, the people divided sharply on the issue of secession. Kean associated with the extreme state rights group, and after Lincoln's election he urged secession. When the first gun boomed out over Fort Sumter in April 1861, Kean had no decision of conscience to make. He was passionately devoted to Virginia; he was already committed; the path of duty led straight to the battle field. Ten days later private R. G. H. Kean proceeded to Richmond where the well-drilled Home Guard was mustered in as Company G of the 11th Virginia infantry regiment. A new phase of his life had begun.

3

Kean's regiment was hurried to Manassas and assigned to the brigade of General James Longstreet. Actual fighting was now close at hand. In late May Federal forces occupied Alexandria, and in June a skirmish took place at Vienna in Fairfax County.

In mid-July Longstreet's brigade occupied Blackburn's Ford on Bull Run, and on the 18th Kean for the first time heard the bursting of shells from a cannonade and the whizzing of balls from rifle volleys, as he faced a charging Federal line. The green Confederate troops stood their ground and repelled the attack in this preliminary battle of Bull Run. Three days later in the major engagement of Manassas, Kean's regiment, in the center of the Confederate line, was slated to take an active part, but was bypassed by the Federal flanking movement. As the enemy fled in panic toward Washington, his regiment was ordered to move forward and collect and guard the spoils of war.

With the rout of the Federal forces at Manassas, the Confederates belatedly moved forward and occupied the row of hills overlooking Alexandria and Washington. Within the Confederate lines at Camp Harrison, Kean wrote the first entry of his Diary on Sunday, September 15, 1861. For the next five and a half months, during the autumn and winter, he chronicled the unfolding events within the army, and his perceptive impressions as well, while participating mostly in routine chores of camp life.

Advancement of course was in the offing. His scholarly and legal abilities were well known among his host of friends in the 11th Virginia; his talents would be hard to ignore. Early in the autumn he began to serve as quartermaster sergeant, and in November his colonel applied for the commission of assistant quartermaster for him. Awaiting the results of this application, Kean aspired to become a lieutenant of the line in Company G, but a still more attractive position loomed up. One evening Kean was called in to attend a conference at the headquarters of his brigade, then commanded by General Richard S. Ewell who had succeeded Longstreet. The purpose of the conference was to discuss ways to induce one-year volunteers to re-enlist for the duration of the war. Though Kean was the only enlisted man present, Ewell insisted on hearing him. Soon thereafter Kean's colonel informed him that Ewell intended inviting him to his staff. Meanwhile, his commission as assistant quartermaster with rank as captain came through. But before accepting this commission and before he was invited to Ewell's staff, he was assigned to the staff of General George Wythe Randolph in command at Suffolk. His title was assistant adjutant general and his rank, captain. On February 24, 1862 he bade the 11th Virginia farewell and departed for Suffolk.

Kean found Randolph, formerly a midshipman, now a military engineer and artillerist, vigorously organizing and effecting plans for the defense of the Suffolk area through which the enemy might easily advance up chains of rivers and seize the railroads connecting Richmond with the south and southeast. Major Isaac St. John, on engineering duty, was helping Randolph map the country, and General Howell Cobb was rushed to the area with six regiments. Although Kean did not record his Suffolk experiences in his Diary—he was probably too busy—in a later memorandum he had nothing but praise for Randolph, Cobb, and St. John. Randolph, he thought, had a sound grasp of military strategy; he could plan brilliantly and execute with dispatch. Kean also admired the harmony characterizing the relations between these three men.

Randolph's reputation in planning coastal defense and his political availability commended him to the attention of the Confederate government. Within three weeks of Kean's arrival at Suffolk, Randolph was appointed secretary of war. Naturally he took with him to Richmond his highly trained and competent young nephew-by-marriage. One week in Richmond, and Kean was appointed Head of the Bureau of War—one of the divisions of the War Department.

The War Department was located in the old brick building at Ninth and Franklin streets which once had housed the Mechanics Institute; its great halls and lecture rooms were now converted into offices. All the other departments also occupied this building except Treasury and State. These, the President's offices, and the Cabinet Room were in the United States Customs House on Main Street.

The War Department, under the direction and control of the President, had charge of all matters connected with the army and the Indian tribes. Kean was now the head of one of the nine bureaus in the department; two more were staffed after he arrived. Samuel Cooper, ranking general of the Confederacy, served throughout the war as adjutant and inspector general. His office was responsible for the Department's orders and commands, army records, installations and supplies, and the inspection of all army personnel. An old army man and an intimate of the President, Cooper was frequently the target of sharp criticism. Colonel Abraham C. Myers was quartermaster general and Colonel Lucius B. Northrop, commissary general of subsistence. Their jobs of furnishing the army with food, clothing, and camp supplies naturally elicited suspicion of graft and profiteering. Their personal conduct and personalities were not conducive to allaying criticism, and they too were constantly under fire. Myers was replaced by General Alexander R. Lawton in August 1863 but Northrop hung on until almost the end of the war.

Dr. Samuel P. Moore was surgeon-general. For a time, Major Josiah Gorgas, a talented administrator, headed both the engineer and ordnance bureaus, but he soon found ordnance a full time job. Thereafter Captain Alfred Lewis Rives and Colonel Jeremy F. Gilmer alternately served as chief engineer. Isaac M. St. John served admirably as superintendent of the nitre and mining bureau until he replaced Northrop as commissary general early in 1865. Indian affairs, the ninth bureau, was headed successively by David Hubbard and S. S. Scott. After the passage of the conscription act, Generals Gabriel J. Rains and John S. Preston successively headed the conscription bureau until it was abolished in 1865. William Morris was later appointed chief of the signal corps.

As head of the bureau of war, Kean succeeded Colonel Albert Taylor Bledsoe, a professor of mathematics at the University of Virginia. Bledsoe had incurred the enmity of the first secretary of war and was given little to do by the second. He was ready to give up this post by the time Randolph was appointed. Kean's immediate superior and the person with whom he worked most intimately was the assistant secretary of war. Bledsoe held this position from the time of Kean's arrival until October 1862. Thereafter it was filled by John Archibald Campbell of Alabama, who was an associate justice of the Supreme Court of the United States when the war commenced.

President Davis gave most of his cabinet members moderately wide latitude in running their offices. He frequently sought their advice and he tolerated opinions contrary to his own. But having been an able secretary of war in the United States government and an experienced military man, the President tended to regard the War Department as his own domain. He carefully scrutinized the activities of this department and kept a tight rein on the secretaries. He was in effect his own secretary of war. Two secretaries had preceded Randolph. Leroy Pope Walker of Alabama, lacking administrative ability, resigned in September 1861. His successor, Judah P. Benjamin, was an intimate of Davis and an excellent administrator, but his ignorance of military procedure, and Confederate military losses, led to bitter criticism and his transfer to the Department of State. Three secretaries of war followed Benjamin—Randolph, James A. Seddon of Virginia, and John C. Breckinridge of Kentucky. Kean served under all three.

The bureau of war was closely linked to the administrative functions of the two main officials in the department, the secretary and the assistant secretary. Its functions were not as sharply defined as those of the other bureaus but it clearly served as a co-ordinating force. Kean therefore was an office manager, an executive secretary, and a research assistant; his duties were manifold, sometimes petty, sometimes vitally important. He supervised the large clerical staff and kept the clerks busy copying the bushels of correspondence that poured out of the War Office. With Assistant Secretary John A. Campbell, he made decisions on routine matters and signed orders 'By the order of the Secretary of War.' He often dug out the correspondence and information the secretary and President used in preparing important orders. He prepared important documents for military investigating bodies set up to place blame for military disasters. He supervised the preparation of evidence to be used in courts martial and of other military correspondence requested by Congress.

No task was more irksome and time consuming than issuing passports. Kean and Campbell were besieged by persons applying to leave the Confederacy. Some were aliens or alleged aliens running from conscription, which for a time was under the administration of Campbell; others were war profiteers flitting in and out of the South; and others were leaving for valid reasons. Decisions were often difficult to make, and the responsibility was shifted back and forth from the War Department to the offices of General John H. Winder, commander of the Richmond police. Winder's detectives were accused of selling permits for personal gain and unintentionally providing the enemy with vital information. In time commanders in the field refused to honor Winder's permits.

Kean was also the watch dog of the secretary's office and sometimes determined who was to see the secretary. This of course was an important function within itself, but it was not a pleasant task to say no to important civil and military persons nor to the endless line of lesser people, some of them women, tearfully begging for the relaxation of the conscription laws.

There were times when Kean broke away from the office routine. Scarcity of troops required that government clerks be prepared to help defend Richmond. Of the some 2000 clerks in all departments, over half had military experience, and they were organized into a local guard unit. As a member of this unit Kean marched and drilled and rushed to the outer defenses when the city was threatened. Moreover, possessing a perceptive and fertile mind, he could not resist offering his superiors suggestions, memoranda, and sketches on problems of defense, war economics, and diplomacy, demonstrating a remarkable understanding of military and political affairs.

When Kean took office in Richmond, he was 34 years old and had almost a year of military experience in the field; he was married and now had four children; he was slender, average in height, and not of robust health. Nature had endowed him with a high intelligence. He was thoroughly educated, widely read, polished in personality, and he had family connections which admitted him to the inner circles. He was highly qualified for his new position and he made it an important one. Serious in purpose, he worked hard and expected hard work of those under him. Efficient himself and somewhat formal, he insisted that the work be done correctly. To the War Office he must have brought order and dispatch.

From his desk in the main reception office of the War Department for the next two and a half years, moreover, he kept keen eyes focused upon coming and going personalities, high and low; upon events bursting about him and on remote battle fields; and upon a constant stream of correspondence crossing his desk and revealing to him things he could not otherwise see and hear of the inner workings of the Confederate government. About all these things he wrote in his Diary, and his observations as head of the bureau of war form the main body of his Diary.

4

Let us now examine in a little greater detail the nature of the Diary. The first chapter covers Kean's experiences while a private and quartermaster sergeant within the Confederate lines between Manassas and Alexandria. There he drilled, stood routine picket duty, took part in dress parades, went on foraging expeditions, and once again faced Federal artillery and muskets in the skirmish at Dranesville. As winter closed in, he chopped wood, sloshed through mud, shivered in sheets of driving rain, snow and sleet, and finally came down with a serious attack of jaundice. Occasionally he attended parties behind the lines at the home of a hospitable family. As a soldier in the field, he let himself be run against strong opposition for a seat in the Confederate Congress, and lost.

All these experiences, and more, he recorded in his Diary. Bored by routine camp life, he fretted at the inaction of the army. Reflecting on the potential strength of the North, he let uneasiness slip in between his lines. With 17000 men, out of a total of 25000 in one corps, sick or on leave, and with a slackening of volunteering, he feared the worst. He recognized the dangers of Southern optimism generated by early victories. He deplored the Confederate strategy of defense which prevented decisive concentration and required victory at all points. Federal victories on the Tennessee and Cumberland rivers underscored the dangers he foresaw, and a note of realism, verging on pessimism, crept into his writing. But this did not mean resignation. He would fight for his 'noble, grand old state' while life lasted. Never, never, he avowed, would he yield to the power in Washington, unless as a captive in chains.

Unfortunately, Kean did not keep up his Diary from mid-February to mid-October 1862, covering his brief Suffolk experience and his first six months as head of the bureau of war. For this interval, he promised to make notes later, on the 'many great events transacted, and some curious matters of inside history,' but no such notes have been found.

The next five chapters cover most of the time he was in Richmond. The range of his subject in this main part of his story is as broad as the events of the war. He took special interest in its economic aspects and details the failure of Congress in the field of taxation and finance; he describes and evaluates conscription, impressment, and price control; he comments on disloyalty, desertion, and the gradual disintegration of morale. As a lawyer, he shows deep concern with the rules of war, the exchange of prisoners, policies of retaliation, and restrictions on civil liberties. As a clerk drawing an annual salary of $3000, or the equivalent of $300 in normal times, he describes the hardships suffered by the white collar workers. He gives excellent coverage to the Hampton Roads Peace Conference.

It was not Kean's intention to record military events, but they could not be divorced from civil affairs, and the attention given them increased as the war developed. He took a keen interest in military strategy and advocated greater integration and concentration of Confederate forces. He decried the strategy of defense, and like Randolph urged co-operation of the Trans-

Mississippi forces with those east of the river. A consistent critic of Davis, he repeatedly complained of the President's penchant for tight departmental organization, his passion for detail, and his failure to delegate authority and responsibility, especially to officials of the War Department.

The leading actors of the Diary are the leading personalities of the Confederacy, civil and military. The President, cabinet members, congressmen, bureau heads, and clerks move back and forth through his pages—Davis, Randolph, Seddon, Benjamin, Memminger, Campbell, Myers, Northrop, Cooper, Wigfall, Hunter, and lesser officials who, like Frank G. Ruffin, were playing substantial roles. Military personnel vie with civil officials for space—Lee, Jackson, Stuart, Longstreet, Beauregard, Bragg, Johnston, the Hills, Holmes, Hindman, and lesser officers such as Captain McKay, who with his cannon on his horse was to attack Federal gunboats on the western waters.

Kean naturally illuminates the inner workings of the War Department, its intrigues, the thrusts of its personnel for promotion, the relationship of its various bureaus to each other, and its relationship with the presidency, with the other departments, and with the commanders in the field. New light is thrown on well-known controversies and personality clashes, and on some not so well known. Davis's feuds with Randolph, Myers, Johnston, Beauregard, Vice-President Stephens, and Congress, Bragg's clashes with almost all his contemporaries, and Benjamin's difficulties with the generals receive attention. Kean's personality portraits are sharply etched, sometimes provocative, and often authentic.

From Kean's pen, Randolph, Seddon, and Campbell take on considerable stature. A strong advocate of the importance of the West, Randolph was imaginative and at one time demonstrated boldness. He ordered General Theophilus Holmes, in command of the Trans-Mississippi, to cross over and help recover Tennessee and hold the Mississippi valley. When Davis countermanded the order, Randolph resigned, refusing to perform the functions of a mere clerk. Seddon was also an advocate of a western strategy, a tireless worker, and an able administrator. But as time went on, he too found himself more and more relegated to the status of a clerk. Campbell emerges as the real power in the War Department toward the end. With him Kean developed a confidential relationship, and his Diary is sprinkled with Campbell's wisdom and reminiscences on inside activities of the Federal goverment.

A few random strokes of Kean's pen illustrate his touch at characterization:

Stonewall Jackson 'knew the country, the people and himself.' 'Quiet, reserved, taciturn, and regarded as executive in his manners,' he rose to every emergency. 'The purity of his principles, the manifest devotion with which he carried on war, as a matter of *Duty* merely, his ardent State Patriotism, his carelessness of what men said of him, his intense purpose' made up 'a character of antique beauty, simple and severe.'

Braxton Bragg's character was marked by the 'repulsive traits' of 'prying, indirection, vindictiveness, and insincerity.' He resembled a 'chimpanzee as much in character' as 'in appearance.' Stammering Sam Melton of the A. & I. office, wanted Bragg as adjutant and inspector general. Bragg would make them all howl, but Melton was 'willing to howl' if he could 'hear some other people howl too.' The easygoing incumbent, General Samuel Cooper (wrote Kean), though 'uniformly courteous and uniformly non-committal,' never decided anything and was '*out* of his office most of the time.' Incompetent and ignorant of Confederate military legislation, Cooper was in frequent consultation with the President, and was kept in office because of

Davis's 'irrepressible *West Pointism*' and preference for 'accommodating, civil-spoken persons of small capacity.'

Davis (Kean quoting Frank Ruffin), thought at first to be 'a *mule*, but a good *mule*,' was turning out to be 'a jackass.' Honest, pure, and patriotic (wrote Kean), he was the 'worst judge of men in the world.' 'Peevish,' 'fickle,' 'hair-splitting,' he temporized and wearied his subordinates with the 'endless tediousness of consultations' which yielded 'no results.' He was neither a 'comprehensive' nor a 'representative' man who as 'a *leader* in *council* as well as in the field' could 'comprehend and express the movement' for Southern independence.

Lee looms up as a colossal general but not without faults. He held mechanics in his army while the railroads wore out. After Gettysburg, he was as 'silent as a grave' and 'nearly as costive as Johnston'; his communications were 'brief and jejune.' He too was not 'a *leader* in the *council* as well as in the field.' Near the end, 'the country by instinct, seeking such a reliance, gave its faith to Lee in vain.'

Joseph E. Johnston was 'a very little man,' 'full of himself,' and 'morbidly jealous of Lee and all his superiors.' He wrote brief, 'captious,' 'ice-tempered' letters, 'never treating the government with confidence, hardly with respect.' He was 'more anxious to make a point than gain a battle, to put the government in the wrong than defend a state'; 'retreat and sacrifice' were 'always strategical.' Yet Kean had confidence in Johnston's 'military coup d'oeil,' and the official correspondence of the Georgia campaign furnished 'powerful ground' for the vindication of Johnston, who here showed a 'mastery of the situation, a sagacity in anticipating the future, and a comprehensive view.'

Secretary of Treasury C. G. Memminger was a 'man of smartness, finesse but tricky, shifty, and narrow.' His 'skin was as thick as a rhinoceros's.' Judah P. Benjamin was a 'smart lawyer, a ready, useful drawer up of papers but perhaps the least *wise* of our public men'—a 'poor adviser.' Senator Wigfall of Texas, a bitter critic of Davis, came and went like 'Saul on his journey to Damascus,' 'breathing out threatenings and slaughters.'

In the last chapter of his Diary, Kean writes down his analysis of the fundamental weaknesses of the Confederacy, the causes for her failure, the invasions of the Constitution by the Lincoln government, and the injustices and follies of military reconstruction. Creeping into the record also are the bitter disappointment and despair which a highly intelligent young citizen of a conquered nation feels. This final chapter, spilling over into the post-war era, puts the capstone on the Diary and makes it the best-rounded work of its kind on the Confederacy.

Without trying to be dramatic, without laboring to achieve effect, Kean at times wrote vivid prose, and unconsciously he captured the flavor of the immediacy of events. Excitement and hope tempered with realism and fear steal in.

But let not the impression prevail that Kean did not make mistakes, that his judgment was unerring, that he was unburdened with prejudice. One is not surprised to find him hating Yankees, but he could also be charitable to some of them. Naturally he admired Randolph, and Davis's treatment of Randolph may help to account for some of Kean's severe criticism of Davis and his intimates. Kean's fierce devotion to Virginia may have colored some of his writing about non-Virginia persons and things, and he had the typical civilian distrust of West Point-trained officers. But on the whole Kean tried hard to be objective. His observations were sometimes brilliant and nearly always penetrating. He was not given to outbursts of false optimism. He succeeded in being realistic if not completely objective. His Diary is neither as full nor as gossipy as J. B. Jones's *A Rebel War*

Clerk's Diary and Mrs. Mary Boykin Chesnut's *A Diary from Dixie*, but Kean was better informed, and his Diary is more reliable, more discerning, and better rounded than either. It is a picture of the inside of the Confederacy that even the assiduous Jones and the ubiquitous Mrs. Chesnut could not know.

5

Disillusioned and despondent at the end of the war, R. G. H. Kean saw moderate reconstruction give way to Radical Reconstruction, whose excesses confirmed his belief that constitutional liberty had perished with the Confederacy. In accordance with a war-time vow made in anticipation of harsh reconstruction, he laid plans to emigrate to Mexico but abandoned them when informed by a friend there that prospects for a man without money were poor. Soon deep personal grief compounded his despair. In 1868, Jane Randolph Kean passed away, leaving her 40-year-old husband with five children to support. His personal difficulties were somewhat relieved by his faithful Aunt Betty Hill who now came to care for his children as she had many years before cared for him.

Radical Reconstruction in Virginia gave way in 1870, and the state was restored to the Union. Lynchburg moreover made rapid headway toward economic recovery. The tobacco business revived immediately, new banks opened their doors, and railroads steamed in. Slowly but surely Kean brought together the loose ends of his broken career, re-established his law practice and his place in the community as a civic leader. In 1874, he married again, and five children were born of this union. In 1881 he was appointed city attorney and held this position during most of his remaining years. Over the state he came to be recognized as a brilliant lawyer, whose 'memory was like an engraving in glass.' He contributed papers to scholarly legal and scientific journals and made many public addresses on the same subjects. In 1890 he was elected President of the Virginia Bar Association.

Although a life-long Democrat and repeatedly urged to run for office, Kean refused; he was content with his 'one good office.' On the other hand he took a keen interest in local and national issues. An advocate of temperance, he opposed prohibition as an invasion of individual liberty. When the Readjusters sought to scale down Virginia's public debt, Kean sided with the Funders who advocated paying the debt in full. He deplored the evils of the spoils system and actively supported civil service reform. Toward the great industrial disorders of his day he took a conservative position, and saw in labor's discontent a class war.

Kean's interest in the University of Virginia never waned. His contributions to it were constructive and substantial. In 1872 he was appointed to the Board of Visitors and at once chosen Rector. For the next four years, among many other services, he formulated and helped execute a plan restoring the University's financial solvency. Again, beginning in 1890, he served four years as a Visitor, helped reorganize the Law School, and played a vital part in encouraging endowments. When he died in 1898 at the age of 70, his son, Jefferson Randolph Kean, had already graduated from the University and was on his way toward becoming a general and a distinguished surgeon in the United States Army.

The Kean Diary was passed on to this son, and when he died it was passed on to his son, Robert Hill Kean, a doctor of philosophy from the University of Virginia and the present owner of the Diary. It is now on deposit at the University Library of which, more than a hundred years before, the Diarist's father served as Librarian.

That R. G. H. Kean's career could have been more spectacular is certain. Politics, for one thing, offered a way to greater fame. But Kean, disillusioned with the politics of sectionalism, war, and reconstruction, did not desire such fame. On December 30, 1874, Kean wrote the following brief introduction to his Diary, which in some measure explains why he never sought the limelight:

> The honorable Charles C. F. Greville in his Memoirs, a journal of the reigns of George IV and William IV, says, 'The more one reads and hears of great men the more one is reconciled to one's own mediocrity.' This sentiment [wrote Kean] of a man of some capacity, but without much of that personal ambition which is ever ready to sacrifice personal and domestic ease to so-called 'distinction,' which fetters one's individual independence in order to compass the favor of the great or win the applause of the multitude, has often suggested itself to my mind before I ever saw it expressed. And it is to no little extent illustrated in the following Journal kept irregularly through two and a half years of the most interesting period of the struggle for Southern independence.

Modest in taste and ambition, he was devoted to his family and preferred a life of simplicity. But competent and constructive, he represents that substantial group of Southerners who unobtrusively but effectively carried on the more permanent reconstruction in the South.

*　　*　　*　　*　　*　　*　　*

Chapter divisions in this Diary are the editor's. Chapter titles are Kean's words chosen from the context by the editor to represent the tone of the chapter. Sub-titles are the editor's, chosen to represent content and chronology.

Identification and explanation in footnotes have been made only when clarity seemed to demand it. In other cases, sufficient information has been inserted in the context to enable the reader to follow up the person or thing in standard histories of the period and in dictionaries of biography.

Materials in parentheses are Kean's; in brackets, the editor's. Words and phrases which Kean unintentionally repeated have been dropped. Where Kean rarely misspelled a word, the spelling has been corrected.

Kean used capital letters excessively and inconsistently. In haste he often used dashes for periods, commas, and other marks of punctuation. For clarity, consistency, and appearance, the editor has made changes in capitalization and punctuation.

INSIDE THE CONFEDERATE GOVERNMENT

1

DANGERS CLOSE US ROUND

After First Manassas

CAMP HARRISON. *Sept. 15, 1861. Sunday.* The 11th Virginia regiment returned at 10 o'clock P.M. to their camp from Mason's Hill whither they marched the preceding Tuesday morning for a tour of five days' picket duty. The prospect from Mason's was very fine. On Tuesday and Wednesday the Yankees put a large camp on Eagle Hill, south of Hunter's Creek. We could see their operations there and also their entrenchments about the [Episcopal Theological] Seminary and their flags at Roach's Mills, the Long Bridge and Ft. Ellsworth. Their pickets have ceased firing, and in an interview near Bancroft's between some of them and two of Captain R. C. Saunders's men (Company B., 11th Va.), they said they had strict orders not to fire. These interviews are recently encouraged by General [James] Longstreet. (Colonel J. E. B. Stuart made himself ridiculous by cutting up at Saunders's first interview down at Upton's ten days ago).[1]

---

[1] After the battle of First Manassas, or Bull Run, the Confederate Army of the Potomac under the command of General Joseph E. Johnston had moved toward Washington and was concentrated in the vicinity of Fairfax Courthouse. General James Longstreet, in command of the 4th brigade, had

On Friday Colonel Stuart took and burned Basil Hall's home which the Yankees used as a look out and picket station. They send up their balloon frequently, but never high enough or near enough to see anything we wish to conceal. It is a wretched humbug, but as Mr. William M. Burwell (of Bedford, Va.) says, Lowe[2] is spending their money. General Longstreet has removed on the 14th to Falls Church, and [General P. G. T.] Beauregard to Fairfax Court House. He whose name L. G. Latham (captain of artillery from Lynchburg) says should be written P. (ea) (St. G.) Cocke omitting the *St. G.* is commandant of this post. We are afraid promotion will lose us Longstreet and perhaps put us under Stuart who openly seeks this brigade.

Sept. 18.   When we got here Sunday Charles M. Blackford[3] had got here from Lynchburg. He brought me the daguerreotype of my wife and children, a great treasure to me. Mary Walker, Tom Randolph's wife (Major T. J. Randolph, Jr. of Albemarle County, my brother-in-law), got to the village last

charge of the line of outposts which overlooked Washington. Among these outposts were such hills as Munson's and Mason's from which an observer could easily view activities in Washington. To the east Federal forces held the area lying immediately around Alexandria including Eagle Hill, the Theological Seminary, Roach's Mills and Fort Ellsworth. The 11th Va. infantry and 'Jeb' Stuart's cavalry regiments were attached to Longstreet's brigade. Robert C. Saunders of Lynchburg, who had helped organize the Southern Guard of Campbell county, later died of wounds received at Seven Pines.

[2] 'Professor' Thaddeus S. C. Lowe, chief aeronaut of the Federal army, was experimenting with the balloon for military observations with more success than Kean realized.

[3] Captain Charles Minor Blackford, Jr., was an original member of the Lynchburg Wise Troop which became Company B of the 2nd Va. cavalry. He was one of five brothers in the Confederate service.

evening. These cavalry fellows have great advantages in their extra horses and Jersey wagons over us infantry men.

Captain Saunders came to our mess breakfast table and began one of his talks about the sick, which spoiled my breakfast. The fever in this regiment is very fatal, and very much on the increase. At dress parade, orders were read from General [Joseph E.] Johnston complimenting J. E. B. Stuart on the affair at Lewinsville on the 12th, which the Yankee papers represent as a success on their part. The truth was they ran like sheep. Colonel Withers's (18th) regiment (R. S. Withers, afterward in the United States Senate from Va.) got in some disgrace down at Munson's a day or two ago by declining an expedition Stuart wished to engage in against Hall's Hill. Some of the company officers seemed to think it was useless expense, the only end of which would be to magnify J. E. B. as an active, enterprising officer, and opposed it. Said to be some courts martial work impending. They may have not been far wrong in anything except the indiscretion of *saying* what they thought. All the rumors of battle between Generals [Robert E.] Lee and [William S.] Rosecrans in the West [western Virginia] seem to be false.

Sept. 24.   On 20th, went with a 2-horse wagon up into Loudoun as far as Aldie to get fowls, eggs, etc. for our sick men. Returned evening of 21st with 42, after visiting perhaps 50 farm houses. Since my return have been quite unwell with dyspepsia accompanied with soreness of the stomach, the first indisposition of any consequence with which I have suffered since I left home in April.

Company G have applied to be transferred to the artillery service. Colonel Thomas Jordan (A. A. G. on General Beauregard's staff) told John G. Meem (first lieutenant, Company G) there would be no difficulty about it, and the paper was prepared by me at Otey's request immediately. Sam Garland,[4] colonel of the 11th Va., I understand, takes it hardly that his old company should leave his regiment, in which he is mainly wrong. If they can better themselves, they ought to do it, as he did in exchanging a captain's for a colonel's commission. Orders have been published prohibiting picket skirmishing; interviews will now be more frequent. I suspect this indicates a desire to avoid active hostilities on this front at present, perhaps because some flank movement is contemplated. *Nous verrons.*

A joke is told by Mr. W. M. Burwell which deserves record. A negro attached to Colonel R. T. Preston's regiment (28th Va.) being asked how he felt in the battle of July 27 replied that 'the bullets come by Zoop! I never mind dat. De minny balls come by Zeu! I never mind dat. De bom shells come by coosh, coosh, coosh, Bang! I never mind dat. But when them things begin to come *Whar ish you? Whar ish you? Whar ish you?* (rifle cannon shot) I tell you dis nigger left.' Colonel Funsten[5] says the only deficit in the story is that it can only be appreciated by persons who have heard the sound illustrated.

---

[4] Samuel Garland, Kirkwood Otey, and John G. Meem were original members of the Lynchburg Home Guard. Garland, a V.M.I. and University of Virginia graduate and a prominent lawyer, was captain of the Guard, Otey a first lieutenant, and Meem a second lieutenant. Upon mustering into service Garland became colonel of the 11th Va. infantry and Otey a captain. Meem, soon promoted to captain, joined General Edmund Kirby Smith's staff. Garland was made a brigadier general the next spring following the battle of Williamsburg. He was killed in action at South Mountain defending Fox's Gap in the general engagement of Antietam. Otey in time became colonel of the 11th Va., and led it under Pickett in the charge at Gettysburg.

[5] This is David Funsten of Alexandria, Virginia, who succeeded Samuel Garland as colonel of the 11th Va. infantry. His brother Oliver R., of Clarke county, Virginia, was colonel of the 11th Va. cavalry.

Oct. 2.   Had Jaundice for the last week, feel very weak and
badly yet, though much better. It was this and not dyspepsia
which was the matter as long ago as September 20. I have met
with great kindness from the Baileys. On Friday night the 28th,
a dark stormy night, the whole line of our outposts were suddenly ordered to fall back by General Johnston, and by day
light we had abandoned to the Yankees the whole range of hills
overlooking the Potomac valley—Mason's, Munson's, Taylor's,
Falls Church, Padgett's. Next day a general order required all
the sick to be sent back to general hospital. These orders produced a general impression that a general engagement, or some
movement of the army was in immediate contemplation. Down
to the present time nothing has occurred to indicate either. The
Yankees have merely occupied the space we abandoned, and
give no sign of advancing in force. They have had just their own
time to prepare for a second invasion of Virginia. God grant
that its issue may be as the former, and more also.

On Saturday night, September 29, James Chalmers (of Lynchburg) was shot by a picket of [General Jubal A.] Early's
brigade. Entering his left fore arm the ball then entered his side.
Amputation of the arm was made Sunday evening, but the doctor could not touch the ball. He seemed to be doing well, but
Monday night grew rapidly worse and expired Tuesday morning, regretted and mourned extensively in the army and the
state. He was a man of unusual, pure character, a true and devoted Christian, a brave soldier, an ardent patriot, a fast friend,
a man of cultured mind and refined taste, fond of curious books
and recondite reading. Major Carter Harrison [6] and Chalmers

---

[6] Harrison was also from Lynchburg and as major in the 11th Va., he
was killed in the skirmish at Blackburn's Ford on Bull Run. Chalmers of
the 2nd Va. cavalry was shot between picket lines near Annandale.

have been the two dearest friends of whom the war has as yet robbed me. It may, probably will, come greatly nearer.

On Monday, September 30, the 11th went out on picket. I was too unwell to accompany them and hung around the lonely camp, or went to the village and to the Wise Troop [from Lynchburg] for society.

Oct. 5. The reports as far back as the 28th are that our battery on Funsten's point, below Occoquan, has virtually closed the navigation of the Potomac; also that the *Resolute* was so hammered by 'Long Tom' in passing down that she sank off Mathias Point.[7] Captain Francis Jordan (of Luray, who married Miss Cornelia Matthews of Lynchburg) told me night before last that the effective strength of Beauregard's Corps is 25,000; the absences and sick, i.e. not for duty, 17,000!! He did not know the figures in General [Gustavus Woodson] Smith's corps. The above are official.

I inserted here General [Sterling] Price's report (by telegraphy) of the capture of Lexington, Missouri.

Oct. 7. Orders have been issued, and are being carried out, for sending all baggage not absolutely necessary to the rear. Some of the regiments are stripping themselves very close. A rumor has become current that the whole army will fall back on Manassas and that it is the purpose to winter there. Captain Frank Jordan told me the other night that the impression at

---

[7] The *Resolute*, a small screw steamer of the Federal Potomac flotilla, was frequently attacked by concealed Confederate batteries on the west bank of the Potomac. The 'Long Tom' was the 30-pounder Parrott, rifled gun captured by the Confederates at Manassas. For a brief interlude the Confederates almost succeeded in blockading Washington by closing the Potomac.

headquarters was that [General George B.] McClellan would advance at 'the fall of the leaf.'

Oct. 11.   On Monday, the 8th, our regiment received orders to move our camp immediately from the brigade drill ground. By the time the ground was chosen and wagons procured, the evening was advanced, and before the tents were raised a rain set in which increased to a prodigious tempest of rain and wind. The men had not over half of their tents up, and none trenched, so that a wet cold night was in store for the whole of us. The rain prevented fire being made, and we had no wood; hence cold and supperless. About 8:30 p.m. J. Lawrence Meem (adjutant of the 11th Va.) and C. V. Cosby (color sergeant) and I went to Mrs. Bailey's to ask a supper.[8] The little branch at the foot of the lawn just did not swim our horses. She received us most kindly and got us a good supper.

Yesterday, the 10th, at 2 o'clock a courier brought an order for the brigade to turn out an hour earlier than usual (at 3 p.m.) in their best clothes and largest numbers, as the drill would be witnessed by visitors of distinction. General Beauregard was on the ground attended by Sir James Furgusson [veteran British officer and military observer], who is said to have approved of the exhibition in terms equivalent to this: 'It was quite creditable, considering all the circumstances!' What we get for our pains! As appears by the annexed extract, the Potomac batteries below Occoquan have stopped the river. We have heard heavy firing in that direction yesterday and today, but no news. Captain Stevens [W. H., engineer officer on Beauregard's staff], speaking of the sinking of the *Resolute*, remarked it was doing pretty well for a *sham* battery. It was the decoy spoken of in

---

8 Meem and Cosby had been members of the Lynchburg Home Guard. Among the attractions at the hospitable Baileys' was a pretty daughter.

the annexed letter, which was no doubt written by one of [Wade] Hampton's Legion, who are there.

Oct. 14.   General Longstreet was published yesterday as a major general. We thereby have lost from the command of our brigade one of the best brigadiers in the army; no one yet assigned to command this brigade. On the 12th a false alarm sent us bright and early down the [Warrenton] turnpike towards Annandale. The whole brigade was out, including [Captain Thomas L.] Rosser's battery.

Yesterday I received the following extracts from the Lynchburg *Virginian* in pursuance of an intimation of a few days before by a letter from William M. Blackford, Esq. I accepted the call and shall see the thing out, although election is hardly probable. I am so little known in Albemarle, Nelson, Appomattox and Buckingham that whoever gets majorities in those counties will beat me. If Messrs. James P. Holcombe, Shelton F. Leake and William Cabell Rives all run they may divide the vote so much as to cause my being returned.[9]

Below is a very sensible article from the Richmond *Enquirer* on the cotton question, also official reports of the fight on the Greenbrier river. The papers this morning report great things of Captain George N. Hollins's iron-covered battery below New Orleans, that he sank the *Preble* and ran the other blockading ships aground. The official report will be seen hereafter.

---

[9] Kean is referring to his candidacy for a seat in the Confederate House of Representatives. William M. Blackford was the father of five sons in the Confederate service and former editor of the Lynchburg *Virginian*. James P. Holcombe was professor of law at the University of Virginia and later a Confederate spy. Leake and Rives were from Albemarle county, Rives a former United States Senator and diplomat and Leake, a United States Congressman.

Wrote to Mr. William M. Blackford, James O. Williams, Colonel [Thomas Jefferson] Randolph, William T. Yancey, and Tom Randolph about candidacy for Congress.[10]

The Yankees are said to be advancing this side of Falls Church in some force, and it is further said that Stuart intends to attack them this evening or tomorrow morning.

Oct. 15.   A little evening party at Mrs. Bailey's, 1st regiment band played on the lawn, and the girls and young men danced. We all got home after 11 o'clock. About 4 in the morning a signal of five rockets, sent up from General Beauregard's headquarters, set off our drums with the long roll, which was taken up all around. It is now 9 o'clock and nothing has come of it yet. A single gun, fired by the Washington Artillery of Louisiana about 8, was probably the signal that all was quiet.

Every indication points to our falling back behind Bull Run for, or perhaps before, the winter. I pity these people who will be over-run as soon as we leave here, by the Vandals. What I shall do about keeping warm this winter I cannot conceive. I am bitterly cold every morning by day break, even now when this weather is just becoming frosty. When the thermometer is at zero I shall perish outright.

About dark today (Oct. 15) we got orders to be ready to march bag and baggage, at 2 at night. Our tents were all struck and the wagons loaded by 1, but by a mistake, forgetfulness, or blundering on the part of somebody at general headquarters, our train under my charge was halted on the road one-half mile from Fairfax Church for five hours.

---

[10] Blackford, Williams, and Yancey were prominent civic leaders of Lynchburg. T. J. and Tom Randolph of Albemarle county were Kean's father-in-law and brother-in-law respectively.

Oct. 19. The whole army has fallen back to and about Centreville and Bull Run at Union Mills. Stuart's cavalry and two batteries are said to have gone up to Leesburg to cover the retreat of General [Nathan G.] Evans's brigade. (A mistake. Evans did not retreat. It was a reinforcement to Evans.) Fortifications are being thrown upon this, the southwest side of Little Rocky Run. We (our brigade) will man those near the village. The meaning of this general movement has not yet reached down to me.

Oct. 20. The army is encamped in order of battle, the 1st corps along the heights west of Little Rocky Run, from Centreville towards Union Mills; the 2nd corps (Smith's) from Centreville back along the turnpike to Cub Run at Suspension Bridge.

Oct. 26. On Monday the 22nd, the 11th went out to picket on the front just west of Fairfax Court House for four days. They held the two turnpikes at Germantown, and on each side connecting with details from [General Milledge L.] Bonham's brigade on one side, the right, and from what was [General Thomas J. 'Stonewall'] Jackson's on the left. On Thursday we had from Stuart's cavalry pickets beyond Fairfax Court House an alarm of the enemy's approach. All hands stood at arms for about two hours. It proved nothing. The scouting parties of the enemy, one of which was said to be a regiment on the Vienna road, went back. The army is enthusiastic at the great victory of General Evans at Leesburg on Monday. With about 2500 men (real numbers 1200–2000) he gave twelve regiments a sound thrashing.

Oct. 27. Sunday. It is said that General Evans fought at Leesburg in direct disobedience of orders, and by checking the enemy there has disconcerted a trap which Johnston and Beauregard had for them. Colonel [William Nelson] Pendleton told me last night that 15,000 of the enemy were said to have occupied Martinsburg; also that it was suspected they might come up the Rappahannock to Essex county and land a force to threaten Richmond.

The new army organization has appeared in the papers before it has been published to the army.

Went to see a new rocket stand for shooting iron rockets, which are on the rifle principle, dispensing with the stick. The rocket is sheet iron with a shell in front, egg shaped. Part of the gases are vented through a hole directly in the rear about one-fourth the area of the cross section; the residue, through small holes drilled obliquely through the iron end. Think the stand will be overset by the impact of the gases in the brass ring at the hinder end of the stand.

Oct. 29.   Friends who were at Leesburg on the 20th say that Evans is not entitled to any credit whatever for the action there; that he was drunk; that he had timely notice of the crossing of the Yankees in the night, turned in his bed, took another drink and said he did not believe it—didn't believe any man who did not have a musket in his hands; that 4000 more of the enemy crossed, were caught by the rise of the river, disorganized by the defeat of the others, and were huddled about Edward's Ferry four miles from him, scattered about getting fence rails, barn doors, etc. to make a raft to get back, and might [have been] easily disarmed and captured. He fell back without even making a reconnaissance. Colonel Micah Jenkins (5th South Carolina) begged to be permitted to attack them but he would not allow it. ([Kean's later comment made in the margin of his diary:] All this is a specimen of what may be heard in camp

among soldiers of the kind that compose the portion of army
with which I am acquainted. Often there was much truth in what
was said, and shrewd criticism of officers. Sometimes the tale
was founded wholly in mistake.) [11]

McClellan must be waiting to hear from his big fleet, which
sailed from Hampton Roads on Thursday last, before doing anything hereabout. The rocket stand was tried yesterday. The
inventor, Captain Duffy [George, expert mechanic and train-
man from Alexandria, Virginia], says it acted well. The frag-
ments are lying about the ordnance yard. It was blown to atoms
by a rocket bursting in it; he says that the rocket was too old
and defective and that it is a success. I could improve on his
contrivance a good deal I think. I am considering the propriety
of withdrawing my name from the people as a candidate for
Congress. Mr. Rives having withdrawn, my chances are I suspect diminished; and the inadequacy of the time for notice of
the fact, through the district and the army, makes it probable
that both the others, who have been longer out and are can-
vassing, have too great an advantage for my friends to overcome.

Oct. 31.   Yesterday evening the Virginia regiments were
assembled around the redoubt in the forks of the road (except
such as were on picket) to receive from Governor [John]
Letcher the state flags. The scene was vastly less imposing than
it ought to have been. The drill after it was over was better.
The troops being crowded in one dense mass as close as they
could stand made simply a great amassed crowd. There were no
salutes fired, no display of lines or columns in order of battle,

---

[11] At the battle of Leesburg, or Ball's Bluff, Evans defeated a Federal
force attached to General Charles P. Stone's command. Colonel E. D.
Baker, Lincoln's personal friend, was killed. Stone, a Democrat and tolerant
of slavery, from this point on was a marked man, and eventually he was
relieved of his command and imprisoned.

'no nothing,' excepting that certain inebriated [men] fired, and several officers made asses of themselves in character.

The following lines we have been altering and copying amongst us for some two months. With some defects, they combine many beauties.

VIRGINIA CHIVALRY
Dr. Ticknor [12]

The Knightliest of the Knightly race
Who since the days of old,
Have kept the lamp of chivalry
Alight in hearts of gold

The Kindliest of the Kindly band
Who rarely hated ease
Who rode with Smith around the land
And Raleigh round the Seas

Who climbed the blue Virginian hills
Amid embattled foes,
And planted there in valleys fair
The lily and the rose

Whose fragrance lives in many lands
Whose beauty stars the earth
And lights the hearths of many homes
With loveliness and worth

We thought they slept—the sons who kept
The graves of noble sires
And slumbered while the darkness crept
Around their vigil fires

But still the Golden Horseshoe Knights
Their Old Dominion keep
Their foes have found enchanted ground
But not a Knight asleep.

[12] Francis Orray Ticknor, poet and physician of Columbus, Georgia, is best remembered for his 'Little Giffen of Tennessee,' a poem about the death of a Tennessee drummer boy observed by Ticknor while supervising Confederate hospital activities in Columbus. The poem here printed is derived from Ticknor's 'Virginians of the Valley.'

Nov. 2.   Went over the battlefields of the 18th infantry yesterday with Mr. Granbery [John C., Methodist bishop from
Lynchburg serving as chaplain] and made a pretty accurate
sketch of the topography which I sent to my wife in a letter.
Last night began the most violent eastern storm of wind and
rain I ever saw, which is still raging (at 2:30 p.m.). Many tents
have been prostrated and the inmates drenched. Have been wet
myself for ten hours. Heaven grant this blow may fight our
battles with the vast fleet of the enemy which sailed last week,
and scatter and overwhelm it as the Spanish Armada was
destroyed!

Nov. 8.   On the 6th, the 11th sent on picket, Colonel Funsten
in command. I did not go, being detained by the duties of quartermaster. Election day. The returns reach us very slowly; my
vote in Lynchburg is very gratifying, 534 to Holcombe's 157
and Leake's 14. I begin to think I stand some chance for election.

Jackson's brigade follows him today to the [Shenandoah] Valley. The enemy are said to be in eighteen miles of Winchester,
force not known. ([In margin, written later:] When General
Jackson was ordered to the Valley, Colonel Garland, an old
pupil at the Virginia Military Institute, went over to his quarters to bid him goodbye, and asked, 'General, what force do you
take with you?' General Jackson replied 'None, except my staff.'
Garland told me this on his return to our camp.)

Holcombe elected. Albemarle, Buckingham and Fluvanna
counties did my business. In the last eleven days nothing of interest has transpired on this line except a sack of [Captain Will T.]
Martin's Mississippi cavalry on a foraging party of the enemy
down at Doolan's [near Falls Church], capturing a captain, 2
lieutenants and 30 men, 6 wagons loaded with corn, and 28
horses. But elsewhere events have been thick.

1. The enemy's fleet have taken the forts at Port Royal, and they now have possession of Beaufort and Port Royal Island [South Carolina], with a splendid roadstead and a district containing 30,000 slaves and $5,000,000 worth of sea island cotton.

2. At Belmont, Missouri, Generals [Leonidas] Polk and [Gideon J.] Pillow with about 4000, after a bloody and desperate, as well as wavering contest, defeated some 8000 under General [John A.] McClernand and ran them seven miles to their gun boats.[13]

3. Old Scott [General Winfield Scott] has 'retired,' and McClellan is made actual as well as virtual lieutenant general of the Yankees.

4. [James M.] Mason and [John] Slidell [Confederate diplomats] have been seized on the high seas by [Captain Charles] Wilkes, who in the *San Jacinto* proceeded and overhauled the British mail steamer in mid-ocean and took them off. This may be an event of great significance; England is bound to complain. Lincoln may disavow the act, make abject apologies and hold the prisoners; or, if England desires a quarrel it is provided; or, as Colonel Funsten suggested, [Secretary of State William A.] Seward, convinced that he cannot conquer a union, may desire to provoke a foreign war as a good pretext for making a general peace.

5. The Unionists of East Tennessee made an insurrection about November 10, and by concert burned several bridges on the East Tennessee & Virginia railroad and the Knoxville & Chattanooga railroad. This, stimulated no doubt by Andrew Johnson, [William G. 'Parson'] Brownlow, [Thomas A. R.] Nelson,

---

[13] Brigadier General U. S. Grant was in command of Union forces in this, his first Civil War battle. The number of troops engaged was more nearly 3000 on each side.

[Horace] Maynard *et al.*, once seemed to have been formed on the expectation of an advance by [General William Tecumseh] Sherman from Kentucky. It was coincident with the attack at Port Royal, the advance at Belmont, and a rumored advance on the Potomac lines.

Nov. 19.   It is said the enemy are massing troops down the [Potomac] river from Alexandria on both sides—on this side toward Occoquan and in Maryland opposite Evansport. An attempt on our batteries at the latter point is said to be anticipated by our generals, and General [Richard S.] Ewell expressed the opinion that the position is weak. It is reported that 20,000 of the enemy were moved down in that direction today. General Ewell took command of the 4th brigade November 8. [General Richard] Dick Taylor's Louisiana brigade was attached to Longstreet's division about the same time.

Conjecture. That McClellan will make a vigorous demonstration here to keep this army in position, make a push on Evansport to open the Potomac, and if successful, march on Fredericksburg. The regiments have been chiefly employed for the past ten days in making field works. The 11th has executed the best work on the line—a double sap on the right of the Braddock road from the little bottom near the road to the west of the hill. The 17th did from the bottom to the road, and the 7th from the Braddock road to the redoubt on the turnpike. The generals are reported on every hand to be in daily expectation of battle here. It seems that the Yankees are under a military and political necessity to fight.

For the last five or six days the weather has been very frosty and windy. On Friday, November 15, the mountains were white with snow. Many tents are destroyed constantly by the high winds, and they are getting very cold quarters at night. The men built themselves chimneys and flues. Fuel is a heavy business. It takes an average of four wagons to supply this regiment, and wood is daily getting further off.

Dec. 8. Sunday.   Nothing of general interest on all this line. Dullness reigns supreme. The picket duty has been changed. Five companies go now for two days, instead of a regiment; A, B, C, D and E went out this morning. The weather for the last three days has been very mild, and today is disagreeably warm. I hear William Blackford is under arrest for having fire at his picket station.

All the generals express the belief that McClellan will advance, is now advancing, and that he will endeavor to open the navigation of the Potomac by shelling out and taking the batteries at Evansport, impelled by a military as well as a political necessity. I sent to Captain Alexander of the ordnance, a few days ago, a little model I had made of a frame to support earthen casemates. (E. P. Alexander of Georgia, a prominent railroad man after the war.)[14] He told me it was the best he had ever seen, that he had carried it to General Johnston, but the latter was interrupted before he had an opportunity to examine it. Alexander said such a protection would have made the Port Royal affair a different sort of thing and should by all means be used at Evansport.

Dec. 21.   Yesterday morning at 3 o'clock this regiment went to General Stuart's headquarters, reporting there at 6 a. m. There they were met by the 10th Alabama (1st regiment) and the 6th South Carolina, which with [Captain A. S.] Cutts's battery

---

[14] Alexander was also chief signal officer of Beauregard's army, and at First Manassas he spelled out the first message on a battlefield with 'talking flags,' warning the Confederates of a Federal attack on their left.

[Sumter, Georgia, Flying Artillery] and 150 cavalry, constituted a force intended to be pushed towards the Potomac in the
direction of Dranesville to protect a train of forage wagons with
which it was designed to sweep the country of forage in that
direction. Near Dranesville they came on the skirmishers of the
enemy, and Companies D and A were deployed from this regiment in front. A got lost and did not see the enemy; B was then
deployed and they, using D, drove the enemy's line beautifully.
As the road approached Dranesville through thick wood, the
regiments had to deploy into line of battle the best way they
could in the thicket, and the artillery occupied the road in the
woods. The enemy were on clear ground just above the crest of
a hill which protected their line very well. With two or three
hundred yards of clear scope in front of them, they soon brought
up artillery which was well posted, and soon silenced our battery, killing the horses, exploding a caisson and killing four men.
The musketry is said to have been very sharp.

The fight lasted about one and one-half to two hours when
our force was drawn off, beginning with the left. Stuart was so
afraid some of the artillery would be left as a trophy of his
defeat that he forgot to inform Garland that he had ordered the
other regiments to fall back, and the 11th stood its ground on
the field half an hour after the fight was over. They did not get
in musket range, behaved with excellent coolness, and retired in
perfect order, leaving 3 men dead, 3 mortally wounded (one
since died) and 15 wounded. The whole loss said to be 35 to 40
killed on the field and 150 wounded. All the dead were left to
the enemy. Our boys heard the enemy's officers ordering them
to charge and urging them forward after the firing ceased, but
they did not succeed in getting them to come. If they came upon
our ground it was long after we had left it. No trophies except
the dead were left. Their force was 6,000 to 8,000; ours a little

short of 2,000. Stuart's comb is cut; the Army of the Potomac had its first check. If these useless forays he is so fond of getting up and which Johnston shows him such partiality in authorizing, are made less frequent by this partial disaster, it may be the means of preventing something worse hereafter.

Colonel Funsten went home yesterday morning on a 30-days furlough, so was not in the fight. It is pretty certain that the enemy had information that this expedition was going out. Country people (women), down to the port, are ascertained to have known it the day before it started. Captain Jamieson [of the Rough and Ready Rifles of Fauquier County, or Company I of the 11th Virginia] and Lieutenant Horton [James C., of the Home Guard] were both wounded in the thigh.

Jan. 28, 1862.　On December 23 I got leave of absence for 20 days, beginning on the 24th. Stayed at Manassas with old Mr. E. Snead (father of J. W. B. Snead of Company G) and on Christmas eve got to Edgehill at 1 a.m. Found a two day old soldier[15] for the Southern Confederacy there. Mother and child doing well. Returned to camp on Sunday January 12. In the interval the regiment had built most of their huts and some were living in them.

General Ewell has been made major general. Beauregard has been for some days expecting orders to Columbus, Kentucky. He and his entire staff are ready to go (at a moment's warning?).

Gustavus W. Smith is next in command under Johnston. For now nearly a fortnight there has been but two days in which the sun has shown. Rain, hail, snow, sleet, mist have succeeded each

---

15 Robert Garlick Hill, Jr., Kean's fourth child and third son. Edgehill in Albemarle county near Charlottesville was the home of Kean's father-in-law, Thomas Jefferson Randolph.

other in dreary round—pitchy dark nights, dismal days, the whole earth one mud hole, the road horrible, wagons and teams rapidly going to wrack and ruin.

On Friday last I received the commission of quartermaster which Colonel Garland wrote for in November. It came just when I wanted it to be slow, for I am now wishing to be elected a lieutenant in Company G in the vacancy occasioned by John Meem's appointment on E. Kirby Smith's staff as aide. My commission is to take pay and rank from December 14. By not accepting I will lose $200 already due on it, and if elected lieutenant get $80 in place of $140 per month. But the more congenial duties of the line will compensate for all the other advantages of quartermaster duty which I cordially dislike, besides it being a complete shelfing of a man.

Per contra, where will the officers of volunteers be when the volunteers muster out of service if they do so! *Sauve qui peut* will be the cry with the members who rush to Richmond for places. God help the country.

The legislature has wasted two months in wretched squabbles over the senatorship while a powerful and actful enemy has been drawing his lines closer and closer around us on every side; has won a victory in Somerset, Kentucky,[16] over a general supposed to have been drunk on the battlefield. The men are disinclined to re-enlist until they see what the legislature will do. The weather perhaps alone keeps McClellan from advancing on us here, or at least at Evansport. John Meem returned from General Beauregard's headquarters last night and said that Captain Alexander, chief of ordnance, in reply to the inquiry whether

---

[16] This is the battle of Logan's Cross Roads, or Mill Springs (Jan. 19, 1862), in which the Confederates commanded by Major General George B. Crittenden were defeated by General George H. Thomas. Accused of being drunk, Crittenden was reduced to the rank of colonel.

he was going to Kentucky with General Beauregard, said he wished he was; he might not be here at the crash; and expressed the opinion that we would be beaten here. I heard another old United States army man express that opinion on July 17, the night before the fight at Blackburn's Ford and three days before the Battle of Manassas. This was Chief Quartermaster Dr. M. W. L. Cabell. This worthy has been ordered to Arkansas with General [Earl] Van Dorn. Nothing certain is even yet known of the [General Ambrose E.] Burnside expedition [to Roanoke Island, N. C.], its destination or fate, in the recent storms. There are rumors that it has suffered heavy losses, being composed largely of old vessels, bought up for the temporary purpose of transporting this expedition.

There seems to me to be a more general feeling of despondency prevailing at this time than ever before since the war began. Nor is it the fruit of the late disaster; it existed before that. I suppose the vast preparation of the enemy, the obstinacy with which they persist in the purpose of subjugating, their success in raising enormous sums of money for the war, and the seeming willingness to go to any length of taxation, has produced a general disappointment of the hopes founded on the late bankrupt condition of their treasury. Many too are disappointed at the stiffness with which McClellan has withstood all outside pressure, and gone on with his plans and preparations developing the vast system of attacks by which he proposes to outflank the entire Confederacy. Some are disappointed that the Mason-Slidell affair was so disastrously managed by Seward and that England seems no nearer our ally than last summer. But the most just cause of alarm of all is the apathy of the people, their anxious desire to avoid military service, and the apparent cowardice of the legislature, which seems afraid to do anything worthy of the occasion. There seems a probability that the men from the

Southern states will go home when their term is out, and not return. The naval expeditions are probably designed to have, and will have, this effect.

Virginia must fight her own battles, defend as best she may her own soil and in so doing defend the whole eastern part of the Confederacy. If the rulers will only bring out her sons and the general government give them back the army she has furnished, they will do it. Noble, grand old State! I love her dearer in her days of tribulation than in her prosperity, and while life is spared me I will fight in her behalf so long as a foe is on her soil, or raises a hand against her; nor if, like Poland it is written in the Book of Fate that she shall 'close her bright eyes, and curb her high career,' will I cease to strive for her deliverance while Life lasts. Never! Never! Never! will I be a subject to the power which rules in Washington, unless as a captive bound in chains. ([Kean's later insert:] January 1866—Alas! Alas!)

Feb. 12.   One disaster after another has befallen our army. The defeat of Crittenden at Somerset, Kentucky; the taking of Fort Henry on the Tennessee river on February 6, opening that stream to the gun boats of the enemy, so that they have proceeded to Florence, Alabama, and destroyed the public stores there, burned the railroad bridges, and thus cut off communication between Bowling Green and Columbus [Ky.]; the capture of Roanoke Island by Burnside's fleet on the 8th with all the artillery and the entire force there, about 2200 men; the closing in of the enemy around Price in Missouri—all these things look dark enough. Then our condition is feebler today than it has been since last July. Relatively we have waned ever since August, that is, since the policy of a *defensive* was distinctly adopted. We have lain still and slumbered and our people have sunk into a false security, while the enemy with prodigal expense and sleepless activity have raised, equipped and disciplined a gigantic host. When history shall record the events of the past six months, mankind will be amazed at the infatuation of our policy, which has made our own soil the seat of war and imposes on us the necessity of being successful *everywhere*—the inherent weakness of Defense. May God forgive us the presumption of the past and make us more humble, more earnest, more devoted, and self sacrificing.

Among our disasters may also be enumerated the recent evacuation of Romney [now in West Virginia] and its reoccupation by the enemy, thus giving them possession of one of the richest and most productive of our mountain valleys and undoing all the work of Jackson's toilsome and costly marches.[17]

Feb. 20. News from Tennessee indicates a great disaster of our arms at Fort Donelson on the Cumberland river. Reports are probably exaggerated. It is said not only the fort is taken but our entire force captured with Generals Pillow and [Simon Bolivar] Buckner, [but with General John B.] Floyd escaping with 100 men. The way is now open to Nashville; Columbus is cut off, and will of course be, probably has been, evacuated. Bowling Green has been evacuated; our western connections are doubtless cut; vast supplies, especially of pork, doubtless lost or destroyed. Dangers close us round on every side. The timid will begin to croak, the half-hearted to quail and suggest submission, the traitorous to agitate. Redoubled effort, nerve, decision, firm-

---

[17] The evacuation of Romney by Brigadier General W. W. Loring came on orders from Confederate Secretary of War Judah P. Benjamin and resulted in the resignation of 'Stonewall' Jackson although it was not accepted. Both Jackson and his superior, Joseph E. Johnston, resented the fact that orders had moved directly from the War Department to Loring and not through army headquarters.

ness are essential in all who love the Southern land, and Freedom. It is amazing to see with what trifling loss most of the conflicts of this war have been attended. The fighting has been child's play on both sides in comparison with the battles of modern, still more, ancient Europe. See [Sir William F. P.] Napier's *Peninsular War* and *Recollections of an Officer of Zouaves*. Our men surrender without an effort to cut their way when surrounded or outnumbered, and the enemy are rapidly acquiring the character of being better soldiers than ourselves.

I received in January a commission as assistant quartermaster with rank and pay of captain from December 14. I have not yet accepted it; the reasons are fully stated in my correspondence with my wife. My first impulse was to escape from the vexations and responsible duties of that office by getting a commission in the line, which I had hoped for at the hands of Company G. This I probably would get; the vacancy has not yet occurred. Meanwhile I have an intimation that General George Wythe Randolph [18] will offer me the position of A. A. G. of his brigade at Suffolk. I have yet had no intimation from official quarters of this. After having indicated a purpose to accept this to Colonel Funsten, he informed me that our present Brigadier R. S. Ewell had intimated to him the intention to invite me to his staff when he takes command of the 4th division to which he has been promoted. This he will probably not do now, having heard an intimation of General Randolph's intention before I did.

[*Feb.–Oct. 1862.*]   On Saturday, February 22, I received a letter from General G. W. Randolph inviting me to be his A. A. G. [and] urging me to report at once at Suffolk. I got leave

---

[18] Randolph was Kean's wife's uncle and later Confederate secretary of war.

detaching me for this purpose on Sunday the 23rd and set out Monday the 24th. Stayed at Manassas with Captain McPhail [John B., 56th Va. inf.] that night and to Richmond on the 25th. Stayed there the 26th and 27th to make arrangements, and reached Suffolk on the 28th. We stayed there only a month, General Randolph being appointed Secretary of War on March 22 and taking charge of that Department on the 24th.

I was appointed Chief of the Bureau of War in April, vice A. T. Bledsoe, who was made assistant secretary of war, vice Robert Ould (Esqr.); and shortly afterwards, on the arrangement of the cartel for [prisoner] exchanges, Colonel Ould was made Confederate commissioner [of exchange].

[*Kean's insert, May 17, 1863:*]   In this interval, from February 1862 to October, I kept no record of events, which I now strongly regret, as there were many great events transacted, and some curious matters of inside history of which I had knowledge. I will some day endeavor to make notes of these latter.

2

INDICATIONS OF FAMINE THICKEN

PERRYVILLE TO CHANCELLORSVILLE

Oct. 19, 1862. Sunday.   Bragg is retreating in Kentucky. No official news of the battle of Perryville at the Department yet. Loring was relieved in western Virginia last week for not obeying orders to march towards Romney. Perhaps bad terms with Virginia authority had something to do with it. He is certainly a weak man.[1] The President considers this the darkest and most dangerous period we have yet had; at least he so said to a committee of Congress. (Wed. General Loring had never received the orders in question.)

Nov. 15.   General Randolph resigned as secretary of war. The immediate occasion was this: He had written a letter of instructions to General [Theophilus H.] Holmes, commander in the

---

[1] After winning a half victory at Perryville, General Braxton Bragg abandoned Kentucky and retreated back into Tennessee. This battle has been called the Antietam of the western theater of war. Subsequent to the difference between Jackson and Loring over the evacuation of Romney, Loring was promoted to major general and assigned command of the army in southwest Virginia. In December 1862 he was sent to command the 1st corps of the Army of Mississippi.

Trans-Mississippi, in addition to one already sent. The first had been submitted to the President; the supplemental one was not. It (the last) contained a clause authorizing General Holmes to cooperate with [General John C.] Pemberton [commander of the Mississippi department] and if need be to cross the Mississippi in order to do so effectually. A copy was sent to the President. These letters were dated Oct. 25 and 27. On [November 12] he received a note from the President saying that it was improper to have authorized Holmes to cross, very essential for each to keep in his own department, etc.—which note (a copy) General Randolph enclosed to General Holmes instructing him to regard it as part of his instructions. On the 13th [14th] the President wrote General Randolph a note, stating in effect that all communications to generals should be through the adjutant general's office, that he [the President] must be consulted as to all instructions as to appointments of *every commanding officer;* that this was what he had no authority to delegate; that he must be consulted also as to movements of all troops and stationing of officers. General Randolph replied inquiring whether this was to be taken literally, and on the reply, [Davis] modifying it *in some particulars,*[2] resigned peremptorily. ([Kean's later comment in the margin:] The President's second note explained that he meant by movements of troops and assignment of officers, the designation of departments and transfer of arms; that he had neither the power nor will, under the Constitution, to delegate the power of appointment; and that embarrassment would be avoided by conference at the earliest stage of appointment. This materially altered his position.)

---

[2] Italics are the editor's. Kean had originally written *little if at all,* but scratched it out and inserted this phrase.

Nov. 25. I believe this issue was intentionally made by the President and that it was induced to some extent by the Adjutant and Inspector General [Samuel Cooper]. The latter applied to me some days before through Colonel Withers [John, assistant adjutant general in Cooper's office] for a copy of the *last* letter to General Holmes. He has been complaining of the War Office in other respects. ([Kean's later insert in the margin:] I incline to think that this suspicion of mine did General Cooper injustice. The application for copies referred to was probably by direction of the President.) This was followed by the temporary assignment of General G. W. Smith as secretary of war ad interim, and this by an attempted reorganization of the War Office and the A. G.'s bureau—which led to great confusion. The reformers neither understood themselves nor each other as the records of the Department from the 20th to the 30th abundantly show.

My own belief is that Mr. Davis became jealous of the independent character of the Secretary; that this feeling was stimulated by others, especially General Cooper; and that the issue made was factitious. Real or pretended, the point was insuperable. No one can administer the War Office, or the Government, on the terms laid down by the President. Conferences as to every appointment for a population all in arms, as to every movement of troops and assignment of officers—in addition to endless talk which General Randolph had—is more than the day of 24 hours will contain. But the physical objection is the least. The President required his Secretary to incur the responsibility of office without discretion, and reduced him in very truth, as the people have long charged, to a mere clerk. General Randolph had not been treated by the President with proper confidence and consideration for sometime. When the western generals were here (in Richmond), sent for at his instance, they—Bragg and

Polk[3] had repeated conferences with the President to which he did not invite the Secretary of War ([Kean's later insert in margin:] The President issued orders, planning campaigns, as in East Tennessee, which he neither consulted the Secretary about nor apprised him of. He appointed general officers, sending their names directly to the A. G.'s office without consultation, the first information the Secretary received being that the commissions were brought to him to sign. For all these acts he was necessarily responsible to the country. Thus the President actually evicted him of his office, exercising it himself without General Randolph's knowledge of the fact till such acts were done. When Mr. Davis was [U.S.] secretary of war, he tendered his resignation because [President Franklin] Pierce was opposed to appointing his nominee to a colonelcy, and the President [Pierce] yielded.)

I am coming to Mr. Ruffin's [Major Frank G., assistant commissary in Northrop's office] opinion. He says he used to think Jefferson Davis a *mule*, but a *good mule*. He has come to think him a jackass.

On November 17 General G. W. Smith was assigned by the President as secretary of war ad interim, and on the 19th Hon. James A. Seddon was appointed. General Smith continued to execute the duties for a week before Mr. Seddon came to take charge of the office. In that time he cleared out the accumulation of papers, not by disposing of the business, but by sending them

---

[3] Following Bragg's retreat from Perryville, Kentucky (Oct. 8, 1862), President Davis summoned him to Richmond and extended the area of his command. Polk, next summoned to Richmond to give his side of the failure in Kentucky, bluntly placed the blame on Bragg. Although Bragg was a favorite of Davis, the President went ahead and promoted Polk to lieutenant general.

pell mell into the A. G.'s office whence they have nearly all been referred straight back again.

Nov. 30.   For nearly two weeks the armies have been facing each other at Fredericksburg with the Rappahannock river between them. The question of supplies is becoming more and more particular. The Commissary General of Subsistence [Colonel Lucius B. Northrop] reported some weeks ago that he could not supply the army unless allowed to purchase bacon from the enemy at Memphis, with cotton. The Quartermaster General [Colonel Abraham C. Myers] says he cannot get blankets except in that way. General Randolph was convinced before he left the office, and was in favor of such a trade exclusively in the hands of those bureaus. The President resisted it in toto. I am told by Judge [John A.] Campbell [assistant secretary of war] that in 1861 there were proposals from the contractors for the Federal army to supply ours, one-half for cotton, the other for Confederate bonds; and it was believed the proposal had the acquiescence of the United States authorities; but was rejected by ours, it seems to me most unwisely. The question is simply whether they suffer more for the comparatively small quantity of cotton, say 100,000 bales, or we for the indispensable articles of salt, meat, clothing, medicines. Besides it would have exerted a good influence to have had a few millions of our bonds in the hands of Northern capitalists.

The French consul, M. [Alfred] Paul, returned from a Washington tour two weeks ago, and was very anxious to take back a message to M. [Henri] Mercier [French minister in Washington] indicating willingness on our part to listen to terms of pacification. Two points were spoken of—slavery which he admitted was out of all question, and the tariff which was equally impracticable, since the North is sensible that our low tariff would ruin them, and we could not think of making it as high as theirs for the converse reason that they would profit at our expense.

Dec. 13.   Day before yesterday Burnside commenced crossing the Rappahannock at Fredericksburg. Banks's expedition was sailing down the coast. The latter is intended to strike at the southern communications of Richmond.[4] General Lee seems to have fallen back at Fredericksburg. The enemy have succeeded almost without resistance; [have] crossed their whole army over the river.

The President went on Wednesday to the South [Tennessee, Mississippi, and Alabama]. Private information from many sources represents the tone and temper of the people of the Mississippi Valley as very unsound. *They are submitting.* Whether he can reassure them is doubtful. The new Secretary [Seddon] staggers under his load. He is physically weak, seems to be a man of clear head, strong sense, and firm character but from long desuetude, wanting in readiness in dispatching business. Judge Campbell is invaluable; his capacity of labor infinite; his breadth of view great. His endorsements are so judicial, deciding questions rather than cases [that] they perplex the red tapists who complain that they do not decide *the case.*

Dec. 15.   On Saturday 13th in battle of Fredericksburg, enemy repulsed with heavy loss. General Lee occupies the range of hills from Marye's [Heights] around towards the mouth of the Massaponax. No fighting since.

---

4 General N. P. Banks was headed for New Orleans to relieve General Benjamin F. Butler, reinforce the Federal department of the Gulf, and help open the Mississippi above New Orleans in anticipation of what became the Vicksburg campaign.

Enemy in stronge force at Kinston [N. C.], whence Evans retreated on Saturday after a very gallant fight. General G. W. Smith is at Goldsboro [N. C.]. He telegraphed that the enemy are reported to be 30,000 strong. If so, Banks is there.

Dec. 22.　　But he [Banks] was not; nor was 30,000 either—a mere raid of some 8000 to 10,000. They [Federals] burned the bridge over the Neuse on the Wilmington railroad and tore up a little of the track.

The President has issued today a long proclamation outlawing Butler for hanging Mumford in April and maltreating Mrs. Phillips *Italia enormia Brutum fulmen*—too late either to scare an enemy or please a friend. This exhibition will produce only a smile of derision in Washington. Unlike the order as to [General John] Pope's officers, which could be executed because some of them were sure to be caught, there is no possibility of anybody hanging Butler, because Butler will take very good care not to be caught.[5]

---

[5] For pulling down the Federal flag in New Orleans shortly before the city's formal surrender to Admiral David Farragut, William B. Mumford, a local citizen, had been convicted of treason. When General Benjamin F. Butler took command he approved the verdict and had Mumford hanged. Mrs. Philip (Eugenia) Phillips, while residing in Washington, D. C., had been detained as a Confederate spy suspect with Mrs. Rose Greenhow in the latter's home. Influential politicians in Washington had arranged her deportation to New Orleans, where she was accused of jeering at the funeral cortege of a Federal soldier and of training her pretty daughters to spit on Federal officers. Butler ordered her sent to barren Ship Island where she was confined for two months.

General John Pope, Federal commander at the battle of Second Manassas, had announced a policy of pillage and severe treatment of noncombatants. In retaliation, Davis had ordered that Pope's officers when captured should be treated as ordinary criminals.

Dec. 22, 1862

Rumored today that Seward has tendered his resignation, in consequence of proceedings of a caucus of Black Republicans, Secretary of the Treasury Salmon P. Chase demanding change of cabinet—doubtful in toto;[6] also that McClellan has been summoned to Washington and is in consultation with Lincoln—more probable. Burnside's official jacket was whipped off at Fredericksburg. The Northern papers are lugubrious about the defeat and criticize the tactics of the battle very severely. They state the loss at 1400 killed and 8000 wounded. We captured some 1600. Total say 11,000. Our loss, *stated* by General Lee at 1800, will reach 3000.

There have accumulated on Mr. Seddon's table since he came in some 1500 papers, *all* touching appointments to officers. He does not look at them because on the terms on which impliedly he took office, he cannot act on them. They are for the President. *He* cannot examine them in less than a week if he did nothing else. Meanwhile the persons interested have just cause of complaint. Many of them are essential to the proper reorganization of the army, in filling vacancies. Such are the fruits of the position taken to get rid of General Randolph. I understand the President says he was taken by surprise in that transaction and that General Randolph's resignation was so tendered as to cut off all explanation. He [the President] had that opportunity, and *used it* to qualify his own position, and make it more plausible, without [saying] more. If he *wished* to have explanations made he should have said so; for General Randolph's note inquiring

---

[6] The rumor was a fact, but Lincoln, summoning a group of the disgruntled Republican Senators to meet with the cabinet (Seward not invited), put ambitious Chase on the spot. In front of his cabinet colleagues and the Senators, Chase meekly said that the cabinet was harmonious. Seward retained his secretaryship.

whether his (the President's) first note was to be taken literally was a plain warning of what the next step would be should the answer not be satisfactory.

Jan. 2, 1863.   Yesterday the new year opened auspiciously with a bright warm sun, and a telegram from Bragg announcing a ten hour's fight with Rosecrans near Murfreesboro [Tenn.]. Bragg attacked, drove the center and right, took 200 wagons, 31 pieces of artillery and 4000 prisoners. The enemy's left successfully resisted the attack. Bragg subsequently failed in an attack and fell back some 40 miles to Tullahoma.

Judge Campbell, who abounds in information of men and things about Washington, told me of a dinner at [Stephen A.] Douglas's at which he met Seward. During the dinner when wine was set on, a lady asked Seward for a toast. He arose, and with much ceremony intended to attract attention, gave (remarking that it was a sentiment in which *all* would unite): 'Away with all platforms, all parties, all previous committees, and whatever else shall stand in the way of a restoration of the Union!'

The Judge told me today of the history of the Indian Trust Fund bonds stolen by Bailey, as narrated by Judge Black. When Judge Black by the President's discretion informed Floyd of the matter, he replied, 'It is all a damned lie' (meaning Bailey's story about the necessity of protecting the acceptances). 'I didn't care a damn whether they were paid or not. He has $2000 and is living at the rate of $10,000 a year.' It was determined by [Buchanan's] cabinet that Floyd should be dismissed, and the President had directed Black to write the letter. Floyd had an interview with Buchanan, and the direction was countermanded. Floyd had bullied old Buck out of it. Previously and down to this time, Floyd had been a strong Union man in the cabinet, opposing Howell Cobb and Jacob Thompson who were secessionists.[7]

I inquired what was the explanation of Buchanan's statement in his recent letter in his reply to [General Winfield] Scott, that the transfer of arms in 1860 to the Southern arsenals was his own (the President's) act. Judge Campbell explained that at the time of the John Brown Raid (Nov. 1859) he (Judge Campbell) was requested to attend the meeting of the Cabinet (the Attorney General being absent) for legal advice. He thus became familiar with the thing from its inception. Among John Brown's papers taken by [Robert E.] Lee and sent to Floyd was a letter to Colonel Craig from Brown, asking when and in what quantities the arms of the United States were stored; and Craig's reply showing minutely where they all were, and that comparatively *none* were in the Southern States—all were in the North. Floyd swore that should not be the case any longer, and the transfers were at once begun and continued all through the year 1860, Floyd being then a Union man. After the Indian bond business, the matter of the Pittsburgh guns was probably designedly in the extent of secession. The other transfers were not, and were merely a just, proper, and necessary distribution of the common arms approved by Buchanan, and this is what the latter meant.[8]

---

[7] John B. Floyd (Va.) was Buchanan's secretary of war; Jeremiah S. Black (Pa.), attorney general; Howell Cobb (Ga.), treasury; Jacob Thompson (Miss.), interior. Bailey, a clerk in interior, had stolen the bonds. Floyd was thought to have profited from the theft but the evidence does not indicate that he received a cent; he was more careless than dishonest.

[8] The South not having received her quota of arms for the state militias, Floyd ordered a shipment from Pittsburgh to the South, December 20, 1860. Hostility in the North was so strong that Buchanan revoked the order. Modern scholarship has cleared Floyd of the charge that he was filling the Southern arsenals in anticipation of secession and war.

Feb. 15. General G. W. Smith tendered his resignation on October 21 [1862] because he had been overlooked in making the seven lieutenant generals, four of whom had been under his command in Virginia, viz. Longstreet, Jackson, E. K. Smith and Holmes. He withdrew it at General Randolph's instance, but a few days ago tendered it again and insists now on action being taken on it. The President made a pretty sharp endorsement on the paper of Smith reciting the causes which led to his resigning.[9]

There is a rumor this morning from [General Roger A.] Pryor that the enemy are transferring their army from the Rappahannock to Newport News and Suffolk. Bragg is said to have lost the confidence of his command completely and Johnston has been called from Pemberton's department to take command in Tennessee in person.[10]

The Arkansas [congressional] delegation, except [Senator Robert W.] Johnson, insist on a change of commanders out there. [Representative Augustus H.] Garland wrote the President a very strong letter on the subject a few days ago, declaring the want of confidence in Generals [Thomas C.] Hindman and Holmes.

Beauregard has got into another controversy with the Government, betrayed into it again doubtless by Jordan [Thomas, Beauregard's chief of staff]. He had arrested [Major H. C.] Guerin,

---

[9] Smith's second resignation followed Confederate defeats within his command at Kinston and Goldsboro, N. C. Davis made it clear that if the only alternative to resignation was promotion to lieutenant general, then the resignation would be accepted. Smith was next assigned as aide to Beauregard who was also at odds with Davis.

[10] Bragg's officers were so critical of him that Johnston, in command of the entire western theater, was sent to investigate but advised against Bragg's removal. Johnston himself did not want the command of Bragg's army.

the post commissary at Charleston [S. C.], for corresponding directly with the bureau. Colonel Northrop got the President to order the release of Guerin. Beauregard sends a very angry and impertinent letter on the subject, which cannot fail to widen the old breach. Colonel Northrop backs up his subordinate and throws the weight of his influence against Beauregard in this matter. The fact is the General is wrong. He insists that all the officers of the staff departments in his military department shall correspond with their chief of bureau through his headquarters. This pretension is not supported by the army regulations, or by common sense. Colonel Northrop has been in a quarrel also with General Lee for sometime. This grew chiefly out of the treatment Captain Crenshaw received when he went in January to General Lee's Headquarters to concert means of getting the wheat of the upper Rappahannock counties to the railroad. Crenshaw's report on this subject, if accurate, was that he was not properly received or treated.[11]

A letter of General Lee's to the Secretary received February 14 shows that he has adopted what the Commissary General desired but that there is no concert of action. The field officers are beginning to complain heavily of their troops' having insufficient food. It is a noteworthy fact that the health of the army is nearly perfect—doubly better than ever before, since the ration was reduced.

The enemy's numbers in the Northern Neck are supposed by General Lee to be very great, at least double his. His are about 50,000 of all arms; theirs, say 150,000. The confidence of our army of their ability to beat them is very high.

Hunter at Hilton Head [S. C.] has announced by a letter to

---

11 W. I. and Joseph R. Crenshaw of the Richmond Flouring Mills were supplying the War Department with flour.

General Mercer [Hugh W., Confederate commander at Savannah] that he will not only hold officers to answer for their officers turned over under the President's proclamation to the states, but that he will seize and hold and deal in like manner with *all citizens* of South Carolina, Georgia, and Florida, he can lay his hands on. This amounts very nearly to the black flag and will lead to it. The futility of the President's proclamation I pointed out the day it was published. The state courts cannot try and punish prisoners of war and no court could permit an indictment to be found on the facts which could be produced. It is not mere *brutum fulmen.* The tendency is to deprive us of the benefit of Lincoln's Emancipation Proclamation by renewing the ferocity of the war and exasperating those who were being driven over to sympathy with us against the Abolitionists. Desertions from the enemy are said to be very numerous especially on the Mississippi.[12]

Feb. 17.   The most alarming feature of our condition by far is the failure of means of subsistence. The Commissary General gets more and more gloomy and complains heavily of department commanders robbing the little stores he is able to scrape together for the future.

The Yankee Army of the Potomac seems to be breaking up. Ours is slowly following. [Generals George E.] Pickett and [John B.] Hood's divisions are on their way to Richmond to

---

[12] As a part of the proclamation directed at Benjamin F. Butler, Davis declared that no commissioned officer should be paroled until Butler met his 'due punishment.' Moreover, captured Negro slaves in arms against the South would be turned over to their respective states for punishment. General David Hunter, a favorite of the Radical Republicans, was perhaps the most hated man in the South next to Butler.

drift south, supplying the place of troops moved to Charleston and Wilmington.

March 7.   Flour in the city is $30; the butchers are closing their stalls—meat at $1.25 per pound. Farmers are making preparations for only so much corn as will suffice for their own use. They resent the Secretary's schedule prices which are often 50% below the market or neighborhood price. The instant impressment of flour, corn, and meat, as soon as they are brought to any of the inland towns to be put in market, is causing universal withholding of surplus—secreting and non-production. The army will be starved, and famine will ensue in the cities unless the Secretary changes his policy and buys in the market for the best price. The Government will have to outbid the traders; else *neither* will get anything of the present scanty stock, and no future stock will be produced.

I had predicted this state of things when Mr. Seddon first adopted the present policy. General Randolph would not have pursued it, and would I think have been greatly more successful. From northwestern Virginia fat cattle have been offered to General [Samuel] Jones in the Valley for tobacco, and the trade has been authorized by the Secretary of War.

Dangerous complications are threatened, growing out of this policy [of impressment]. The merchants of this city whose flour was impressed on the 5th inst. have determined to obtain injunctions from the *state* courts. If the judges grant them, the Government has to elect between a total abandonment of the policy at once and under all circumstances, or the disregard of the authority of the process of the courts—a dilemma sufficiently embarrassing from the Secretary's point of view.

There is a manifest uneasiness in the public mind different from anything I have noticed heretofore. The recent legislation by the United States Congress—their conscription bill, bank bill, and *habeas corpus* bill—passing as they did without opposition except from members representing the slave states (except in the Senate, [James Walter] Wall of New Jersey) indicates a truculent determination to crush us at every hazard, which has not been without effect here. The recent demonstrations in the Northwest appear to have been quieted by the dispersion of the Frankfort convention, at the bidding of a column of cavalry.[13] The abject facility with which that people has laid its liberties at the feet of a buffoon [Lincoln] is the most extraordinary spectacle the world has ever produced. Men like Peisistratus, Sulla, Caesar, Cromwell, Napoleon, have assumed absolute power because they had the ability to wield it. It has been reserved for Yankees, first and alone in History, to confer absolute power voluntarily and by law in manifest violation of their Constitution, upon a man whose administration they confess to have been marked only with failure and blunders—whose character they despise and caricature, and whose manners are the laughing stock of all mankind.

Bragg's report of the battle of Murfreesboro has been received but not yet published. It bears very hardly on [General John C.] Breckinridge attributing the failure on the right to his blundering. It is quite manifest that there are deep quarrels in that army, and that Bragg is cordially hated by a large number of his officers.

A piece of tyranny, such as should never have occurred in Virginia, has recently been developed—as exercised by A. T. Caperton (now Virginia Senator) as provost marshal of Monroe

---

[13] A convention of the State Rights party in Kentucky had been broken up at Frankfort by the fixed bayonets of Federal infantry led by Colonel E. A. Gilbert.

county [now West Virginia] in not only arresting and sending to Richmond (where he died in custody) a man named William Ballard, but actually confiscating and selling at auction his personal objects. The beginning of the mischief sprang from the unutterably silly order or proclamation by General Henry Heth in May 1862, requiring all of conscript age in that county to report in his camp or be deemed deserters after a certain day, and shot on sight. Ballard's crime was 'harboring' his son and nephew who fled from the tyranny of Heth. General Randolph reversed Heth's order as soon as it became known to him, but this and other mischief resulted. (See the curious history of this thing in the papers recently enclosed to the Department by General Samuel Jones, who was called on for a report in the case of Ballard.)

I recently made a rough calculation to compare the present currency with a sound one in the matter of my household expenses. The result is that my salary of $3000 will go about as far as $700 would in 1860. Then, flour $28 against $7, tea $15 or $1.25, bacon $1.25 or 20¢, fresh meats $1.00 or 8 to 10¢, wood $15 per cord or $3 to $4, coal $1.00 per bushel or 20¢, and other things in proportion. A coat costs $120, calico $2.50, unbleached cotton $1.00, bleached $2.00 to $2.50, linen $7, etc.

March 9.   General Bragg was relieved this morning by telegram to General Johnston, directing the latter to take command of the army in Tennessee. The order is to report in Richmond for conference.[14] The truth probably is that the dissatisfaction

---

14 Again Bragg retained his command, and he did not report to Richmond. At Tullahoma, Tennessee, at Bragg's headquarters, Johnston found Mrs. Bragg ill and used her illness as an excuse for not relieving him. Davis acquiesced and by the time she recovered, Johnston himself was sick.

of his subordinates has impaired confidence in his capacity for usefulness. There seems reason to doubt his capacity to deal with large affairs.

March 15. General Pemberton reports the enemy's dredge-boats half way through the canal at Vicksburg. He fears they will get through. They have gunboats and transports into the Talla-hatchie by Yazoo pass. This line of attack General Loring has to meet near Greenwood, just below the junction of the Tallahatchie and Yallabusha. The Yankees are also ditching through by way of Lake Providence into the Tensas, whence they may make their way down into Red river.[15]

I hear that the House of Representatives are at a deadlock (in secret session) on the revenue bill, the cotton states going for apportionment according to representative; the others for ad valorem taxes. Some are said to be uneasy about it, the split being supposed to be very deep and wide. This is a fresh instance of the *smallness* of this Congress. Certainly no deliberative body ever

---

[15] Reference is made here to three unsuccessful attempts of Grant's forces to get in the rear of Vicksburg. (1) Sherman's corps was constructing a canal through the peninsula formed by a bend of the Mississippi in front of Vicksburg. Floods and Confederate batteries forced the abandonment of this project. (2) L. F. Ross's division at Helena, Arkansas, crossed the Mississippi, and through Yazoo Pass entered the headwaters of the Yazoo river in order to descend upon the Confederate right at Vicksburg. The Coldwater, the Tallahatchie, and the Yallabusha flow southward along the Mississippi and converge above Vicksburg to form the Yazoo. North of Vicksburg where the Coldwater and the Yallabusha converge, Loring constructed Fort Pemberton and stopped the Federal advance. (3) Meanwhile, James B. McPherson's corps, operating north of Vicksburg and west of the Mississippi, were trying to turn the Confederate left by means of a passage from Lake Providence through two bayous to the Red river, to the Mississippi, and up the Mississippi to Vicksburg—a flanking route of about 400 miles which was abandoned.

met in this state with less of statesmanship in it. They have feared to deal with the question of finance till, leaving it untouched for a *whole year*, the evil is past any remedy they can now apply. My own belief is that before July 1, unless we have great success and a prospect of peace, treasury notes will *cease to have general circulation.* I do not know that I lost anything in not being elected to Congress. The share in the responsibilities of this body is more than I care to do.[16]

The President has yielded at last on the subject of getting meat from the enemy for cotton (See letter to General E. K. Smith of about the 15th inst.). Too late to do much good. When Butler was in New Orleans and Memphis was acceptable for such trade, something worthwhile might have been done in it. Now it is very doubtful whether it can amount to much.

March 21.   Snow nine inches deep by careful measurement fell the night of the 19th and on yesterday. Last night another one and one-half inches was added, the clouds not having broken away since it began. This will postpone military operations in Virginia for at least three weeks.

There are indications that Arkansas is in a state of great irritation and disloyalty. Their delegation in Congress show many indications of dissatisfaction with the Government and complain of neglect of the Trans-Mississippi.

March 22.   A warm sun today is thawing the snow with wonderful rapidity. In 24 hours the nine to ten inch [snow] had been reduced to three (at 1 o'clock) and by night four-fifths of

---

16 Egged on by public demand, Congress the following April (1863) passed its first comprehensive tax bill, which, limited by the Constitution, was so confusing and complicated that it was never very successful.

the fall will be gone. High water and deep mud will be the consequences which will postpone military operations until in April.

General Johnston has written another of his brief unsatisfactory, almost captious letters, protesting against Bragg's removal, against any detachment of troops to meet the movement of the enemy towards Corinth, and reiterating the assertion of his former letter that the Army of Tennessee is too weak by 20,000 men to meet Rosecrans with confidence. He never treats the Government with confidence, hardly with respect. A quarrel in which, as usual, Pillow is instrumental, is brewing in the disregard of a general order by Bragg and Johnston in establishing a bureau of conscription under Pillow, unconnected with the Department and overriding that under General Rains. The latter has submitted a very strong letter on the subject showing the evils and confusion which result from this state of things.[17] The Commissary Department have entered into some sort of arrangement to get salt meat from Nassau for cotton.

General Order No. 31, March 19, is a manifest yielding on the part of the Department on the subject of indiscriminate impressments.

March 28.   Major Ruffin informed me last night at his home [that] *the late* impressment policy was adopted in point to cause Congress to legislate on the subject, and so far is not a success; that Mr. Seddon did not use it as they wish *in terrorum* by publishing a general order that impressments *would be* made—which he thought would cause holders to sell.

Pemberton [in Mississippi], who sometime ago asked leave to

---

[17] Brigadier General Gabriel James Rains was director of the bureau of conscription for the entire Confederacy. Operating independently under Bragg and Johnston, Pillow and his agents naturally came into conflict with Rains and his agents, culminating with Pillow's resignation.

be allowed to shift for himself in providing food, has starved his army and cries out lustily to the Commissary General for aid. I heard a day or two ago that the army at Vicksburg had not tasted meat for nine days. (William Price of Mobile said so.) A queer contract has been made: a fellow has been found who *contracts to be captured* with a cargo of supplies. (Major Ruffin told me this.)

April 1.   Indications of famine thicken. Judge Dargan writes that the contest between Pemberton and Buckner has brought things in Mobile to such a pass that a few nights ago placards, 'Bread or Peace' were stuck up at the street corners.[18] The Commissary General is in low spirits and looks haggard. General Lee writes anxious letters to which he endorses that he has long foretold the scarcity, that transportation is the present difficulty. The railroads are worn out. Wadley[19] says he can do nothing unless he is allowed to have mechanics. General Lee has fought all winter *against* this, and now the evil, which much might have been done to remedy during the winter months, is nearly irremediable, and the campaign about to begin. The truth is the Secretary has been too deferential to the army officers. They have thwarted whatever of policy then was in supply by their clamor against details, and Mr. Seddon has 'recommended, to favorable consideration of' where he might and should have given

18 Edward W. Dargan of Mobile, former chief justice of Alabama and House member of the 1st Confederate Congress, referred to a dispute between Pemberton and Buckner over the transfer of troops to Buckner's command in East Tennessee at Knoxville.

19 William Morrill Wadley, New Hampshire-born former blacksmith, had come to the South as a young man and made a reputation as a builder and operator of railroads. In December 1862 he was given supervision and control of government rail transportation for the entire Confederacy.

instant orders. The Department has been energetic only in the very doubtful policy of impressments. The Secretary (like General Randolph) has been overruled upon the question of supply from the enemy, by the cabinet: Watts, Reagan, Benjamin and the President have overruled the officers responsible to the country.[20] This division (if accurate) makes it virtually the President's individual responsibility.

Now a little gossip. The President seems recently to be in a very bad humor. He has returned a number of papers referred to him by the Assistant Secretary with sharp petulant endorsements addressed to the Secretary. Relations between the Secretary and President are I think cordial and confidential, and hence when the latter feels fretful he frets at Judge Campbell. A pretty savage case of a 'tut to the whale' occurred today in the official execution of Major D. H. Wood, transportation quartermaster [responsible for management of military traffic through Richmond]. The Quartermaster General [Colonel Abraham C. Myers] wrote Major Wood a note saying he had heard that he (Wood) was bringing sugar from the south on private account and asked a report. Wood replied that he had bought fifty barrels in Augusta and delivered them to the Southern Express Co. to transport. Myers referred the matter expressing the opinion that an officer in the transportation service had no right to press on the narrow and inadequate resources of the railroads with private speculation. The Secretary referred to the President, and he *dismissed* him. Now Wood has no control whatever over the railroads, still less over the Express Company. His business was issuing coupon transportation tickets for carrying persons and

---

[20] Thomas H. Watts of Alabama was attorney general; John H. Reagan of Texas, postmaster general; and Judah P. Benjamin of Louisiana, secretary of state.

keeping the account between the railroads and the Government
for transportation done. There was no moral wrong in his act,
no direct injury to the country. There has been great clamor,
however, against other quartermasters, and as soon as a man is
found who owns his transaction, believing it harmless, his head
goes off—a sacrifice to public wrath and official purity. Wood is
spoken against in other connections and may be an offender. In
this matter he seems to me to have had very harsh justice.

April 7.   From 2 to 5:30 p.m. the iron clad fleet [under
Admiral Samuel F. Du Pont] attacked Forts Sumter and Moultrie
[S. C.]. At 5:30 they retired, two appearing to be damaged.

April 8.   At 9 o'clock one iron clad sunk—the *Keokuk*.

April 9.   No disposition on part of fleet to renew the attack
though they remain within the bar. The enemy have abandoned
the siege of Vicksburg. The Tallahatchie expedition is a failure
and also the Duck river and Rolling Fork expedition.[21]

April 12.   No attack at Charleston yet. Indications are that
approaches will be made landward by Bull's bay and Stono river.
Beauregard wants reinforcements. Longstreet yesterday proposed to cross the Blackwater at or near Franklin [Va.]. He
proposed to drive the enemy in so as to recover the productive
country on the Chowan river [N. C.] and perhaps expel the
enemy from Suffolk. He is very anxious that the *Richmond* shall

---

[21] The real siege of Vicksburg from the rear by Grant had not yet
begun. The Duck river and Rolling Fork expedition was an unsuccessful
attempt by Grant to land a force on the banks of the Yazoo below Fort
Pemberton, by ascending Steele's Bayou and moving eastward to the Yazoo
through cross streams or bayous including Rolling Fork.

go down the [James] river and co-operate by preventing re-inforcements from coming over from Newport News. The engineers oppose making an opening in the obstructions to allow the *Richmond* to pass. The matter is referred to the President but progresses very slowly. Nothing is likely to come of it, I think. Longstreet expects to be down below for a fortnight, and thinks that will give sufficient time for the 'naval' co-operation.[22]

General Johnston has written another sharp captious letter, quarreling because [General Humphrey] Marshall had been authorized to advance into Kentucky without the matter having been referred to him. In substance he is clearly right; yet the letter in manner and spirit is of a piece with his jejune and ice tempered character of correspondence. He treats the Department as an enemy with whom he holds no communication which he can avoid and against which he only complains and finds fault. He is a *very little man*, has achieved nothing, full of himself, [and] above all other things, eaten up with morbid jealousy of Lee and of all his superiors in position, rank, or glory. I apprehend the gravest disasters from his command in the western department. Time will show.

April 16.   Judge Campbell not yet confirmed [as assistant secretary of war]. Opposed vehemently as I hear by [Senator William L.] Yancey. I had heard, by [Senator C. C.] Clay also, but today I am told that Clay will vote for him. ([In margin:]) Judge C. was confirmed on Saturday the 18th. I have not heard the vote.)

---

[22] Built in the Richmond navy yard, the *Richmond* was the first fully armored ship put afloat on the James river. The engineer bureau refused to remove obstructions in the river in order to let the ship pass, on the ground that she was defective and not worth the risk of exposing the city to enemy ships by breaking the obstructions.

There is a matter assuming a troublesome shape, viz., the restrictions put by military officers in Texas on the cotton trade with Mexico. The resolution of Oldham [William S., Texas Senator] that the orders from the Department countermanding them be communicated to the Senate, was less from any difficulty he would have in seeing the Secretary of War, than because the Secretary had written declining to furnish him a copy of the letter to General Holmes and assigning a reason for it. He has now written declining to look at the order on the records of the Department. The Secretary will probably decline furnishing the correspondence called for, or advise the President to do so. The truth is the Secretary thinks the orders beneficial though they are diametrically controverse to law. The cotton trade has got into the hands of speculators who are selling it for specie in large quantities, and threaten to absorb not only all the transportation of the country, but to exhaust this means of supplying the army of the Trans-Mississippi country—[a supply] which has been greatly relied on through Brownsville and Matamoras. If Mr. Oldham carries his point, he not only throws this door wide open, but puts Generals Holmes, [John Bankhead] Magruder, and H. P. Bee in a position to be run down by those who now are kept under by the restrictions. The Department, thanks to the wisdom of the Assistant Secretary, is right on the record. See the letter to Holmes drawn by him.

April 19. Sunday.   Today a year ago we got official news of the surrender of New Orleans. (A mistake of just a week. New Orleans capitulated on the 25th.) This morning we had the intelligence that five of the enemy's gun boats passed the batteries at Vicksburg on Friday the 17th, also three store ships with supplies; also reported that the *Queen of the West* has been recaptured.[23] Congress proposes to adjourn in a few days until next

December. Members are leaving now. The tax bill has not been finally passed, nor the appropriation bill for the first half of the next fiscal year. These will be crowded through at the shank of the session.

On Saturday the 11th, General Longstreet crossed [the Black-water] in force at Franklin and after taking possession of the roads to Norfolk invested Suffolk except as to the Nansemond river. The object of his expedition is to forage for his army in the unexhausted and productive country between the James and the [Albemarle] Sound, especially on the Chowan. In this he reports himself very successful. He was anxious the *Richmond* should go down and co-operate with him by holding the mouth of the Nansemond. If this were done he would probably capture the force in Suffolk. As it is he thinks he could take the place, but at a heavy loss [of] probably 3000 men, but does not think it worth the cost. The *Richmond* is such a stupid failure, drawing fourteen feet of water [so] that she cannot get up and down the river even if the obstructions were opened to let her pass; and as she can only steam about three knots, being worthless as a ram and her machinery very defective, it is deemed unsafe for her to go down.

April 21.   The engineer bureau has today reported against opening the obstructions for the reasons above mentioned.

The new impressment law bids fair to ruin the country and

---

²³ McClernand's corps of Grant's army was making its way to New Carthage below Vicksburg, and across the Mississippi. Rear Admiral David D. Porter's river fleet then passed the Vicksburg batteries to join the forces down the river. The *Queen of the West,* a ram converted from a river steamboat by the Federals, had been captured on the Red river by the Confederates. In March 1863 she was destroyed by the Federal river squadron.

the cause. Appraisers in Powhatan the other day put the 'just compensation' for hay at $20 per cart and in Hanover wheat at $6.00 per bushel. The farmers are the worst extortioners we have to deal with and at this rate will wholly break up supply of the army. This incident caused an important amendment to be passed giving an appeal to the appraisers.

General Lee writes, enclosing a general order of [General Robert C.] Schenck [commanding in Maryland] requiring all our men caught with Yankee clothes or accoutrements to be tried as spies and declaring that the fact that they have on Yankee uniform or accoutrements shall be sufficient evidence for court martial or military commissions, that they are spies. This is part of a system—Porter's 'notice' about firing on transports, Rosecrans' orders as to partisan troops, etc.—all indicate a settled purpose to outlaw us as belligerents, disowning the application of the laws of civilized war to us.[24] I hope the President will do something more than make a *brutum fulmen* order. He should collect all these things together and give notice that the rule will be *two lives* for one; that any credible report of the outrage designed to be suppressed will be acted on; that the war shall not be conducted on any terms intermediate between the fullest recognition of civilized rules, both as to soldiers and citizens, and a war without quarter. A little *real* shooting of prisoners will I think do good, prevent suffering and save life.

April 30. Yesterday General Lee telegraphed that [General Joseph] Hooker under cover of a dense fog had thrown bridges over the Rappahannock at Deep Run and was crossing. Later in

---

[24] Porter's notice warned that all persons firing from the river banks on unarmed vessels would be treated as 'highwaymen and assassins,' and no quarter would be shown. Rosecrans ordered all Confederate soldiers wearing Federal uniforms to be treated as spies.

the day he telegraphed that the enemy were crossing at Kelly's Ford, turning his left. Today he informs the President that Stuart attacked north of the Rapidan and took prisoners from three army corps, v, xi, and xii, Generals [George Gordon] Meade, [Henry Warner] Slocum and [Oliver O.] Howard commanding. He closed by saying, 'If Longstreet's corps were here I would feel safe.'

There seems great uneasiness on account of the failure of the supply of meat arranged two weeks ago to be brought from the stores at Atlanta. The railroads have made default for a whole week, when they were under engagements to deliver 120,000 daily. The Secretary, Judge Campbell thinks, was in bad spirits today. General Pemberton announces an attack on Grand Gulf by six gun boats; cannonade lasted six hours, three killed, fifteen wounded; transports loaded with troops in sight but no attempt to land; expects a renewal of attack today. Western matters are in a sad way. Banks is reported to have occupied Alexandria [La.]. They have Louisiana pretty well under their heel, and Red river, so that the Trans-Mississippi country is wholly cut off.

Orders were sent yesterday to Longstreet and D. H. Hill to forward all the troops they can possibly spare at once to the army of Northern Virginia. This will doubtless bring Longstreet back behind the Blackwater with his whole force and put a stop to his foraging on the Chowan.

May 3. Sunday.   General Longstreet cannot move any portion of his force without endangering his [forage] train on the Chowan and the Sound. The last reports from the Rappahannock are that General Lee has marched towards Chancellorsville leaving Generals [Lafayette] McLaws and Early in the lines at Fredericksburg. Mr. Benjamin circulated a story last night of a telegram from Colonel R. H. Chilton [Lee's chief of staff] to

Jackson that the Yankees were fighting badly, that we had driven them five miles and held the fords by which they had crossed the river. Mr. Seddon does not believe this. Mr. Benjamin is the most unreliable of news reporters, believes anything, and is as sanguine as he is credulous. The enemy were repulsed by General Bowen at Grand Gulf after a bloody fight.[25]

The Secretary has great difficulty in saving the railroad bill from the President's veto. He is said to have vetoed quite a number of the less important acts. Mr. Seddon has drafted the railroad bill himself. [26]

Governor [Zebulon B.] Vance has written a querulous letter complaining that North Carolina is neglected, that her rivers are undefended, and that Wilmington would be safe with one-fifth the armament expended to make Charleston impregnable, etc. General [William Dorsey] Pender has sent up a letter [from Lee's army] disclosing a most disgraceful spirit of desertion among the North Carolina troops, which he attributed to a dictum of Judge [Richmond] Pearson [North Carolina chief justice] that the conscript law is unconstitutional. They think when they get there they will be safe from re-arrest and desert in squads, with their arms.

May 6. Wednesday.   Sunday afternoon couriers from Hanover announced appearance of enemy's cavalry[27] in Louisa on the [Virginia] Central railroad and in Hanover, advancing towards

---

[25] Actually, John S. Bowen had been outflanked by Grant's forces which had crossed to the east bank of the Mississippi below Grand Gulf. Bowen was forced to evacuate Grand Gulf, and Vicksburg would soon be enveloped from the rear.

[26] A bill placing the railroads under strict government control under the supervision of the quartermaster general.

the city [Richmond] on the Mountain Road. The excitement was great. There were no troops here except General [Henry A.] Wise's brigade down at Chapins [Chaffin] Bluff. The people went to church as usual knowing as yet nothing of the stir. Then the clergy requested the men to meet the mayor of the city at the Town Hall. A crowd assembled there and little appeared likely to be done till General Randolph was requested to organize a force of citizens. He succeeded in getting up eight companies of infantry and one company and a section of artillery, who were armed and stationed by 11 o'clock.

The Secretary was in his office all night. I stayed there till 4 a.m. Monday. The confusion about Department headquarters was excessive. General Elzey [Arnold, in command of the department of Richmond] told Barton [Major William S. Barton, assistant adjutant general under Cooper] he wished he was dead; that the Yankee cavalry would certainly take the city. On Monday the enemy were reported on the Bordentown pike five miles from the city, approaching. The bells were rung, the citizens again turned out and were marched to the batteries. General Randolph visited the batteries and found no powder in any of them. Powder was sent for and when late in the evening it was obtained, there were no friction tubes. If the enemy had come not a gun could have been fired on Monday! Some 1500 under Colonel [Hasbrouck] Davis of the 8th [12th] Illinois passed by Ashland pulling up the track and cutting the wire. Connection was lost on both lines, to Gordonsville and Guiney's at 6 p.m. Sunday evening.

Meanwhile on the Rappahannock General Lee has been struggling with a vastly superior force. He sent Jackson to flank the

---

[27] This is General George Stoneman's cavalry raid designed by Hooker to get in the rear of Lee's army and destroy supplies and communications.

enemy on the left. He gained the rear and drove them on Saturday from the Wilderness to Chancellorsville. The battle was renewed on Sunday and they were driven from their position at Chancellorsville, falling back to U. S. Ford where Hooker fortified. Meanwhile at Fredericksburg the enemy got possession of Marye's Hill. On Monday General Lee sent Early reinforcements, and the Yankees were driven beyond the river. In these battles General Lee's force did not exceed 65,000 to 70,000. Estimates founded on the letter of Dr. [Jonathan] Letterman, medical director of Hooker's army, make his force about 160,000. One of the Northern papers states it as 159,000 and some odd hundred. Dr. Letterman states the sick at 8000 making a clear total effective strength of 150,000, or at least 2 to 1. We have no exact statements yet of casualties on either side.

Prisoners and wounded have come in in large numbers. Dr. [William A.] Carrington, medical director here, told me last night he had received 8000 of our wounded, and that Dr. [Lafayette] Guild, medical director of General Lee's army, had informed him there were 2000 yet to come.

General [Robert Emmet] Rodes has stormed the President's penchant for West Point imbeciles in preference to volunteer men of capacity. General Lee insisted on his being made a major general on the spot for his great gallantry and conduct [at Chancellorsville].

The country is deeply anxious for Jackson's fate. He was fired on at night by one of his own brigades in front of which he was galloping with all his staff, after a reconnaissance beyond his lines, between them and the enemy who were not over 200 yards distant. One ball broke his left arm, shattering it from the wrist to the elbow making amputation necessary and the ball went through his right hand. Several of his staff were killed. The fire drew out the enemy, who advanced and at one time actually passed him lying on the ground, but they were repelled and he brought off. He is at Guiney's in a critical condition.

May 10.   On the 6th instant General Earl Van Dorn was shot and killed at [Spring Hill] in Tennessee by a Dr. Peters. The cause is said to be the seduction of Dr. Peters's wife by Van Dorn who has the reputation of being a horrible rake. The divisions of Hood and Pickett are moving towards the Rappahannock.

The New York *World* of the 7th concedes a defeat [at Chancellorsville]. It says, 'our general has been outgeneraled, and our army has been outfought.' The same paper says that [General Samuel P.] Heintzelman with 30,000 men has been sent from Washington to reinforce Hooker. It contains a debate in Parliament on the Adams Matamoras passport, the seizure of British vessels, the *Alabama*, the *Alexandra*, etc. Mr. Roebuck made a very fiery speech against the United States, which was cheered at every sentence. Palmerston and Russell were very mild upon every point except the passport which they utterly condemned, and said Seward must disavow—which he will of course disavow. It is rumored from Paris that the Emperor will take in high dudgeon the excuse of Adams that the passport was to secure the transmission of arms to the Mexicans to be used against the French.[28]

---

[28] Charles Francis Adams, U. S. minister in London, had issued certificates which would enable certain individuals in England to have insured by Lloyd's of London specified cargoes destined to Benito Juarez of Mexico. The certificates would ensure safe passage through the Federal blockade into Matamoras, Mexico. Since Matamoras was a neutral port, the British accused Adams of presuming to license British trade. The *Alabama* and *Alexandria* were famous Confederate commerce raiders. John A. Roebuck was a vociferous spokesman for Southern independence in the House of Commons; Viscount Palmerston, prime minister; Lord John Russell, minister of foreign affairs.

Stoneman's expedition into Louisa appears to have been barren of results. Except very partial injury [to] the Central railroad, and horse stealing, it has done nothing. Compared with what he might have done with such a force, it is ridiculous. He had 4 divisions, 28 regiments and 20 forces of artillery. He was on the Central railroad on Saturday. By following it to Beaver Dam, crossing the North Anna there and passing by Ball Church over to Milford, he would have come upon the vital communications of General Lee, might have destroyed the Mattaponi bridges, got the transportation and ammunition trains and some seven or eight railroad trains at Guiney's, and ruined General Lee's army, which he might then have compelled to fall back rapidly and disastrously on Richmond. By destroying all the county bridges he might have made this inevitable retreat a rout and converted the victory, over which all now rejoice, into a terrible disaster. I do not know what force General Lee had about Guiney's, but I presume it was not very great nor sufficient to resist 8000 cavalry with artillery, if well handled.

The details of the [Chancellorsville] fight come in slowly. It is reported by General R. H. Chilton that the enemy lost six generals killed—[Alpheus] S. Williams, Berry, Howard, [Daniel E.] Sickles, and two others whose names I do not remember. This is probably not true.[29] A few days ago General [Nathan Bedford] Forrest captured 1600 of the enemy's cavalry [Colonel Abel D. Streights' raid] who were making for Rome, Georgia, after a five days' chase. Forrest had between 500 and 600 men.

A very important communication from General Magruder on the cotton trade with Mexico, acknowledging receipt of orders for rescinding their regulations, etc. came on the 7th. He says if the control of this is taken away, he must have $100,000 in

---

[29] Generals Hiram S. Berry and P. W. Whipple were killed.

specie every 60 days or evacuate the country on the Rio Grande. The treasury notes are not current there or in Mexico, and the force there cannot be maintained, except by controlling the cotton or making disbursements in specie. The letter is in excellent spirit and very sensible. It is an important document in the history of the war in the Trans-Mississippi.

May 11.   Lieutenant General T. J. Jackson died at Guiney's, Caroline county, yesterday afternoon, of *pneumonia* (together with his wounds) caused by the application of wet cloths to his body, which he caused to be done.

No man in the nation would be so universally regretted, for he was almost without enemies. In November 1861 when he was detached from the Stonewall Brigade and sent to command in the Valley, the general opinion of his friends and old pupils was that a separate command might cause the loss of the laurels he had won as a subordinate. On that occasion Colonel [Angus W.] McDonald, who was very much alarmed about the advance of the enemy in the Valley and had come over to beg General Johnston to send troops, asked Jackson what force he would carry. Jackson replied calmly, 'No physical force, Colonel, except my Staff.' There was no presumption in this. General Garland, who was present and told me of this the day it occurred, said it was said with the most perfect quietness. The hero knew the country, the people, and himself. The last was not known to any other in the country. The splendor of his subsequent military career, down to the very hour when he received his fatal injury, made the above anecdote highly characteristic.

No name in the states was so electrical to troops as his, none so terrible to the enemy, so inspiriting to his own. He has left a name second to none these times have evoked. Quiet, reserved, taciturn, and regarded as executive in his manners, he had never given promise of greatness. He served in the Mexican war as a subaltern of artillery and was brevetted for gallantry. But no emergency in which he has been placed found him unready or unequal to meet it and he has perished at that stage of his career in which it might be fair to suppose him equal to any untried test. He was a devoted Christian, austere in life and doctrine, yet not deficient in charity, as such are apt to be. The purity of his principles, the manifest devotion with which he carried on war, as a matter of *Duty* merely, his ardent State Patriotism, his carelessness of what men said of him, his intense purpose, make up a character of antique beauty, simple and severe.

3

OH, FOR A MAN AT THE HELM!

VICKSBURG AND GETTYSBURG

May 17, 1863.   J. E. Johnston got to Jackson, Mississippi, on the 13th and telegraphed that he was *too late*. Communication with Pemberton had been cut off. On the 15th Grant occupied the capital of Mississippi [Jackson]. Johnston had retired toward Canton. His 'strategy' seems of the mind Yankee correspondents ascribe to all their commanders—retreat and sacrifice is always 'strategical.' I have little confidence in the General who came near losing Richmond and who thinks so much of himself. Grant is now in a position where a man of daring energy like the lamented 'Stonewall' Jackson would destroy him. He is far inland from his base. Johnston has a force of not less than 15,000 collecting in his front. Pemberton is on his flank with 30,000. His force is not known, but it is not believed to exceed 50,000.[1] Beauregard

---

[1] Grant on April 30 crossed to the east bank of the Mississippi with some 25,000 men and struck out to clear the area of Confederates immediately east of Vicksburg. Johnston, sent to take command, arrived at Jackson to find the Federals between him and Pemberton's army. Repeated attempts to unite Johnston's and Pemberton's armies failed. In a series of engagements Grant defeated each force separately, drove Pemberton back to Vicksburg, and invested this fortress on May 19. By the time the siege ended Grant's forces had increased to 75,000.

and the Charlestonians are in a furious passion at the detachments which have been sent from the department to Pemberton. These amount to about 20,000 men. Hunter is still active on the island below Charleston, and Beauregard is apprehensive [that Hunter] will make another effort before the season of fever drives him off or suspends his operations.

Vallandigham has (as is reported) been sentenced by court martial to two years imprisonment at Tortugas for his speech to his constituents at Mt. Vernon in which he denounced the conduct of the War.[2]

This, only, was wanting to demonstrate how utterly that people have lost every pretense of civil liberty. Against this very thing, Magna Charta was re-enacted 30 times and the Petition of Right was leveled, which the framers of the United States Constitution incorporated bodily into that instrument. Shades of John and Samuel Adams! To what have your descendants come? Yankees though you were, you at least had some Roman virtues and loved the essentials of Liberty without licentiousness. How amazing has been the rapidity with which free society and universal suffrage have utterly debauched that race. No hand will be lifted to stay this fatal stroke. *Fear* will make slaves even of the unwilling. They have sought to trample our rights into the dust and have filled the continent with outrage and blood, and behold their 'violent doing they have plucked down on their own fate.'

---

2 Clement L. Vallandigham, leader of the Ohio Peace Democrats, or Copperheads, had been condemned to imprisonment by a military commission for declaring disloyal opinions. Lincoln, instead of imprisoning him, banished him to the Confederacy, whence after a brief stay he made his way to Canada. Dry Tortugas was a barren isle in the Carribean, west of the southern end of Florida.

May 20.   News comes slowly from Mississippi. Grant left Jackson on the 15th and marched to attack Pemberton at Edward's Depot near the Big Black. Johnston telegraphed that after a fight of 9 hours Pemberton fell back behind the Big Black. This means that Pemberton was whipped and we have nothing taken.

Judge Campbell has prepared a very able letter to Governor Vance reviewing the disorganizing opinion of Chief Justice Pearson, in the *habeas corpus* case of [*in re* Bryan]. The local judiciary are doing what they can to defeat the conscription and encourage desertion in many places, especially Georgia, North Carolina and Tennessee. These states have the largest infusion of dissatisfaction, the former source of Unionism, a great deal of faction, and the two latter any quantity of Reconstructionism.[3] I mistrust that these feelings have a good deal to do with these decisions by which they thwart and obstruct the execution of the conscription.

May 24.   Still no news from Mississippi. Plenty of Sunday rumors as usual. The complexion today is *couleur de rose*, that Grant has been defeated in an attack on the defenses of Vicksburg with great loss. There is a possibility that the newspaper account of Pemberton's defeat west of the Big Black [Edward's Depot] was a sugar speculation story.

Commissions as lieutenant general have been signed for General *R. S. Ewell* to take rank from May 23 and *A. P. Hill* to take rank from May 24. So Lee is to have these corps I suppose, or else Ewell remains in command here and south of James river to the Cape Fear, as Longstreet has lately commanded. Henry Heth

---

[3] A term used during the war to indicate a peace movement, a means of reentering the Union.

has been promoted to major general. General Ewell [who lost a leg from a wound received at Groveton in August 1862] is still unable to take the field, not having sufficiently learned the use of his false leg. His general health is also feeble.

May 26. Tuesday. Vallandigham has been sent into our lines in Tennessee. I understand it was a cabinet question a day or two ago whether this should be allowed. I have not heard the result, but the Yankees have thrust him over the lines before (as it would seem) any conclusion was reached, at least if it was adverse. I think this is probably a fortunate event. If he lives quietly in exile among us and through counsel appeals next winter to the Supreme Court from [Judge Humphrey Howe] Leavitt's decision refusing a writ of *habeas corpus,* he cannot fail to create a powerful reaction against his arbitrary oppressors. Nothing like this has occurred in two centuries in any country save Russia and France during the madness of the Reign of Terror. There appears to be great stir among the opposition newspapers in the United States. Lincoln has been guilty as usual of a great blunder. Had he quashed the whole proceeding with a contemptuous phrase like Seward's on surrendering Mason and Slidell, he would have been politic. As it is, it looks as if he feared to take his victim to Fort Warren [Boston, Mass.] through the great cities. Brooks at the meeting in New York offered to lead an army to put down such tyranny. His turn will possibly be next.[4]

Still nothing official from Mississippi. Press telegrams from Jackson represent that repeated assaults on the lines about

---

[4] In the Vallandigham case, the U. S. Supreme Court in 1864 declared that its jurisdiction did not extend to the proceedings of a military commission. James Brooks, newspaper editor and soon to be U. S. Congressman from New York, was a hard-hitting Peace Democrat.

Vicksburg have been repulsed with great slaughter, the casualties on our side being small. We hear nothing whatever of Johnston, whether he has effected a junction with Pemberton, or where he is and what doing. The crisis there is of the greatest moment. The loss of Vicksburg and the Mississippi river are allowed to be events which would wound us very deeply in a political as well as a military point of view.

Colonel [Briscoe G.] Baldwin, chief of ordnance, Army of Northern Virginia, reports 26,000 small arms taken from the battlefields above Fredericksburg and counted, besides small lots still coming in and such as regiments keep in their wagons as a reserve: 13 cannon, 9 caissons, 4 battery wagons, 2 forges, etc. He deducts 10,000 as our own muskets. Majors [Charles S.] Venable and [T. M. R.] Talcott [aides on General Lee's staff] think this excessive, since many of our men exchange on the fields, and the custom with our wounded is to bring their arms off with them.

May 29. There is a strong suspicion that Pemberton's men behaved badly at Edward's Depot [Baker's Creek or Champion's Hill]. General [Carter Littlepage] Stevenson's division broke, and officers of different grades were heard to say that they were betrayed. It has long been well known that that army and the people of the country, whether for or without cause, disputed Pemberton both in point of fidelity and capacity—many as to the latter, some as to the former. There is no reason to doubt his fidelity whatever. The objection turns on his Northern birth. If Vicksburg is lost it will ruin Pemberton at any rate. If it is lost without a desperate battle to save it by Johnston, he will be ruined too, and justly. The stake is worthy a desperate throw. Such venture is inconsistent with Johnston's character as I understand it, and I greatly fear he will not make it.

Judge E. S. Dargan wrote a most despondent letter to the Secretary of War today, which I placed in his hands without its going the usual round of the office. He urged the absolute necessity of purchasing the intervention of France and England by any conditions they demanded, and declared he would accept gradual emancipation as one of them—this as the only means of escape from extermination. Judge Campbell told me that Judge Dargan was not always responsible, being given to intemperance (which I had never suspected), and that ill health and liquor made him crazy.

I got a good jest on Colonel Thomas H. Watts, Confederate attorney general, who is a candidate for governor of Alabama. Some days ago he endorsed and sent to the War Office a letter from a friend in Alabama, asking his influence with the Secretary of War as to some matter. At the end of the letter the writer informed Colonel Watts that his chances were fair but would be improved if Colonel Garrott was out of the way, as he (Colonel Garrott) would take off a number in northwestern Alabama who would otherwise support Watts. About a week afterwards, there was received from the executive office a letter from the Attorney General to the President, urging in the warmest and most enthusiastic terms of admiration and commendation, the appointment of Colonel Garrott as brigadier general to succeed Tracy, killed at Grand Gulf, on which the President has endorsed an order for the appointment. I told the Attorney General of this last night much to his amusement, and he did not deny the impeachment.[5]

---

[5] Under Brigadier General Edward Dow Tracy, Colonel Isham W. Garrott participated in the engagement against Grant's forces at Port Gibson near Grand Gulf. Here Tracy was killed. Four days before Grant invested Vicksburg, Garrott was promoted to Tracy's place and himself died during the ensuing siege.

The memorandum here inserted of the correspondence in respect to stripping prisoners shows that the devilish malignity of the Federal 'instructions' prepared by Lieber and published as General Order No. 100, is bearing fruit. I have some extracts from the demoniac document, of which as mild a man as the Assistant Secretary said it was 'a lie enacted into a law'; and he said that in its infernal suggestiveness of what it did not enjoin it was equal to King John's dealing with Hubert, for the death of Arthur. Act III, Scene III.[6]

May 31. Sunday.   This is the anniversary of the battle of *Seven Pines* which occurred on Saturday May 31, 1862.

Governor Pettus [John J., of Miss.] has telegraphed from Jackson that the enemy's dead strew the fields before Vicksburg and that he does not doubt that Pemberton will hold the city.

Now that Grant has a convenient base at Snyder's [or Haynes's] Bluff on the Yazoo (where the range of heights strikes that river), his communications are as perfect as he could wish them, and are quite unassailable to us. He is just between Vicksburg and the upper Big Black, from which direction alone the relieving army could approach. The want of water alone can remove him, unless before the supplies of provisions and

---

[6] The memorandum is an abstract of correspondence between General Henry W. Halleck and Bragg, Halleck demanding to know whether it was true that Bragg's men had stripped certain Federal prisoners of their overcoats and blankets. Bragg replied that it was true and was a retaliatory measure against similar action within Rosecrans's command. Francis Lieber, noted German-American jurist and former professor at the University of South Carolina, at Lincoln's request had sought to codify the laws of land warfare in the famous General Order No. 100, entitled *Instructions for the Government of the Armies of the United States in the Field* (1863).

ammunition in Vicksburg give out, an army sufficient to dislodge him can be collected by Johnston. I do not see whence this can be drawn, and look for Vicksburg to capitulate some time during the month of June, for Grant can be indefinitely reinforced by water and can get unlimited supplies. If Bragg's force moves in that direction, Rosecrans if not strong enough to fight him, can either penetrate into Georgia or East Tennessee, or if required can reach Grant earlier than Bragg can. Under these circumstances, it seems to me that it is necessary for Bragg to fight a battle without delay and by beating Rosecrans, compel him to retain all his force in Tennessee while a part of the army can be thrown into Mississippi. ([In margin:] Note whether these speculations are borne out by events, May 31, 1863.)

Vallandigham is to be notified, if he holds himself as a loyal citizen of the United States and a loyal enemy of ours, that he cannot be allowed to reside among us, but will be furnished with a safe conductment beyond our lines by way of one of the seaports, say Wilmington. The best place for him is supposed to be Canada, where he can hold unrestricted intercourse with his friends.

June 7. Sunday.   The indications from the Northern accounts are that the enemy suffered very severe punishment in their assault on Vicksburg and are quite sick of storming. The armies on the Rappahannock are in motion, up towards Culpeper where a battle will probably be fought soon. [The fateful Gettysburg campaign is about to begin.]

From every side evidences of the barbarity, savageness, and insolent assumption of the Yankee government in the policy on which they have resolved in the conduct of the war, thicken.

We have in the last few days:

1. the deportation from New Orleans to Pascagoula of 5000 persons, men, women and children [mostly women] who would not swear allegiance to a hostile government.

2. the execution by Burnside of two recruiting officers captured by him in Kentucky. See General Bragg's letter enclosing Burnside's to him, received on the 4th inst. Burnside declared if the hostages we selected for these men suffer he will put to death 10 for each, and so on, *and if he has no captives, will retaliate on the sympathizers and relatives of Southern men who may be in his lines.*

3. the orders of Brigadier General Roberts, at *Weston*, Lewis county, Virginia, a number of *ladies*. See copy here inserted.[7]

4. Rosecrans's declaration (and Schencks's) that they will put to death men who wear any article of the enemy's uniform, or accoutrements. (See communication of General Bragg some days ago, copy three pages back, and Brigadier General William E. ['Grumble'] Jones's some months ago.)

This catalogue might be swelled by thousands of special cases. The policy fully disclosed is to trample out opposition in all places which come into their possession, even if it leads to a deportation of the whole population. They have negro regiments in every military department except Hooker's, mostly enrolled in the South. Massachusetts (Boston) with characteristic regard for consistency, principle, and thrift is sending her *resident*-free negroes to the wars *to be killed off*, a clear gain every way. A letter (circular) was captured on a vessel taken on the Neuse (N. C.) some days ago, addressed to General

---

[7] Benjamin S. Roberts, commanding a brigade at Weston (now in West Virginia), on May 16, 1862, had banned from his army lines all pro-Confederate families, narrowly limiting the luggage each family could take from their homes.

June 14, 1863

[John G.] Foster by [Augustus S. Montgomery] dated Washington City, which proposed a plan for organizing a general insurrection on August 4 next throughout the Confederate states to be supported by the United States armies. The slaves were to be informed through the contrabands, and the circular was to be passed from one military commander to another, each writing below, *without his signature,* the word 'approved' so that the friends of the enterprise might know how far it had the support of the military authorities, and that they might each be aware that it was generally known and approved. Copies of this letter were sent by Governor Vance to the War Department and to General Lee. This diabolism was not authenticated by any government authority, but bore internal evidences of having the countenance of the United States Government.[8]

There is nothing which they suppose tends to the destruction of the South which they are not prompt to embrace, and this published code of [Lieber's] 'Instructions' implicitly avows this in the most odious and crafty manner. The Earth contains no race so lost to every sentiment of manliness, honor, faith, or humanity, at once so servile and so tyrannical, so mean and so cruel, such willing slaves, and so bent on destroying the independence and existence of their enemy.

June 14. Sunday. The siege of Vicksburg has progressed regularly since the last assault in May. Its fall I regard as certain. Johnston writes that it will require a force from two to three times as large as he has to effect anything, and telegraphed on the 12th that he has not considered himself as in command over Bragg since he was ordered to Mississippi; that the Government

---

[8] Lincoln himself was consistently opposed to a servile war of blacks against whites in the South.

decide between him and Bragg in respect to the transfer of troops; that the withdrawal of a sufficient force from Bragg would be the evacuation of Tennessee; and [that] the Government must decide which state shall be defended, Mississippi or Tennessee. This is precisely what I have foretold and expected ever since Johnston went there. He seems more anxious to make a point than to gain a battle, to put the Government in the wrong than to defend a state (See ante March 22, April 12, and May 17). It is very clear to me that the *Mississippi will be lost.*

Judge Campbell tells me that the Secretary and President are at their wits end and seem to have no plan, to be drifting along on the current of events. This is characteristic of the President. He is not a comprehensive man. He has no broad policy, either of finance, strategy or supply. He had none for recruiting until General Randolph infused some vigor and consistency into the chaos which reigned in the War Office on March 24, 1862. ([In margin:] Hon. L. T. Wigfall. I was told by Mr. Chapman [Alfred, disbursing clerk in the War Department.] 9) Mr. Davis's friends say that he is honest, pure, patriotic but no administrator—the worst judge of men in the world, apt to take up with a man of feeble intellect or character, and when he has once done so, holds on with unreasoning tenacity—for instance, [General Benjamin] Huger, [General] Holmes, [Stephen R.] Mallory, Benjamin, [C. G.] Memminger, etc. etc. It is the same way with *ideas.* The fatal notion of making each military Department a separate nation for military purposes without subordination, co-operation, or concert—the same on which in point the President and General Randolph split—has lost us Mississippi.

The cavalry affair at Brandy Station appears to have been dis-

---

9 Senator Louis T. Wigfall of Texas became one of Davis's severest critics.

graceful to our officers. Stuart is so conceited that he has got careless, and while he and his staff and general officers were having a frolic with Colonel Rosser's wedding party, the enemy crossed the river and surprised him with horses grazing and guns empty. They fought after being rallied with the most determined valor. ([In margin:] Since proven to be a mistake. [written in 1867:] This statement was vehemently denied at the time. Von Borcke's book has since proved it to be substantially true.) [10]

General Ewell's corps are in the Valley about Front Royal. I have as yet no idea why the army is thrown across there. They have a pontoon train along and may be on their way to Pennsylvania or Baltimore.

A curious affair has come to light in North Alabama and in the army in Tennessee—a secret society called the Washington Constitutional Union, with oaths, signs, grips, etc., the object of which is to put a stop to the war. It had its origin in some local politicians in North Alabama. It is not thought to be very extensive in the army and is confined to the most ignorant, who now that it has been ventilated are very much ashamed of it and appear shocked that it should be deemed treasonable.

---

[10] Early in June 1863, following Chancellorsville, Stuart had staged a massive cavalry review at Brandy Station near Culpeper. On June 8 a second such review was staged for General Lee. The next morning, without warning, Stuart's force was vigorously attacked by General Alfred Pleasanton's cavalry which were driven away only after severe fighting and some serious losses. Worse still, Pleasanton had discovered that Lee's army was moving north. In his *Memoirs of the Confederate War for Independence* (London, 1863), Heros von Borcke, a Prussian officer on Stuart's staff, charged the surprise more to the grand reviews than to the wedding party of Colonel Thomas Rosser, who was married the preceding May.

General [Archibald] Gracie reports it, as also Colonel J. T. Morgan [later United States Senator from Alabama], commanding, Camp of Instruction at Talladega. See their letters for an account of it.

June 15. Monday. Lieutenant Colonel [Hugh Lawson] Clay, A. A. G., told me yesterday that a note had been read from E. K. Smith's engineer's office in the last few days, in which he said he could [not] state what they were going to do [in respect to relieving Vicksburg] because his letter might fall into the enemy's hands, but that we would hear from them in a few days.

June 17. Mr. Seddon has telegraphed Johnston to attempt the relief of Vicksburg with the force he has. He did this on his own responsibility. It is an error. Napoleon in one of his maxims states the precise case, and decides that the general should not obey against his own judgment (See Max. LXXII.) I expect Johnston will follow Napoleon's advice. ([In margin, written later:] I felt so anxious about this that I took the book, Napoleon's *Maxims*, to the Department, with the leaf turned down. Hesitating to show it to Mr. Seddon as a warning, I did show it to Judge Campbell who read it, walked backward and forward a while, and went into the Secretary's office with the book in his hand. Presently he came back and said he concluded to let it alone; it would do no good.) Johnston has replied that he thinks the Secretary does not appreciate the difficulties of executing his orders, that Grant is strongly fortified towards the Big Black, has obstructed all the roads, etc., and that the most that he can hope to do is to assist in getting the garrison out of Vicksburg. He also says he has received a telegram from [Major General Franklin] Gardner in Port Hudson that the garrison is in fine spirits but is getting short of ammunition and provisions.

June 21. Sunday.   Yankeedom is in a great fright at the advance of Lee's army to the Potomac, and considers this part of Pennsylvania south of the Susquehanna as good as gone. The public records have been removed from Harrisburg. I hope they might be destroyed, and all the public buildings also, as they did at Jackson. General Lee's plans are still wrapped in profound mystery, at least to us in Richmond except doubtless the President and Secretary. Hooker is reported to be with his army on the north side of the Potomac. This is just where General Lee does not wish him to be, I presume. There are two plans which General Lee may have in view, 1st, to occupy the passes in the Blue Ridge in Maryland with the body of his army and send the cavalry and one corps into Pennsylvania. This will compel Hooker to come out and fight him on his own ground with his communications open, and Hooker's a good deal exposed, and long. 2nd, to march from Frederick on Baltimore. This also will compel Hooker to fight but on more even terms and a shorter line, while General Lee will have the long line, but to gain a battle would give him Baltimore, and if the overthrow was complete, perhaps Washington.

General Lee has doubtless matured his plan of campaign. He saw last year what was lacking and will provide against it. Harpers Ferry is much more feebly garrisoned than then. I can hear nothing of A. P. Hill's corps for a week. They left Fredericksburg just a week ago. The Northern papers of the 18th represented Hooker at Dumfries [Va.] on the 16th with his rear guard.

Ewell has made a brilliant start as Jackson's successor. The capture of Winchester and most of Milroy's force (the miscreant[11] himself escaped) in a fortnight after he reported for duty at Fredericksburg is doing well. Why some energy cannot be infused into the western operations is hard to understand. The President is said to be furious with Johnston. Bragg is lying still, at Tullahoma [Tenn.] while Rosecrans reinforces Grant. Yesterday it was telegraphed from *Knoxville* via Chattanooga that the enemy after a fight in the suburbs had been driven off and had gone eastward. It was an office message to Dr. Morris, which he sent to the Secretary; character and amount of force not stated. [General John] Pegram I suppose has had his usual luck of being second best.

June 28. We are still without distinct news from either Vicksburg or Lee's army. The latter is smaller than I supposed. The infantry is 55,000. The source of this information is the ordnance returns. The cavalry I suppose is about 8,000 and the artillery not over 5,000—aggregate effectives say 70,000. The general impression is that it is 90,000. Bragg has some 50,000 infantry, 15,000 cavalry, and say 3000 artillery—aggregate 50,000. He and General [Simon Bolivar]Buckner are engaged in some enterprise the nature of which I am not informed of. It is a profound secret.[12]

There have been great efforts made to get the citizens of Richmond to organize for local defence, but with very indifferent success. The clerks in the departments have organized; also

---

[11] Because of his harsh measures against alleged guerrillas, the Confederate Congress had passed a bill offering a handsome reward for the body of Major General Robert H. Milroy, dead or alive.

[12] Pressed hard by Rosecrans in Middle Tennessee, Bragg was on the point of being maneuvered out of Middle Tennessee into Chattanooga. In the reorganization of Bragg's army, Buckner was sent to Knoxville and given command of East Tennessee, still under Bragg's department.

the operatives in all the shops, making an aggregate of over two thousand men, half of whom have served in the army. The Governor [John Letcher] and Mayor [Joseph Mayo] have made very inflammatory appeals to the citizens, but I believe they have not got out over five or six companies—about 300. Finally the Governor has required the militia to turn out tomorrow *to a man* on penalty of being treated as deserters. The occasion of all this is the information received from the lower James that the enemy have concentrated 25,000 men at Williamsburg and [that General John A.] Dix has taken command. Five thousand landed on Friday at the White House, and two regiments of cavalry went up and burned the bridge over the South Anna, of the Central railroad.

June 29.   General Humphrey Marshall, with whom I had a long conversation tonight, told me that the Yankees stole his library (which he estimated as worth $12,000) and sold it at auction in Cincinnati, sending him a copy of the notice of sale; also that they arrested one of his sons on his riding horse at the village of Warsaw and whipped the horse to death in the street, because it was his! He further told me the history of his connection with our service; also his theory of General Lee's campaign, which is that he will take a position on the Monocacy [in Md.], draw Hooker over there, and then recross rapidly and advance on Alexandria and Arlington.

General Lee wants Beauregard to collect an army in Virginia to protect his communications. It will hardly be attempted.

There is some stir about the command here. The Secretary has directed an order assigning Hill (D. H.). General Cooper brought it back and told him he had better see the President before issuing it as he thought the President had other views. I have not heard the issue. Mr. Seddon *knows* by personal observation at the time of the Stoneman expedition that General Elzey is wholly incompetent.

July 7.   On the 2nd inst. all the clerks and government employees, some 2000 in number in five battalions, were ordered out under arms to the outer line of earth works, to support D. H. Hill's command. It was reported that Dix with 25000 men was advancing from the White House. The War Department clerks went out on the Darbytown road, some eight miles. I went with them as a private not in ranks. Friday night we were marched back through Richmond to Meadow Bridge, starting at 10 A.M. and marching all night. Saturday night at 1:30 we were moved over to the Brook road and Monday came back to the city. [General Micah]Jenkins had felt and driven in the enemy at Tunstall's Station, and he [the enemy] had been repulsed at South Anna bridge Saturday night and retreated into King William county by Littlepage's bridge which he burned behind him. It is doubtful whether the force this side the Pamunkey river exceeded 5000 at any time.

On the 4th inst. Vicksburg capitulated, the men paroled, the officers leaving with their side arms. This reached the Department by a press telegram, which caused Mr. Seddon to call on Johnston for the facts. He replied as above. This is a mortal blow in that quarter—[E. K.] Smith, Taylor and Magruder had just reconquered Louisiana, relieved Port Hudson, and got to the river below. Johnston has attempted nothing. See ante June 16 and May 31 [for Kean's prediction of the loss of Vicksburg].

General Lee has delivered a great battle at Gettysburg, Pennsylvania with Meade's army, lately Hooker's. It began on Thursday, July 2. We have only Yankee accounts, but these inspire hope of a victory. The battle has evidently lasted several days, the last struggle probably taking place on Sunday, July 5.

A telegram from the operator at Martinsburg states on the 6th that General Lee has captured 40,000 of the enemy; that [A. P.] Hill in the center fell back as if borne back by the enemy who fell into the trap, while Longstreet and Ewell closed in on the flanks and made this capture; and that the prisoners were under escort of Pickett's division, having refused to be paroled. This I do not yet believe. We have no official news from this great battle.

July 12. Sunday.   This week just ended has been one of unexampled disaster since the war began. Besides the surrender of Vicksburg and the retreat of Bragg behind the Tennessee river, which opens the whole Southwest to the enemy who now have two powerful armies opposed to two feeble ones, it turns out that the battle of Gettysburg was a virtual if not an actual defeat. Lee has written to the President that he was successful on Wednesday and Thursday, July 1 and 2. On Friday the right and left wings carried the ground to which they were opposed, but the center of the enemy resisted successfully all of Longstreet's efforts, and as this position commanded the right and left, the successes went for nothing. He retreated on Friday night toward Hagerstown leaving many severely wounded in the enemy's hands, paroled his own prisoners, and left in the hands of the enemy an equal number of his men. All accounts represent this as the most sanguinary battle yet fought. The details have not yet reached us but the loss of general officers is unprecedented.

The enemy attacked at Charleston again on Friday last. The 10th they effected a landing on Morris Island after severe fighting. They are also in strength on James Island. Yesterday morning they engaged Fort Wagner on Morris Island with four monitors and made an assault, which was repulsed with the loss of 95 killed and 130 captured besides the wounded whom they removed. Casualties on our side 6.

The radical vice of Mr. Davis's whole military system is the separate departmental organization, each reporting only to him. It makes each department depend only on its *own* strength and deprives them of the mutual support and combination which might else be obtained. It appears from a recent report of Richard Taylor that Vicksburg *might* have been relieved from that side; that the whole situation was treated with a levity incomprehensible when the vast stake is considered! Mr. Seddon remarked yesterday that he thought there was more blame on the command on the west than on the east side of the [Mississippi] river for its loss.

It was a difference on this very principle of co-operation across the Mississippi, at this very point, Vicksburg, in connection with which General Randolph's resignation was brought about. His instruction to Holmes, who then had the command Smith now has, to cross over when necessary to produce the best results, and by virtue of his rank to take command of the combined force, was the thing of which the President so pointedly disapproved, and *countermanded*. See ante Nov. 15, 1862.

The enemy, while concentrating upon Lee's shattered army all the force they can collect, are making demonstrations in some show of force in every department along the Atlantic to keep us from sending him reinforcements. They have threatened the Charleston and Savannah railroad, attacked at Charleston harbor, made a raid in North Carolina, and one in this neighborhood, and now the information is that 2 monitors, 3 wooden gunboats, and 5 steamers—the two last crowded with troops—passed up by Sandy Point last evening at 6 o'clock. I hope the reinforcements will be sent to Lee notwithstanding, but fear it will not be done.

In this crisis of our affairs the prospect for recruiting our wasted armies is very poor. The conscription up to 40 is about exhausted. Between 40 and 45 it will not yield probably over 50,000 men and will take 6 months to get them out. We are *almost exhausted*.

July 14. There are signs of great trepidation in high quarters. Port Hudson surrendered on the 9th unconditionally.[13] That is all we know of it. D. H. Hill has been made a lieutenant general and sent to Mississippi. A worse appointment could hardly be made for a people whose loyalty is shivering under the pressure of expected occupation. Harsh, abrupt, often insulting in the effort to be sarcastic, he will offend many and conciliate none. Nor has he talents to reduce this disadvantage, though brave and loyal. There is talk of calling Congress together in order to bring into service all the present exempts, including those who have substitutes. By a crude estimate it is thought 50,000 men can be got by the measures. I do not believe any thing like it can be obtained.

July 19. A great riot in New York on the 13th and 14th raised in resistance to the draft. It does not appear however to possess any consistency or organization and will probably be suppressed. Lincoln at Governor [Horatio] Seymour's instance suspended the draft, the latter promising the people that they should have justice done them. [General John Hunt] Morgan's raid into Indiana is one of the most remarkable smaller events of the war. He has been on the north side of the Ohio for several

---

13 Port Hudson, above Baton Rouge on the east bank of the Mississippi, commanded the entrance to the Red river. Its fall to Banks was the last effective link to the Trans-Mississippi; the Confederacy was severed.

days, riding about very nearly at will. He will be captured. [He was, near New Lisbon, Ohio.]

General Lee has withdrawn his army, or rather the remnants of it, to the south side of the Potomac. He reports that it was effected safely. Meade reports the capture of a brigade of 1500 men, two pieces of artillery, and several caissons.

In the present state of our affairs it would seem to be worthy of consideration whether it would not be well to obtain the assistance of some powerful foreign state, even at the expense of some pride and independence. It might be expedient to sound the Emperor of the French on the basis of large commercial privileges, a sort of protectorate guarantee of our territory, say 11 states, and entire freedom of domestic administration as to all laws and institutions, etc. This accepted would involve him at once in war with the United States but would give him control of cotton, abundance of ship timber and naval stores, and make France a first class naval power. War with Great Britain we would have to apprehend, but *per contra*, Great Britain would be benefitted by a hook being put in the nose of the United States. It would require a good deal of time for any such arrangement to be worked out.

July 26.   A week ago I submitted a brief memoir on the subject of an arrangement with France. I handed it to the Secretary of War who read it and endorsed it to the Secretary of State. What the further fate of it will be is not doubtful. I have conversed with several thoughful persons who agree with my ideas on the subject.

Grant has returned from Jackson to the Mississippi. A part of his army has gone to reinforce Banks, and Sherman's corps [has gone] up the river, deserters say, to come to Richmond, i.e., reinforce Meade. The attack on Charleston progresses slowly.

Beauregard continues to beg for more heavy guns. His requests find small favor with the President who seems generally on the lookout for some objection. Johnston has not yet been removed. I have positive information that such was the President's purpose in the appointment of D. H. Hill a lieutenant general and sending him to Bragg, and Hardee to Mississippi.[14] There is believed to be a split in the cabinet on the subject. Johnston has very influential supporters and more real popularity in the country than the President has. It [Johnston's removal] would be a first class disaster. Colonel E. J. Harvie, who is on his staff [as assistant inspector general], sent a telegram to Mr. L. E. Harvie, his father [president of the Richmond and Danville railroad] yesterday that Sherman's corps was coming to Virginia, that it was all important for the best men to be here; who they are, it was for the government to decide, etc.

Johnston [Davis] has no command which could be given him [Johnston]. If he and the President were not on bad terms, he might be taken as a military adviser of the Government, but that is impossible. He would in my judgment be a great improvement on the President if he could have any weight. While I do not trust him because he is timid and because he hates Davis and Lee, I have a high opinion of his military coup d'oeil, derived however mainly from public reputation; for I do not think he has done anything worthy of a second rate officer during this war.

[14] Lieutenant General William J. Hardee was sent to the shriveled Mississippi department commanded by Johnston, who was relieved of responsibility over Bragg's Army of Tennessee. Daniel Harvey Hill replaced Hardee in Bragg's army. After Chickamauga, Hill joined with fellow officers to request Bragg's removal. As a consequence Davis did not submit his promotion to the Senate for confirmation and he was relieved of his commission, which was not restored until 1865.

Gettysburg has shaken my faith in Lee as a general. To fight an enemy superior in numbers at such terrible disadvantage of position in the heart of his own territory, when the freedom of movement gave him the advantage of selecting his own time and place for accepting battle, seems to have been a great military blunder. The battle was worse in execution than in plan. The different corps did not move at the right time. The battle which was to have been taken up in echelon from right to left was not taken up promptly in the center; the supports were out of place, failed to engage when it was necessary they should, and the result was the worst disaster which has ever befallen our arms—the loss of 15,000 to 20,000 men and all the prestige of the Army of Northern Virginia. This last is an immense loss; the former cannot be replaced. ([In margin, written later:] It turned out that my criticism was unjust in large part. The battle was fought *when*, and it was, *in* consequence of Stuart's disobedience of orders. Instead of finding the enemy and keeping Lee advised, he went off on a raid towards Washington, and the armies *blundered* on one another.)

In October last (1862), the President considered that the darkest period we had had (after Sharpsburg and the other 'invasion'). Our strength was all put out, the enemy's not. The present is infinitely more critical for that very reason. I have a vague suspicion that the Secretary has little or no influence with the President and is getting tired of it. He constantly speaks to Judge Campbell of pressing things, which have not been adopted.

Colonel John S. Preston of South Carolina has been appointed chief of the bureau of conscription, a very good appointment; that concern has been weak. Lay has been the chief man, and through Judge Campbell (his father-in-law) has been kept on very sound principles of administration but there has been little *vim* in the head.[15] Some of the state chiefs have been very efficient, of whom Preston has been very much the best. He will have hard work to make much out of the late call, which I am satisfied will be very unproductive.

General Richard Taylor has sent a report of his operations west of the Mississippi for the relief of Vicksburg and Port Hudson. It is enough to make a man sick to read it. [Major General John G.] Walker's division of three brigades was to take Milliken's Bend and Young's Point. The brigade to take Milliken's did so, but after running the Yankees and negroes to the river, saw a transport steamer, which they took for a gun boat and could not be got to hold the point. Perry's brigade which was to surprise Young's Point delayed nine hours on the march and came near the camp unperceived, when they were drawn off without making an effort or any attack at all, the brigadier sending word that 'he did not think it would pay.'

On this report the President made an endorsement highly approving General Taylor's operations. It was this report which Mr. Seddon had just received and read when he made the remark mentioned July 12 that there was more blame on the west of the river than on Johnston.

Lee is at Culpeper Court House. He is as silent as the grave, has become nearly as costive as Johnston. When he deigns to make a communication of any importance it is a letter to the President, or telegram—always brief and jejune. Beauregard is the only general who keeps the Department advised *fully* of affairs in his department, of his plans and prospects.

---

15 Preston succeeded General Charles W. Field, who had replaced General Gabriel J. Rains on the preceding May 25. Campbell, in some measure directing conscription through his son-in-law, Colonel George W. Lay, was accused of being too liberal and judicially profound with exemptions.

The Commissary General has written to tell General Lee that during the time he was in Pennsylvania, he was only able to get together here 500,000 pounds of meat, and to urge a reduction of the ration to one-fourth of a pound as it was last winter. This is a most alarming state of the supply question. God help this unhappy country!

July 27. Judge Campbell told me this morning that a member of the Cabinet and an intimate friend of the President told him that Mr. Davis *despairs* of success in our struggle. Oh, for a man at the helm like William of Orange, a man of steadfast calm temper, heroic character and genius, a man fertile in resources, equal to emergencies. This, it is quite evident, Mr. Davis is not. He is liable to exultation and depression. He was very low down after the battle of Sharpsburg. See ante October 19, 1862. I remember the then Secretary of War told me that he said our maximum strength had been laid out, while the enemy was but beginning to put forth his.

> Oh God for a *man* of heart, head, hand
> Like one of the simple great ones gone
> Forever and ever by.

July 28. It is quite manifest that the Yankees are after some deviltry about exchange of prisoners. *Twice* recently they have sent large steamers up to City Point under flag of truce, empty, to take their men off, when Tennessee papers announce that 10,000 of ours are in their hands at the fort [Fort Delaware on Pea Patch Island] in the Delaware.[16] They now have the balance in their favor and are preparing to cheat in some way. If they

---

[16] Exchange of prisoners was carried out by a flag-of-truce boat, which plied the James river between Richmond and City Point.

deigned to adhere *honestly* to the cartel as to enlisted men, they would have returned those prisoners who have all been in their hands, the latest taken, at least 20 days. They have systematically violated that provision of the cartel which requires parole in ten days after capture, have generally kept our men from 30 days to six months, in order to demoralize them and to prevent their return to service, where (as has been generally the case until July) the balance was in *our* favor.

It is regarded by some as not at all improbable that Texas, being now severed from the Cis-Mississippi, will throw herself into the arms of *France*, become her neighbour by the occupation of Mexico. As the principle on which this government is constructed is that any state may secede at will, nobody can gainsay her right to do so. Nor would it be a bad thing for the rest if she was accepted, since it would ensure war between France and the United States, or the recognition by the latter of the right of secession which would amount to a concession of the injustice of this cause.

I have several times intimated my opinion of the incompetency of the Adjutant and Inspector General [Samuel Cooper]. It is so manifest that nothing but the irrepressible *West Pointism* of the President, and that other peculiarity of preferring accommodating, civil-spoken persons of small capacity about him, can account for his retention. As *Inspector General* one would suppose that the office highest in rank, the official keeper of the rolls whose specific duty it is to *know* the state of the army and *compel* proper returns, would in two and a half years have got some complete returns. Yet it is notorious that the returns are not complete even from the nearest and most stationary army, while of the Trans-Mississippi forces, they have almost no account whatever. There has never been a time when the A. I. General could give even a tolerably close *guess* of the whole force on the rolls of the army, still less of the *effective* force. He is most of the time *out* of his office. There is not one paper a week which bears evidence of his personal examination. He never decides anything, rarely ever *reports* upon a question, and when he does the report is very thin. Yet he is said to be in frequent consultation(!) with the President.

Aug. 2.   It is now said (I have not learned whether truly or not) that General Lee was ordered back from Hagerstown by the President, his own judgment being to remain there and let the enemy attack him. This would have had the advantage of enabling him to draw his supplies from the enemy's country.

The New York *Herald* of the 20th ult. prints a letter from General Cooper and one from the President to General Lee, dated (about) June 28, both very confidential and the latter especially giving details of the strength, position, and plans of all the armies as a reason why a reserve cannot be collected as Lee wished. This letter will, I fear, do us more injury abroad than anything which has yet appeared. It reveals our feebleness and shows our defenses to be, as the *Herald* has said, a mere shell with nothing inside.

The [Richmond] *Enquirer* of Saturday states upon what it says is high authority that Mr. Slidell has not only not been instructed to offer commercial advantages to France, but has been instructed *not* to do so. If this is true it strikes me as the smallest kind of statesmanship. Why we should stand off on our dignity and be done to death, when a little policy, [foreign aid] such as William of Nassau used, might with the same result work out our deliverance by gaining us powerful allies, is hard to perceive. I do not understand how it is that the *Enquirer* with the reputation of a court journal should scorn the State Department.

I have understood (from Judge Campbell) that in February

1862, just after his inauguration, the President talked seriously of resigning in consequence of the opposition in the Congress and his unpopularity in the country.

The Surgeon General [Dr. Samuel Preston Moore] has reported that he has information that our prisoners at Fort Delaware are dying very rapidly from their crowded condition, bad water, and unwholesome fare and asks that proper steps be taken to procure an amelioration of their condition. He speaks in justly strong terms of the diabolism of this *policy*, for such it undoubtedly is, to destroy our soldiers by the most miserable of deaths. The devilish malignity of that people passes belief and comprehension—from the driving a negro broken out with smallpox to swim the Rappahannock in January, whence he was rescued in a drowning condition by our pickets, to whom they called 'there was a nigger worth $2000,' to the horrors of Camp Chase [in Columbus, Ohio], Fort Delaware and the other Black Holes to which in defiance of good faith they have systematically sent prisoners. ([In margin:] See letter of Dr. Guild [Lafayette, medical director of the Army of Northern Virginia,] to the Surgeon General.)

Judge Dargan has written again that we are ruined unless we get foreign aid and urges that we offer to England and France to go into prospective gradual emancipation. People on the street corners are talking very much as if they thought we had about enough of the war. I once heard something of this sort last evening, the parties being two men who looked like laborers.

Aug. 9. The event which has put the gossips agog in the last two days is the taking off of the Quartermaster General's head. Myers, the incumbent, has long been the object of the President's dislike. Why I never learned. Under the law of last winter which was passed *for the purpose* of making Myers a brigadier general, he is removed and [Brigadier General Alexander R.] Lawton put in his place. Myers has a good deal of popularity in Congress and this will make his friends furious. The uncharitable ascribe this change to a quarrel between the ladies some year and a half ago. It was reported to Mrs. President by a gentleman who himself told me of it, that Mrs. Myers had called her a *SQUAW*, Mrs. Davis being of very dark complexion. The lady President sought her out and charged her with it, Mrs. Myers denied it, burst into tears, and a high scene ensued. The late A. S. W. told me of this; he was the person who told Mrs. Davis that Mrs. Myers had made the remark above mentioned.

It is also rumored that Stuart is to be relieved of the command of the cavalry of the Army of Northern Virginia and Hood put in that position. Cause: absence of the cavalry before and at battle of Gettysburg against orders, to which absence General Lee in his report of that battle is said (I have not seen it yet) to attribute the loss of the battle or rather of the campaign.

I have observed recently that the Adjutant General in connection with the President acts *independently* of the Secretary of War. He refers papers for appointments directly to the President when the Secretary has never seen them. This was so of the recommendation on which Colonel Eppa Hunton was ordered to be made a brigadier. I received from the President's office another of the same sort the same day. I ought to say however that the old gentleman is always a gentleman in his manners—uniformly courteous and uniformly noncommital, rarely venturing an opinion outside of the 'custom in the old service' and ignorant of the military legislation of the Confederacy to a marvellous degree.

Aug. 13.   I have been recently getting up documents for the court of inquiry on the conduct of affairs in Mississippi in the months of April, May, and June.[17] From all I hear the incapacity of Pemberton was as glaring as the President's abusers allege. It comes in every shape and especially from some of the general officers under his command.

General Lee's report of the Pennsylvania campaign has been received some days. It is as jejune and unsatisfactory a document as I ever read. The fact stands broadly out that, as at Sharpsburg, the enemy were more vigorous than he calculated and were amongst his troops before he was aware of their near approach. Stuart was behind the Yankee army which was between him and Lee, instead of between the two armies, so that information of their movements was not complete or timely. Hence a battle was fought without due concentration or preparation, and at a time and place, when and whereas General Lee says he had not proposed to deliver one.

The gravest question now demanding solution is that respecting the employment by the enemy of our slaves as soldiers, and their further assertion of the purpose to *protect* them as persons entitled to the right of war. The first error committed by this Government was President Davis's proclamation of last December, whereby he declared that all *officers* serving with negro troops would be turned over to the state authorities to be dealt with by them under the laws touching insurrection of slaves. There are three questions: 1. as to Northern free negroes enlisted by the United States. 2. as to *slaves* enlisted by them. 3. as to white officers serving with the latter.

It is very clear that the United States have the right to enlist any of their own citizens. They have long in those states regarded

---

[17] The court of inquiry was set up at Pemberton's request. Though elaborate materials were assembled at the War Department, the court never met.

negroes as citizens even, as in Massachusetts, to allowing them the right of suffrage. Free blacks served in the army on the Northern frontier in the War of 1812 and in the navy as sailors. The French enlisted, as soldiers during their occupation of Egypt in 1800-1801, negroes whom they purchased for that purpose.

As to the 3rd question it is quite clear that the enlistment of our slaves is a barbarity which no people, who regarded anything save the gratification of a devilish lust of revenge and hatred, could tolerate on the principle, the use of savages, which Chatham denounced and the Declaration of Independence recorded as infamous. It is also contrary to the public law, since the Pandects. We cannot on any principle allow that *our property* can acquire adverse rights by virtue of a theft of it. The right of postliminy applies by express law as ancient as Justinian; and when slaves are captured in arms against their lawful owners, it becomes a mere question of domestic administration whether they shall suffer the penalties of the municipal law for their revolt, or this [the penalty] being remitted out of consideration of the temptations, seduction, and force to which they are subjected, they shall simply be returned to their masters.

The 2nd question as to officers serving with slaves is one of more doubt as to the legal solution—whether an officer can in conscience obey an order of his sovereign *in foro conscientiae* and is outside the public law. But it may be competent for a belligerent to say to an enemy, 'All officers who obey your orders in making war in a manner revolting to humanity, I will cease to treat as prisoners of war.' This is in the nature of retaliation.

That officers so obeying orders put themselves out of the pale of the public law is a grave error. It was doubly an error when the President, abandoning the only ground on which they could be dealt with properly—the high executive prerogative of the war-making power—proposed to turn them over to the local municipal authorities. Upon this whole subject we have great need of a policy at once resistant and wise. We have already taken one false position for which the Congress by a joint resolution extricated the President, and now we do not seem to have any settled clear rule of action. Meanwhile all exchanges are stopped and each side is hoarding up prisoners as the subjects of retaliation. We have about 5000, and the enemy at least double that number. [End of Kean's Book I]

Upon the whole subject of the relations with the enemy the President has seemed to me to be wanting in firmness. The benevolence of his disposition would appear to stand in the way of such measures as would have resolved these questions (treatment of prisoners, citizens, and violation of the laws of war) heretofore when the balance of captures was in our hands. I think it is quite clear that he has little skill or knowledge as a publicist, and also that the Secretary of State (Judah P. Benjamin) is a poor adviser. He is a smart lawyer, a ready, useful, drawer-up of papers but perhaps the least *wise* of our public men.

The Attorney General (Thomas Watts) too, while a most amiable gentleman, is hardly qualified to assist to sound conclusions (to judge by his opinions). He has had but little experience in dealing with the large questions of administration and public law, having been conversant only with such as arise in a provincial sphere. Nor should I take him to be much read in the law of nations.

When the Attorney General resigns (as he has been elected governor of Alabama), the wisest thing the President could do would be to call to that post the present Assistant Secretary of War, Judge J. A. Campbell. But I fear there is little chance of such a selection. Judge Campbell's mature wisdom, vast learning, experience of affairs, acquaintance with administrative questions raised and settled in the United States Government, and especially his perfect knowledge of the business of the War Office, which is now the whole business of the Government (nearly), would make him greatly the best appointment in the whole country. If I knew how to insinuate this suggestion into the President's mind I would try to do it.

4

INFATUATION RULES THE HOUR

CHICKAMAUGA AND CHATTANOOGA

Aug. 16, 1863. Sunday.   Yesterday it was reported an attack
was making on Charleston Harbor. No news from there at the
War Office this morning. The signal scouts report from Meade's
army that a large force has been sent to Charleston, and also that
10,000 New York troops have gone home, their period of service
having expired.[1]

The first distinct submission proposition I have seen was a
letter yesterday from a man named Graves, near Jackson, Mississippi. He is thoroughly conquered and proposes that we shall
throw ourselves on the *mercy* of the Yankees!! Poor spiritless
wretch. I agree with the Secretary that it is better to be destroyed
than to submit.

---

[1] After Gettysburg, Lee's army had returned to Virginia and was
behind the Rapidan. Meade's army had followed, crossing the Rappahannock to Culpeper. Soon both Lee and Meade would be reducing their
strength, Lee sending Longstreet with Hood's and McLaw's divisions to
Bragg at Chattanooga, and Pickett's division to the south bank of the James;
Meade sending Hooker with two divisions to Rosecrans at Chattanooga,
sending some detachments to South Carolina, and sending others to New
York to quell draft riots.

Colonel Richeson of the Tennessee Partisan Rangers sends an interesting report of his recent doings in West Tennessee. He is conducting a real partisan war there, just such a war as made Spain so terribly destructive to the French. Cavalry parties are collecting behind the enemy's lines and making their way out, and Col. Richeson speaks with great confidence of *enforcing the conscription* act in West Tennessee. In Alabama, Mr. Anderson [J. W., recording clerk of the C. S. Senate], who is (Judge Campbell says) one of the ablest and most sensible men in the state, says the people are becoming thoroughly aroused to the issues before them. Heretofore a negro could not be got for work connected with the army for any price. Now men are offering them and are proposing to use them as soldiers. The latter seems to me to be bad policy. I would make laborers of them to build fortifications—teamsters, cooks, all the menial offices of the army I would discharge by them, thus leaving every white man with a rifle or musket. But I would not use them [as soldiers], chiefly because if we do so it will counteract the wholesome effect which Port Hudson, Milliken's Bend, Fort Wagner, and every where existing on them, to make them flee Yankee enlistment. If we use them in the same way there will be nothing to induce them to remain faithful, the danger being the same and the hope of freedom with the enemy the determining motive.[2]

Roger A. Pryor has resigned his commission as brigadier general. To the Secretary yesterday, he insisted on a brigade or resignation, was told then in frankness he could not get a brigade, then asked 30 days to select the company in which *to serve as a*

[2] In the Vicksburg campaign, at Port Hudson (May 27, 1863), and at Milliken's Bend (June 7, 1863), Federal Negro regiments engaged in fierce action and suffered heavy losses. At Fort, or Battery, Wagner on Morris Island, S. C., in July 1863, Negro troops were also under severe fire while they made repeated assaults.

private, which was granted him. So he is going to serve as a private. I do not think he will do so long.

Since the court of inquiry has been constituted to investigate the fall of Vicksburg, the matter of the removal of Johnston seems to have been laid to rest. It is very fortunate that it is so. His removal would have produced an explosion against the Administration which, taken with the restlessness produced by disasters, might have become formidable.[3]

A gentleman of high character and position (Judge Campbell) told me the following of Mr. Benjamin, present secretary of state. Some years ago a clerk of a house in New Orleans defrauded the customs and his employees by false extension in the invoices of goods. By the law the goods were forfeited. The court made a certificate showing the fact that the merchants were innocent and that the fraud was wholly on the part of the clerk who stole the amount of which the customs were cheated. Mr. Hunt [William Henry, later Garfield's secretary of the navy] and Mr. Benjamin were counsel for the merchants. The judgment amounted to over $200,000. Upon the certificate of the court, remission of the penalty was a matter of course. Benjamin, who was then in the United States Senate, was paid $5000 for getting the bill passed [to remit the penalty.] Mr. Hunt, his associate counsel, told my informant that he had this from his client at the time they paid his fee of $1000.

Aug. 18.   Major Barton told me he had read a letter from the President to General Johnston of July 18 last in reply to Johnston's communication in which he pretended that his control in

---

[3] The court of inquiry, first slated to be held in Montgomery, Alabama, and later Atlanta, was called off by President Davis who reported that all officers involved were needed in the field.

the West was fettered; that the letter (evidently written by Benjamin) reviewed the whole correspondence, disproved the pretense, and was most severe in the tone of dignified rebuke with which it scattered the unworthy subterfuge. I am very glad such a letter was written, for I have heard that there was received in Richmond in May or June a letter from Johnston, which was substantially the leading article of the *Examiner* on that subject, being dressed up for publication without even a change in the order in which the points were presented.

Aug. 21. Fast day by the President's proclamation; public offices closed. These occasions are popular with the clerks who get a holiday. The clerks in the Richmond post office have '*struck*' for higher wages. They are paid only $700 to $800, it is said equivalent to less than $100 in ordinary times.

Had a talk on this subject with Mr. Seddon. He thinks that it was a fatuous policy which did not get cotton abroad last year as a relief to the currency. It is pretty evident to me that he thinks the Secretary of the Treasury an *ass*. Northern papers are publishing letters taken from Mr. Davis's private papers in Mississippi. I see none which amount to much. There is one curious letter of Buchanan written in 1850, regretting that the South should have abandoned the Missouri Compromise and taken up with 'non-intervention' instead.

Mr. Miles [William Porcher, member of Confederate House from South Carolina] wrote a letter received yesterday, earnestly asking that Jenkins's brigade might be sent to Charleston to reinforce Beauregard. The Secretary unhappily has taken it in dudgeon (Mr. Miles's letter was in excellent spirits) and written at length to show that the present distress of Fort Sumter was due to negligence in allowing the enemy to get on Morris island and Folly island. Suppose this were so, it would be a poor reason for allowing Charleston to be taken. This misunderstanding on the back of all the numerous imbroglios which surround the administration is unfortunate. They are all unfortunate, and whenever unnecessary are a fault in statesmanship. The Government, i. e. the President, is so bitterly prejudiced against Beauregard that it seems impossible for that feeling to keep out of the way of the public good.

Aug. 23. Sunday.   The bombardment at Charleston continues. Fort Sumter is pretty well reduced. Yesterday the enemy threw several 200 pound shells into the city from their batteries on Morris island, a distance of five and one-half miles, a range unprecedented in gunnery. The French and Spanish consuls protested against this being done without notice. A fico for the protest.

Rosecrans has advanced threatening Chattanooga in force, and Burnside is advancing on East Tennessee with a heavy force. He [Burnside] will get it; Buckner has only about 8000 available troops. There are numerous passes by which the enemy may advance, so that to defend them would be to scatter and squander his force without effect.

It appears there is no purpose to reinforce Charleston. This seems to me to be wrong. It cannot be done from the western army because of the threatening position of affairs there, but it could and I think ought to be done from Virginia. If Charleston is taken, all South Carolina will be bitterly hostile to the Government. The letter referred to on the previous page will then be published and make an irreconcilable breach. I hear there are two parties in Charleston, one charging Beauregard and the other Ripley [General Roswell Sabine, under Beauregard] with the fault of allowing the enemy to get a footing on Morris island. This wretched jangling is a bad sign.

The part of the Confederacy we still hold is in the shape of a boot, of which middle Virginia, North Carolina, South Carolina, and Georgia to the Gulf is the leg and Alabama and part of Mississippi the foot; besides this, the Trans-Mississippi. Nearly half the whole area is in the hands of the enemy, or outside of our lines. We have never substantially recovered any territory once lost, have never retaken any important strategic point once occupied. I do not regard Louisiana as yet recovered, nor Winchester as constituting an exception. Galveston comes nearest to it. The signal scouts below report that the yellow fever has appeared at Norfolk and Portsmouth, also in the enemy's camp at Yorktown; that the latter has been removed to Newport News. An epidemic like that of 1857 might do us a good deal of good all along the coast.

Colonel Northrop, whom I regard as more nearly reflecting the President's opinions than any of his other friends, speaks of our soldiers as less disciplined than the enemy's and of Lee as the only officer we have capable of conducting a campaign or fighting a battle. It might be well for the President in person to try *once*. If he would join the western army with Bragg and Johnston for lieutenants, it might have a good effect. Certainly the style of business with which his time is now consumed is in our present circumstances almost a scandal—little trash which ought to be dispatched by clerks in the adjutant general's office. This absorption of the President's time in trifles (comparative) is due to two facts: 1st, his own desire to be personally conversant about everything. 2nd, the weakness of some of the men he has about him, who have accustomed him to have them run to him for instructions about every little matter. This was General Walker's habit [Leroy Pope, former secretary of war]; also Mr. Benjamin's (in his case well enough, for I have understood he took the War Office with hesitation and stipulated that the President should do the military part of the business).

It is persistently true of Cooper. Napoleon gave attention to details. But he dispatched them; he touched and the work was done; he spoke and the question was solved. Mr. Davis is a slow, very slow worker. Both the Secretaries [Randolph and Seddon] under whom I have served, complain to their intimates of the endless tediousness of consultations which yield no results. Hence a total absence of vigor; all the revolutionary vigor is with the enemy, in legislation and execution. With us timidity, hair-splitting, and an absence of all *policy*. No line of action tending to foreseen results.

Major Barton tells me that Lovell's vindication before the New Orleans court of inquiry was complete; that he comes off with flying colors. Barton made an abstract of the record for the President recently. The finding has not yet been promulgated. Lovell shows well in the correspondence with the War Department, which I had made up for the court martial.[4]

Aug. 26.   Commissioner Ould returned yesterday from a conference with Meredith [Brigadier General Samuel A., at Fort Monroe], the new commissioner on the Yankee side. Nothing was done towards the very desirable end of settling arrangements for exchanges of prisoners and re-establishing the cartel. Meredith, who Ould says makes a bad impression on him every way, could do or would do nothing. He must refer every proposition to his

---

[4] Major General Mansfield Lovell, commanding at New Orleans upon that city's capitulation, was relieved of his command in December 1862. Demanding and getting a court of inquiry, he was absolved of blame for the loss of the city but censured for minor faults incident to the evacuation.

government. The great difficulty arises from the heinous conduct of that foul Government and people in respect of arming slaves. They cannot, without a meanness *avowed*, do anything else but protect as far as they can the victims of their evil policy. If it was convenient, and any way of doing the thing *sub rosa*, they would not hesitate for an advantage to sacrifice them [the slaves] in the cabinet as they do on the fields; but Yankee conscience consists in *keeping up appearances*. Hence, the question has no solution.

Had a conversation with Commissioner Ould on this subject this evening. He says there is no prospect of a solution. The President, he says, feels bound by the resolutions of Congress as to United States free negroes, which in the terms of the joint resolutions on retaliation [read as] 'all negroes or mulattoes.' This is wrong. See my ideas on this subject about the end of the previous book. [April 13, 1863]

Aug. 30.   Buckner has evacuated Knoxville and is now at Loudon, on the road to Chattanooga. This is not generally known here. I suppose he will unite with Bragg, and they will endeavor to give battle to Rosecrans before Burnside comes up.

The clerks of the departments turned out under arms again on Friday, in consequence of a cock and bull story from Wise's pickets at Bottom's bridge. [General Henry A.] Wise's brigade has long since come to be called by the people 'the Life Insurance Company.' Never having effected anything, they are like their commander, somewhat given to sensation making. This war has produced no more emphatic failure than *Wise*, not even in the regular army.

My observation throughout the army has been that the officers of the United States army (regular) as a class are the most inferior men in their profession and the most ignorant out of it, of any profession with which I have ever come in contact. This is also the verdict of several judicious persons to whom I have made the above remark, whose opportunities and capacity for judging have been of the largest.

Sept. 1.   A very savage attack on the President in the *Examiner* of this date in a long ironical letter signed 'Orient,' the text being the removal of Myers as quartermaster general. The article is written with a good deal of sprightliness but can tend to no conceivable good. The *Examiner* and *Whig* in their persistent malice towards the President do only less harm than the Raleigh *Standard*. By the way, the followers of the latter in North Carolina are throwing off all disguises and have begun to hold 'Union' meetings in some of the western counties. What the *Examiner* and *Whig* propose to themselves as the good to be produced by stirring up opposition, distrust, and hatred towards the President, I can not imagine. I am far from being a universal admirer of the President as these pages attest, but I see no conceivable end but harm from such attack and such a policy.

Sept. 5.   The *on dit* in 'official circles' now is that General Lee with a part of the Army of Northern Virginia is going to Tennessee, and [that] Johnston has been relieved and has reported to the court of inquiry at Montgomery. This last is a very decisive step at the present junction. Lee and the President have been riding around inspecting the fortifications of Richmond for a week past. Bragg and Hardee command in Alabama now.

Sept. 20. Sunday.   I have been absent in Albemarle and Lynchburg from the 7th to the 19th and have somewhat lost the thread of events. Since I left Richmond, Longstreet's corps or rather McLaws's and Hood's divisions have gone to reinforce

Bragg; Elzey with Jenkins and Wise to Charleston,[5] and Pickett's divisions hold Richmond and Petersburg. There is a rumor among the *few* that the President thinks of taking personal command in Georgia. Success would be all the more important if it restored to him the confidence and good will of the country, which he has deplorably lost in some way. Failure would destroy his administration and perhaps the Confederacy. The trouble in North Carolina grows apace. The Reconstruction is openly advocated in many counties. In Alabama the same spirit begins to show itself. Mississippi beyond the Big Black is conquered. I find an imbroglio in my office between the principal clerk and Mr. Seddon. It is not yet fully developed but must result in Joynes's leaving the Department [Edward Southey Joynes, later a prominent educator at Hollins and Washington colleges, and at the universities, Vanderbilt, Tennessee, and South Carolina]. I have heard only one side as yet and cannot fully judge of the matter, but so far as appears to me the Secretary's course seems rather harsh.

From what I hear Rosecrans maneuvered Bragg out of Chattanooga very handsomely. It may be that a part of Bragg's plan was to *avoid* a fight until Longstreet reached him. The surrender of Cumberland Gap[6] seems the most atrocious piece of infidelity and cowardice that has yet disgraced our arms. The *court of inquiry* on the Mississippi campaign has been dissolved, the

---

[5] Hood and Jenkins accompanied Longstreet to Chattanooga. Elzey remained in the department of Richmond.

[6] Burnside in late August 1863 headed out from Lexington, Ky., with 20,000 for East Tennessee. Bypassing Cumberland Gap, he reached Knoxville via Big Creek Gap to the south. Buckner with only 6000 evacuated Knoxville, leaving the detachment at Cumberland Gap under Brigadier General John W. Frazer to almost inevitable surrender. Thus direct rail connections between Virginia and Chattanooga were severed.

officers being required for other duty. Pemberton is shelved; Johnston's position I do not precisely know.

Sept. 22. Tuesday.   Bragg has fought a great battle on Chickamauga Creek, result as yet indecisive. A member of the cabinet, the Attorney General, told me last night that the ironclads [Laird rams] in England were nearly done, had been launched *under the French flag*, and this was with the Emperor's sanction; that the title had been transferred to a Frenchman and *this* was with his knowledge and *at his suggestion;* also that Mr. Mallory represented them as perfectly sea worthy and strong enough to handle the enemy's ships and sweep the ocean. The papers say that the ironclads will not be allowed by the English government to sail but will be escorted out by a ship of war and delivered to their French owners in a French port! [See below, Oct. 18, 1863.]

Sept. 27. Sunday.   Bragg, i.e. Longstreet and Breckinridge, drove Rosecrans back to Chattanooga. ([In margin:] For 'Bragg' here read 'Longstreet.' It is now, July 1864, abundantly shown and conceded by all the world save a very few that a great victory was won without Bragg's knowledge and wholly lost by his incapacity.) His trophies were 7,000 prisoners, 36 guns, 15,000 stand small arms, 26 stand of colors. Losses on each side not known. The relative position of the armies is not known here. I greatly fear that the defensive works about Chattanooga out of which Rosecrans maneuvered Bragg will enable the former to hold the place until reinforcements make him strong and safer. The Yankee papers admit a defeat and a severe one.

One good result of this victory will be its ameliorating effect on the question of exchanges of prisoners. Mr. Ould thinks these are approximating a settlement, or at least a partial adjustment by which not all prisoners will be retained, but only so many as each side may take as a sufficient equivalent for such as are claimed to be improperly detained by the other. General Hood, reported killed, has lost a leg above the middle of the thigh, and is reported as doing well. Our best men fall in every battle. We shall soon have none but the scrubs of West Point left in high command. One of the ablest of our officers and statesmen, General Randolph, is practising law in this city.

Oct. 4.　　It seems pretty well settled that the attorney general to succeed Governor Watts will be from Tennessee. Governor [Senator Gustavus A.] Henry and Mr. Haynes [Landon C., Confederate Senator from Tenn.] have been here this week in consultation with the President, doubtless on this subject. ([Later insert:] Henry, G. A., declined, and George Davis of North Carolina was appointed.)

It is pretty certain that General Lee meditates a forward movement this week. Hard bread and bacon in large quantity have been sent up to him in the last three days.[7]

Our intelligence from every quarter is that the enemy are bending every energy in every direction for the relief of Rosecrans. Two corps of Grant's army are on the way, one by way of Corinth, the other by the road north of the Tennessee from Memphis. Troops have been sent from the East also, besides all which were in East Tennessee. Bragg holds both railroads, on the east at Cleveland [Tenn.], on the west from Lookout Mountain. Rosecrans gets his supplies by wagons from Stevenson [Alabama], and doubtless from the Sequatchie valley. Johnston sent Major General Stephen D. Lee with 2000 cavalry several days

---

[7] Lee was planning to flank Meade out of his position at Culpeper and force him to recross the Rappahannock.

ago in the direction of Murfreesboro. There is great danger that the great reinforcements which are moving to his [Rosecrans's] assistance will reach him before he is compelled to evacuate Chattanooga, or if not, [they will] soon after put him in a position to resume the offensive with a superior force. A victory to yield fruits must either be more decisive on the field or be pressed to better results. I greatly fear it will prove rather a barren one. ([Later insert:] See Oct. 8, 1863)

Bragg has relieved from duty Generals Polk and Hindman for disobedience of orders. Longstreet and Bragg have united in an earnest recommendation that Hood be made a lieutenant general. The Secretary has added his emphatic recommendation and sent it to the President. ([Later insert:] Nothing done, Oct. 7).[8]

The Virginia legislature are about to pass a law of maximum [prices]. It fills me with terror to think of the effect on this city. It will have one feature which will relieve it in some degree of the swift ruin such measures inevitably bring, viz. that they adopt the sliding schedule of the Confederate commissioners under the impressment law. But they have pretty well settled on the policy of making little change as the currency declines. Flour they put at $22.50 to $28 according to quality, when it is selling on the street here for $40. Hay baled at $3 when in this city it brings $11.00 per cwt. Production and movement will be so cut off and curtailed that there will be great danger of famine here.

To these causes are added the persistent folly of the com-

---

8 On October 1, Bragg removed Polk, Hindman, and Daniel Harvey Hill for alleged misconduct at the time of battle. Davis restored Polk and transferred him to Mississippi under Johnston. Bragg relented and restored Hindman. But Hill remained inactive till near the end of the war, having been charged with authoring the 'round robin' letter of Bragg's officers requesting Bragg's removal.

missariat, which systematically seizes everything which in any quantity starts to market. ([In margin, written Oct. 25, 1863:] This is generally accepted and believed, [but] has been officially denied by Majors [S. Bassett] French, [Larkin] Smith, and [B.P.] Noland of the Commissary Department. They qualify their denial, however, by restraining it to the impressment of provisions on 'first hand,' i.e. the producer's. *He* is a 'speculator' and the property is infallibly seized. Hence all the movement of trade by which supply is ordinarily and naturally produced is crushed, and scarcity and high prices result.) A butcher who has the enterprise to collect 20 or 30 head of cattle cannot get them to his slaughter pen before they are snapped up. Bacon is now $2.50 per pound by wholesale. My salary of $3000 goes about as far as $300 would do in ordinary times in purchasing all the articles of household necessity, the average of prices being about ten fold. The consequence is that with an income from all sources of at least $6000 and a good deal of help from my father-in-law, my family is reduced to two meals a day (since May last) and they are of the most plain and economical scale. Wood for fuel is $38 per cord, butter $4 per pound, coal $1.25 per bushel, calico $4.50 a yard.

The wages of a journeyman saddler are from $10 to $12 per day, more by 30% than the salary of a head of bureau or assistant secretary in one of the departments. There is already great suffering among the clerks, who get $1500. Those who have families are reduced to the most desperate straits; yet Congress is afraid to increase salaries.

Oct. 8.   General Longstreet has written to the Secretary of War a letter which has filled me with concern. He says Bragg has done but one thing he ought to have done since he (General Longstreet) has been out there and that was the order to attack on September 18. After the battle he lost two days by contradictory orders, which Rosecrans used to strengthen his position; and he [Longstreet] expressed the opinion that nothing will be effected under Bragg's command. He says the army is equal to any achievement and urges in conclusion that General Lee be sent there to command, the army in Virginia being left to act wholly on the defensive. ([In margin, written Oct. 1865:] This letter made Bragg a bitter enemy of Longstreet and strange to say President Davis sided with Bragg, and subsequently to the end of the war showed strong personal dislike of Longstreet.)

Yesterday the President set out for Chattanooga, no doubt to make up the difficulties between Bragg and Polk and Hindman. It is said (by Mr. Burnett of Ky.) that Bragg has also quarreled with General Buckner. Longstreet's letter seems to me to be written without feeling and purely from a sense of duty. I scarcely hope anything from the President's visit. He temporizes too much, takes too long to make up his mind, is as much wanting in vigor as his enemies say he is in amenability to public opinion. Pemberton has gone out to Georgia with the President. It will only require for him to be put in command of a corps to break the public patience down entirely, and almost to break the public heart and hope. The President's dislike and distrust of Johnston will probably prevent his being called to the command of that army.[9]

---

[9] Henry C. Burnett was a Confederate Senator and Theodore L. Burnett a member of the House, both from Kentucky. Buckner, as well as D. H. Hill, is alleged to have authored the 'round robin' letter urging the removal of Bragg. At Bragg's headquarters in the presence of Davis, Bragg, and the complaining generals, the last mentioned recommended a change in commanders for the Army of Tennessee. Davis the next day offered the command to Longstreet who turned it down. Bragg was left in command but the quarreling between him and his officers went on. Davis had taken Pemberton and his staff along, with the expectation of giving

There is a report of a cavalry raid preparing at Yorktown. The enemy have been landing cavalry there from transports; also they are reported to be making some demonstrations in North Carolina. General Lee gives no sign of moving, as I supposed a few days ago he would do.

The secret arrangements which have been made for burning steamboats on the Mississippi river are working pretty well. Nineteen have been wholly destroyed and many more injured. One method is to fire into them from the shore with a small two pound shell filled with a phosphoric liquid which burns in spite of water. The gun weighs only 240 pounds and is carried on horseback. A Captain [John C.] McKay is in charge of this enterprise.

Oct. 11.   Lieutenant Colonel [John N. Galleher], General Buckner's chief of staff, is here and gives a glowing account of things about Chattanooga. Bragg is as badly off for provisions as Rosecrans, and the position of the latter is impregnable. He confirms what General Longstreet's letter (Oct. 8 ante) said, and says Generals Longstreet and Buckner are of the same opinion. General Polk thinks he has been made a scapegoat of, to atone for the want of results. On the whole it seems pretty certain that Rosecrans will winter in Chattanooga, and the conquest of Tennessee be thus consolidated.

The question of the French tobacco may give rise to some complications between France and the United States. The Secretary of State assured Count St. Romaine that the tobacco could go out only in French bottoms under convoy; that it could not be allowed to be liable to capture. The United States are said to have refused peremptorily to allow it to go out, as it would give us a large foreign credit. As this tobacco is owned by the French

---

Pemberton Polk's corps, but hostility to Pemberton in Bragg's army led the President to drop this plan.

government, the Emperor may insist on having his own; whence an imbroglio which may benefit us.

Oct. 18.   General Lee is said at last to be in motion. The Army of Northern Virginia is at or near Manassas. There are plenty of rumors as usual about battles and prisoners taken, none of which are authentic. I think Meade has gotten safely away.

General Samuel Jones is hard pressed in Southwest Virginia. The enemy under Burnside are at Bristol, and Hooker [is] said to be supporting him with a heavy column. [Hooker was at Chattanooga.] The salt works [at Saltville in Smyth Co., Va.] are in great danger. Governor Letcher is bringing up his militia here, to send out there. I doubt if he gets a corporal's guard of them. A difficulty has arisen between Mr. Seddon and Roger A. Pryor about the circumstances of the latter's resignation (See Aug. 16). Mr. Seddon has heard of Pryor's complaining heavily, and S. B. French wrote to the President making Pryor's complaint known to him. The letter was referred to Mr. Seddon who told French it was not true, and this French has written to Pryor, sending his letter to Mr. Seddon to read.

The President has gone to Mississippi. What for, I have not heard. Hardly to confer with his friend Johnston, I should suppose. No fruits of his visit to the army at Chattanooga have yet transpired. I confess I do not look for any. He is not a man of quick and vigorous resolves and none others are likely to yield fruit worth the plucking. The army will probably fall back to get wood and subsistence, go into cantonments, and a general court martial sit to try Polk and Hindman. It is one month tomorrow since the battle of Chickamauga and the fruits are almost *nil*. The enemy are rapidly confining their hold on Tennessee, its *flour* and *meat* so much needed by us. Alas, for our prospects this winter.

The dismissal of the English consuls,[10] the withdrawal of Mr. Mason from England and the late declarations of Lord John Russell, hostile to us and very friendly to Yankeedom, indicate the loss of our iron rams now nearly completed. ([In margin, written July 17, 1864:] Nearly a year after this note, the rams were lost by a compromise of the suit in the court of exchequer vs. Lairds, by which the ships were *purchased* by the English government in May 1864.) England has not in years gained as much benefit by her own arms as she has gained by ours during this war, in transferring to her the whole carrying trade intending to make her independent of Southern cotton in exhausting the resources of the United States.

Oct. 22. Had a long conversation with Judge Campbell, who told me he thought of resigning. It would be a great loss to the Government to lose him. He went over the transactions with Seward in 1861, and told me he had changed his opinion as to Seward's intention to deceive. (He had formerly told me in reply to the direct question, that he did not think Seward was insincere with himself [Campbell] and Judge Nelson [Samuel, Campbell's colleague on the U.S. Supreme Court], but that he had not been able to control events in respect to relieving Sumter. This was many months ago.)

The things which [now] satisfied him of Seward's intent to cheat and deceive were: 1st, a statement in Dr. Russell's diary

---

10 Exercising consular functions without exequaturs from the Confederate Government, the British consuls were a source of irritation because of their constant efforts to keep former British subjects out of the Confederate services. In late 1863, as Confederate-British relations deteriorated, the Confederate Government effected the withdrawal of the offending consuls. In one sense, this act was Confederate recognition of the futility of efforts to obtain British recognition.

under date of March 22 [26], 1861 that Seward had said to him, that nothing would be given up, nothing surrendered, that the *message* was the declaration of policy, nothing contrary to it would be done. On the 21st the very day before, he [Seward] had said to Judges Nelson and Campbell that there would be no attempt to reinforce Sumter and that the order to evacuate would be given in three days; 2nd, on the day of [Lincoln's] inauguration Holt, secretary of war, on Judge Campbell's saying he regarded the inaugural as a war paper and that he would resign, urged him not to resign, that his information was that the message was not so intended, and begged him not to take any steps until he saw him again.

Subsequently Holt came to his [Campbell's] house and had a long conversation urging against his resigning, in the course of which he said in a manner which produced the impression that he was quoting Seward's words, that the inaugural had served its purpose and would never be heard of again as authority or indicating the policy for any purpose. This declaration taken in connection with that to Russell, and with the events themselves, satisfied him that Seward was deliberately and intentionally *false*. I urged Judge Campbell to make a full and accurate memorandum of the whole of his intercourse with Seward and the Southern commissioners, he and Judge Nelson being *the only witnesses* of what passed at a point whence the original of the war took its rise, and [a memorandum as] to transactions which settle the question as to the justifiableness of firing on Sumter. He promised to do so. This is the more important since Seward has boasted (as stated by W. B. Reed of Philadelphia) that he had put the South in the position of taking the aggressive.[11]

---

[11] These paragraphs throw light on Seward's part in the much disputed question of whether Lincoln and Seward deceptively maneuvered the

Oct. 25. General Lee's recent advance to Manassas has been as fruitless, more fruitless than Longstreet's to Suffolk last spring. Meade got away from him with ease, and succeeded in drawing Cooke's, Kirkland's and Posey's brigades into an ambuscade at Bristoe Station where they suffered terribly. On the whole while we have most prisoners, we have doubtless lost more in killed and wounded than the enemy.[12]

Our troops are barefooted too. The failure to provide shoes and blankets—shoes especially, during all this year—after the troubles and suffering of last winter is to my mind conclusive of the mismanagement of the quartermaster department. Other things may have been greatly needed, but shoes are as absolute a necessity to an army as provisions. It is a great failure to duty or enterprise. The ordnance branch has been conducted with greatly more energy and enterprise than the others, and so has got control of the foreign importations. The quarter-

---

Confederates into firing on Fort Sumter, in order to put on the South the onus for commencing the war. Fearing that the Confederate Commissioners, in Washington seeking recognition, would precipitate a crisis, Seward, in a series of conversations with Supreme Court Justices Samuel Nelson and John A. Campbell, both Southerners, pledged the Lincoln administration to evacuating Fort Sumter. At the time plannning to become premier of the administration, Seward thus in the spirit of gambling opportunism made an unauthorized pledge which he could not carry out. William Howard Russell was a British journalist who published his *My Diary North and South* in 1863. Joseph Holt of Kentucky was Buchanan's secretary of war and held the office under Lincoln for a few days after the inauguration.

[12] In a broad flanking movement, Lee was trying to turn Meade's right and get between the Federals and Washington. At Bristoe Station, A. P. Hill's corps ran into concealed, fierce opposition and was repulsed at great loss. Brigadiers John Rogers Cooke, W. W. Kirkland, and Carnot Posey were wounded, the last mentioned dying from his wounds. Following this repulse, Lee withdrew to the south bank of the Rappahannock.

master department complains of this, which is due to their own deficiency in enterprise. Another of the Collie line, the *Venus*, was lost last week by being run ashore near Wilmington.[13]

Oct. 31. Saturday.   It has come to light that one [John] Claiborne as agent for the Belgian government has been purchasing cotton in Mississippi and shipping it, under a permit given by Butler and Farragut, to that government. In point of law this is an end of the blockade. See Pufendorf and Lord Stowell and all the modern writers on international law. But the *law* being with us is nothing. There is no law for the *outlaw*, and the nations have outlawed the Southern Confederacy. See Lord John Russell's late speech.

Accounts from Bragg's army are worse and worse. Colonel St. John [Isaac M., supt. of the nitre and mining bureau] showed me a letter from Captain Clark of the engineers, expressing in the strongest manner the same state of hopeless distrust and disorganization in that army stated by so many others, foreboding nothing but evil from Bragg's command of it. Yet the President seems fatally bent on retaining him now that the enemy have resumed the offensive just below Lookout Mountain, having crossed over three corps. I expect the next intelligence will be that our army has fallen back as it did before the battle of Chickamauga. All that bloodshed has been *in vain*. Clark mentions that on the day after the battle, perhaps on the field itself, Breckinridge rode down his line and was vehemently cheered. His reply was 'Longstreet is the man my boys, Long-

---

[13] The Collie Line was a blockade-running company formed by Alexander Collie of Liverpool and James R. and W. G. Crenshaw of Richmond. In October 1863, this company contracted with the War Department to put five ships in operation out of Wilmington, North Carolina. Of these five, the *Venus* and *Hebe* were soon captured or sunk.

street is the man.' I think there is an evident disposition on the part of the friends of the latter to make him the man to supplant Bragg. The inability of Bragg to be further useful there is manifest to nearly all. The President's solution of the Polk difficulty is to send Polk to Johnston and Hardee [from Johnston] back to Bragg.

The estimates for the first half of the next fiscal year are beginning to come in. The present legislation restricts the issues of the treasury to $50,000,000 per month. The Quartermaster General's estimate is for $320,000,000 being by itself $20,000,000 over the whole issue allowed. All the bureaus together will probably reach the neighborhood of $500,000,000 for six months. This is the great rock on which we are splitting. The currency is *hopelessly bankrupt*, the total of the War Department [being] $450,000,000 for six months.

Nov. 2.   The Commissary General of Subsistence was at the Secretary's office this morning before 10 o'clock urging him to retract the license to the city council to purchase for the city warehouses provisions to be retailed to the destitute. The Secretary declined and went out. Colonel Northrop then came to me and asked me to urge the thing on the Secretary. I told him I did not agree with him, that I thought it of very great importance that the city should be fed. He said very earnestly that the alternative was between the *people* and the army, that there is perhaps *bread* enough for both but not *meat* enough, and that we have to elect between the *army* and the *people* doing without.

This made such an impression on me that I went this evening and stated it to the Secretary with this further, that the problem seemed to be the *recovery of Tennessee*. To do this, suppose Lee relieved of a departmental command and the whole military strength east of the Mississippi put in his hands, with this instruction: *Tennessee to be recovered,* with as little sacrifice elsewhere as may be, but Tennessee *to be recovered.* Mr. Seddon said that was not the problem; that there would be a great pinch for meat till hogs were killed, undoubtedly, but the subsistence department had a number of hogs, enough to last some months; that Colonel Northrop's statements were exaggerated to make an impression for his present purpose; for if the worst came to the worst, hogs could be slaughtered and pork supplied for the present. But the *problem* was to strike vital blows at the enemy, and that was to be done in his opinion only by invasion, by conquering, say Pennsylvania, and holding it by an army of say 120,000, with 50,000 more to keep open communications. Such an invasion he thought the only road to peace.

The Assistant Secretary told me today he had pressed on the Secretary the financial question with a view to seeing what the cabinet proposed, or whether they have any scheme. He ascertained that they have digested a scheme, which is designed to reduce the circulation to $130,000,000. Practically it is equivalent to a forced loan. Judge Campbell told the Secretary he did not think the present Secretary of Treasury had enough of the confidence of the country to carry through any radical measure. The scheme has to be urged by an unpopular President on an angry dissatisfied Congress, half of whom represent no real constituencies, and half the rest of whom have lost their seats in the late election. They are consequently sore and angry. Under these circumstances it is hard to see how it is to be done.

Nov. 5.   Flour is $100 per barrel of 196 pounds in this city of great flour mills. I had a conversation with the Secretary of War last night about the condition of the $1500 clerks. Those who have families are reduced to great straits. He said the only effectual relief will be a reformation of the finances.

But how is this to be done? How in the midst of a war, re-quiring the expenditure of $600,000,000 per annum of a cur-rency equal to species, is the change to be made from one currency in the hands of the people to another, without pro-ducing starvation in the interval before prices would readjust themselves, to great numbers who are dependent on their daily labor for their daily bread? Even if the existing circulation were swept out of existence, any new one which did not represent an actual equivalent of value would rapidly depreciate to the present rate of Confederate money. There is no surplus *capital* of which to get loans. It remains therefore to base the new issue on *property* specifically pledged for its redemption. For this, the property must belong to the Government.

The following appears to me to be the only adequate measure: to lay a tax of such a percent of all the taxable property of the country as will raise $600,000,000, payable in money, bonds, cotton, tobacco, wheat, corn, flour, forage, meat, negroes, and perhaps real estate. So much as is paid in money will be so much circulation retired, that paid in bonds so much debt cancelled, that paid in provisions and forage so much less to purchase, that in cotton, tobacco, slaves, real estate so much property of per-manent value on which to base a substantial new currency. The present system of assessors and collectors could collect this. The negroes would be highly valuable for labor on fortifications, mines, etc., and also in the army. By allowing a certain latitude of choice to the taxpayer as to the subject in which to make payment the burden would be lightened.

There is no news from Bragg. The telegrams to the press and the Yankee papers of October 31 indicate that we have materially lost ground near Chattanooga, the enemy having established themselves on the south side of the [Tenn.] river below Lookout Mountain. This gives them water transportation, and railroad also, to within four to five miles of Chattanooga. Very little seems to have come of the Presidential progress except, as Judge Campbell expressed it, 'composing quarrels which are not composed.'

Nov. 6.   Today I made to Major Barton and Colonel Clay this prediction, that on the 20th of this month Bragg will have fallen back to Rome, Georgia. Grant will be where Rosecrans was before Chickamauga and with a vastly stronger army. Infatuation rules the hour. I have never actually despaired of the cause, priceless, holy as it is, but my faith in the adequacy of the men in whose hands we are, is daily weakened. Men are getting tired of it. Steadfastness is yielding to a sense of hopelessness of the leaders. The irretrievable bankruptcy of the national finances, the tenacity with which the President holds to men in whom the country has lost all confidence, the scarcity of means of support, and the oppression which impressment engenders— those things are producing a deep disgust.

North Carolina has elected several men who I am told ran for Congress as Union men, i.e. reconstructionists. Then Governor Vance is said to be more and more intimate with that party who vaunt that [William Woods] Holden, the traitorous editor of the Raleigh *Standard,* will be the next governor. The prospect grows more and more gloomy.

There is but one way to retrieve our affairs, as it seems to me; that is to garrison Richmond, or rather cover it with one corps of the Army of Northern Virginia and send Lee with the other to Georgia. See ante Nov. 2. The [financial] estimates for six months are in except the Commissary General's; they are over $500,000,000.

Nov. 7.   A telegram from General Samuel Jones announces the severe defeat of General [John] Echols by [General W. W.] Averill in Greenbrier [now West Virginia], and calls terribly for reinforcements. He states the loss in killed, wounded, and prisoners as *heavy* and expresses doubt of the escape of any considerable part of our force. The enemy are put at 7000 mounted infantry and cavalry. A [Federal] force has landed at Winston, North Carolina and is making towards Weldon, said to be 2000. General Lee in a letter respecting two cavalry regiments which he wished to withdraw from General Samuel Jones to Stuart, speaks of his army as greatly smaller than Meade's, putting the latter at five corps.

It is very obvious that Grant now greatly over matches Bragg in numbers. The same is true in the Trans-Mississippi. It is hard to say what has become of our forces.

I estimate them to stand about as follows: [14]

		Effective	
Army N. Va.	Infantry	30,000	
	Cavalry	6,000	
	Artillery	3,000 say	40,000
Western Va.	Infantry	5,000	
	Cavalry	3,000	
	Artillery	1,000	9,000
About Richd & N. Carolina	Infantry	15,000	
	Cavalry	3,000	
	Artillery	5,000	23,000
S. Carolina & Ga.	Infantry	20,000	
	Cavalry	3,000	
	Artillery	5,000	28,000

[14] Kean's estimates here are not generally at great variance from those of Colonel Thomas L. Livermore in *Numbers and Losses in the Civil War in America, 1861–1865* (1901), pp. 45–6.

Bragg's army			
	Infantry	50,000	
	Cavalry	8,000	
	Artillery	5,000	63,000
Genl J. E. Johnston in Ala. & Miss.			
	Infantry	10,000	
	Cavalry	3,000	
	Artillery	3,000	16,000
Partisan Corps east of Miss., say			10,000
Aggregate east of Mississippi			189,000
Trans-Miss., wholly conjectural, say			40,000
Grand total effective strength			227,000

Now the Commissary General estimates for 400,000 men, and the Quartermaster General for 175 regiments of cavalry and over 500 regiments of infantry.

To this force the enemy have opposed not less than 400,000 in their armies, forts, and garrisons, of which at least 300,000 are east of the Mississippi. It is obvious that the conscription does not nearly repair the waste of our force and that a steady decline of effective force has been going on all this year. The abrogation of the cartel [to exchange prisoners] by the enemy is telling upon us; that was a smart thing in Stanton [Edwin M., Lincoln's secretary of war]; it cuts us keenly.

Nov. 9. Monday. The President reaches home tonight. *Quid nunc?* The Cabinet has been in session all day. Truly they have much to do.

On Friday General Lee suffered a severe loss in [Generals Harry T.] Hays's Louisiana and [Robert F.] Hoke's North Carolina brigades, which were overpowered and captured at Rappahannock Bridge. This again must have been the result of bad management; General Lee's losses of late have greatly exceeded what he has inflicted. A battery of artillery was lost at the same time.

Snow fell today the first of this season, not enough to lie on the ground. The prospect is very gloomy. Men of the most hopeful temper are getting discouraged, and I believe nothing will arouse the spirit of the people fully without a change in the cabinet. The people seem to think that Mr. Benjamin has the President's ear more than any of his other advisers, and him nobody appears to trust. Mr. Memminger and Mr. Mallory have long ago lost every particle of the public confidence as fully as Bragg has done or more so.

Governor Isham G. Harris [of Tennessee] told Mr. Seddon that Sunday night of the battle of Chickamauga General Bragg did not know that a victory had been won, and when told that Rosecrans would escape during the night, would not hear of it, but insisted that a severe battle would have to be fought the next day. This is authentic.

Nov. 15. Sunday. Judge Campbell has gone to Mobile to look after his private affairs. It is doubtful whether he will return to the War Department. He has all along been dissatisfied with his position, the duties of which not being defined by law, he was constantly liable to be disavowed. The Secretary told me he thought the Judge was dissatisfied at not being made attorney general, a position for which his qualifications eminently pointed him out. But the difficulty was that it was believed he could not be confirmed, and this was not susceptible of being explained to him. The duties of assistant secretary have devolved on me and give me a very busy time. I would not have the office if it was offered to me for the very reasons Judge Campbell disliked it. This is a bad time to lose the right arm of the Department. The Judge told me he felt that in the present state of the country to resign looked like desertion, and this was the chief consideration which made him hesitate.

I don't believe the difficulty about his confirmation [as attorney general] so great as is supposed. Yancey, his special enemy, is dead—the only man in the Senate who actively opposed him. The office has been going begging. It was offered to Senator Henry of Tennessee and to Judge [Charles Jones] Jenkins of Georgia, who [both] declined. Hon. John Bell of Tennessee is now under consideration.

The President got a letter from General [Howell] Cobb a few days ago about the condition of things in Bragg's army, where he and Hardee had been trying to accommodate matters. He thought all but Buckner and [Franklin B.] Cheatham would co-operate usefully, Longstreet especially; but Buckner certainly and Cheatham probably, he thought, would have to be relieved. The latter has been done.

Nov. 23. On the 6th inst. I predicted that by the 20th Bragg would have fallen back. He has not yet done so but has telegraphed to the President that Sherman's reinforcements to Grant, 25,000 strong, have arrived and are making a demonstration on his left, that it *may be necessary to play the same game over again.* He complains that Longstreet who is in or near Knoxville does not communicate with him at all. So it goes—no confidence or concert. Only mischief can come of it.

The financial scheme is leaking out. It is to make the present issues unreceivable for public dues after a certain near day. They would still be fundable. It is said the President is opposed to this as bad faith. An expedient to get over his scruples is to tax them 5% a month. This is Benjamin's suggestion. Mr. Seddon is opposed, as it would leave them in circulation and at a further depreciation, thus increasing the mischief. It seems to me this objection lies against both plans equally, since in either case they would fall into the hands of the brokers who would fund them after buying them up at a great depreciation.

The grand jury of this city presented to the President the condition of the supply of provisions yesterday in a very able paper, stating the cause of scarcity and their ideas of the means of relief. The Secretary don't like it much.

Dec. 6. Since the last entry, Bragg has been wholly defeated by Grant at Chattanooga and [has] retreated in confusion to Ringgold [Georgia]. From there he telegraphed requesting to be relieved of command. The pursuit was checked by [General Patrick R.] Cleburne, who turned on the enemy and inflicted some chastisement. A large quantity of artillery and material was lost. Our troops were not defeated but ran away in the center and on the left, disgracefully as Bragg says. The right stood and fought well till all was lost on the left. Hardee is for the present in command. Whether Johnston will be trusted with the army is not yet decided. Meade on the Rappahannock advanced with eight days rations on November [26], crossed the Rapidan at Germanna, and turned up on the plank road. The two armies came face to face on Mine Run, lay in line of battle for two days, and on the 2nd Meade retired in the night and recrossed the river. There was no fighting except an affair between Edward Johnson's division and one corps of the enemy on Friday November 28, in which some loss on each side was inflicted and the advance checked. Longstreet, who was investing Knoxville when Bragg's army ran away at Missionary Ridge, is now in a critical situation. By last advices he was supposed to be retreating towards Virginia. [General Robert] Ransom has gone to reinforce him. [Ransom did not go.]

Congress meets tomorrow. It has the destinies of the country to dispose of. Is it equal to the emergency? I fear not. Mr. Seddon has been greatly afflicted. He lost a daughter, 12 years old, on Sunday, and his brother, Major John Seddon, died on Thursday.

5

UNEASINESS PERVADES THE ARMY

FROM THE WILDERNESS TO PETERSBURG

Dec. 14, 1863. Congress met on Monday the 7th. They are in a very bad humor. The most significant measure so far is the proposition in the Senate by R. W. Johnson of Arkansas to change the tenure of cabinet officers so as to make a fresh nomination to every new Congress, thus giving the Senate a fresh chance to overhaul them. This is a direct attack on Mr. Davis, so intended and regarded. If it passes, as Mr. Wigfall told me yesterday it probably will, it will be a radical change in the system of government. The most obvious objection to it is that it will tend to make heads of departments too dependent on the Senate, too compliant towards the requirements of individual senators, too fearful of giving offense. The mover of this proposition has taken very foolish offense towards the Secretary of War because the Trans-Mississippi was not referred to in his report of last year, prepared a few days after he came into office.

The Myers case has come up, by a rule in the Confederate States district court for a *mandamus* on the Quartermaster [Lawton] to pay Myers's account as quartermaster general, and in the Senate by what Mr. Seddon called a 'curious' resolution of inquiry, whether the Quartermaster General is discharging the duties of that office, and if not, who is; whether that person has given bond; whether he has been confirmed by the Senate; and whether he is an officer of the Confederate States army. This resolution was referred by the President to the Secretary of War for reply in the usual way—a cool proceeding, the effect of which is to put upon the latter the whole onus of a measure which is the President's own.[1]

Lincoln's message [to Congress and his lenient reconstruction] proclamation is published in the morning papers. Our newspapers treat it with derision. It is an able and crafty paper. The proposition to recognize any state organization by one tenth of the legal voters who at the same time accept the emancipation policy, with amnesty to the rank and file and lower officers, is a cunning expedient to divide the lower orders from those in position and power, and to consolidate the conquest of the states overrun. Our officers jest about being excepted out of the amnesty.

Dec. 27. Sunday.   In the last fortnight nothing noteworthy has occurred in the field. The President yielded about a week ago and ordered Johnston to take command of the Army of Tennessee.

As the session advances the President loses friends and now hardly has any. He affronted Mr. Hunter [Robert M. T., of Virginia, former C. S. secretary of state and now president of the Senate] a few days ago by entertaining him with abuse of Virginia instead of conversing on important business, to discuss which Mr. Hunter went to his house but came away without

---

[1] Seventy-six members of Congress signed a letter requesting Davis to retain Myers, and the Senate approved a resolution, 15 to 9, declaring that Myers was still quartermaster general. The President stood his ground and the Senate eventually confirmed Lawton.

mentioning. When the response to the resolution about the Quartermaster General went in, Wigfall made a speech in which he took the view I had suggested to Judge Campbell, that the President was putting the Secretary of War forward. He [Wigfall] told Mr. Seddon that 'the President would not make anything by that shuffle.'

Melton [Major Samuel W., assistant adjutant general under Cooper] has suggested to the Secretary to make Bragg inspector general of the army. He told me of it, and added in his stammering way, 'He would make us all howl but I'd be willing to howl if I could hear some other people howl too. We'd be a perfect menagerie.'

No Attorney General yet. The acting Attorney General [Wade Keyes of Alabama], not having a library, cannot do himself justice in his opinions. He sent in one on the question whether a state may make it penal to execute a contract to distil whiskey for the commissary department, which was very elementary in its argument. One said to me in speaking of it that it was like a scene in one of Molière's plays, *The Pleaders*; when the advocate commenced his speech with 'When the world was created,' the Court interrupting, directed, 'Begin at the deluge.'

Jan. 3, 1864.   Events move slowly. The campaigning seems over for the present everywhere. In Northern Virginia both armies are kept still by the severe cold. In East Tennessee Longstreet can do nothing because his men are suffering for shoes. Johnston is trying to reorganize the Army of Tennessee at Dalton [Georgia]. The siege of Charleston drags its slow length along without visible progress. The shells from Morris Island have burned a few houses in the city and killed and wounded a few persons, but Sumter is still as defiant as ever. In the Trans-Mississippi little is known to be going on at present. [Thomas] Green

129

who is the hero of the war there has been recommended by General [Kirby] Smith for major general.

Mr. J. E. Ward [of Georgia] (formerly U. S. commissioner to China) has brought a proposition from the bondholders in the Exchange loan, which promises well. They propose to subscribe 10% in the amount they hold as a fund to build or buy fast steamers for running the blockade; that the Government shall have all the inward cargoes; and then send out cotton in return of which a definite proportion shall be for the repayment of the 10% subscription and another part to constitute a sinking fund for the bonds. This they argue will bring the loan up to par again and will make further negotiations practicable—[negotiations] which with it [Exchange Loan] at 35% discount are hopeless. Mr. Ward informed me that he had met no Englishman who did not wish us success and none who was willing for Great Britain to interfere; that the commercial classes have largely the control, and they prefer peace on almost any terms to war. He thinks Parliament will sustain Russell by overwhelming majorities and that the rams will not be let out under any circumstances.

It is a matter of congratulation that our Government refused to have any dealings with Butler as a commissioner of exchanges.[2] Mr. Ould thinks we will have general exchanges reinstated before very long, and meanwhile the enemy [will] do just as they please as to those of our people who fall into their hands who

---

[2] After nearly a year of military inactivity following his removal from New Orleans, General Benjamin F. Butler was assigned to command the department of Virginia and North Carolina and was stationed at Fort Monroe. Late in December 1863 he was made special agent of prisoner exchange also. Immediately Butler initiated an exchange, but for a time the Confederate Commissioner, Robert Ould, avoided direct relations with Butler himself by negotiating with Colonel John Mulford, in charge of the Federal truce ship.

for any cause are obnoxious to them. Captain [F. B. Gurley], who killed General McCook in Tennessee because he refused to surrender, has been recently captured and tried and condemned by a military commission. They will put him to death while we are demanding and protesting and threatening, and that will be the end of it.[3]

The House committee on the finances has reported in secret session. It is understood their scheme is a total abandonment of the Secretary's plans [Memminger]. Surely if they pass one wholly different from his, he ought to resign if he has any sensibility. But his skin is as thick as a rhinoceros's. He is a man of smartness, finesse, but tricky, shifty, and narrow. It is to be hoped he may be got rid of in some way less radical than the change of tenure for cabinet officers. It is suggested that if this passes, the President will veto it. He ought not, I think, unless at the same time he reorganizes his cabinet. The Myers matter is not yet disposed of. Wigfall expects to carry a resolution of censure in the Senate.

Jan. 5.   Mr. Hunter told me tonight he did not think the proposition to limit the term of cabinet officers would pass the Senate now, but if it had been pressed when first proposed he thinks it would have passed. Mr. Wigfall told me the day before that it *would* pass the Senate. Hon. J. E. Ward's proposal will be adopted, and letters have been written to Mr. McRae accordingly [Colin J., of Alabama, co-ordinator of Confederate purchasing abroad.] Mr. Beverly Tucker has been trying hard to get em-

---

[3] Brigadier General Robert L. McCook was killed in August 1862 by Confederate scouts while commanding from an ambulance near Decherd, Tennessee. Captain Gurley was not executed, but he was imprisoned for several months.

ployment. His present effort is to be sent to Canada on some sort of quasi-mercantile mission.

It has been determined, as I am informed, to send a minister to the French *in Mexico* with a proposal of alliance between the Southern Confederacy and Maximilian. I doubt if that card will win. How feeble all that appears of our foreign policy (?) is! There may be something behind but the *results* certainly are pitiful enough.[4]

Longstreet is getting into trouble with his subordinates in Tennessee. He has relieved McLaws, sent him to Atlanta, and preferred charges for neglect of duty in not attacking at Knoxville. He writes of 'combinations' among his subordinates and says he is willing to be relieved, or to remain there as the adviser of any junior who may be assigned to command. So it goes.[5]

Jan. 9.   General William Preston of Kentucky has been appointed envoy to Mexico. He is one of the handsomest men I have ever seen. What advantage this enterprise is to win is hard to see. The French in Mexico are doing very little more than maintaining their hold on the capital and the road thence to Vera Cruz.

A remarkable historical parallel is found between the law pro-

---

[4] William Preston of Kentucky, Confederate major general and former U. S. minister to Spain, was sent to Maximilian's puppet government but the latter, hoping to obtain recognition from Washington, would not receive the Confederate envoy.

[5] Longstreet preferred charges against his division commander, Lafayette McLaws, for not co-operating in the attack on Fort Sanders near Knoxville and for general unwillingness to support Longstreet's plans. McLaws was ordered to Augusta, Georgia, later court-martialed, and found guilty in part, but the findings were disapproved on technical grounds.

posed in our Congress to prevent trade with the enemy and one enacted by the United States Congress in 1815 to stop the Yankees from trading with the British—a business in which New England was largely and constantly engaged. Judge Campbell tells me he knew intimately an old gentleman, who lived at that time in the same house with Amos Lawrence and who narrated to him particularly how that pattens Yankee and his brother brought vast quantities of goods from Canada to Lake Champlain in enormous trains of sleighs. The country was a wilderness and there was small risk of detection, except by those who sympathized with the trade. At the same time Yankee rebels were carrying supplies to Wellington in Spain under licenses from the British Admiral on the North Atlantic station. Cases were tried before Sir William Scott, in which the rascals produced such licenses to escape condemnation. See the report of his decisions.

The exemption law [from military service] reported by Mr. Miles [William Porcher, of South Carolina] in the House, I was surprised to hear the Secretary say last night, was the President's idea. Why he should desire a power which will cover the Executive with fresh odium, increasing that already existing to a point under which the Government can scarcely exist, passes my comprehension. Judge Campbell has drawn up a frame of bill, at the request of Mr. Lyon of Alabama, [Francis S., C. S. Representative] which is a vast improvement on the sweeping one of the House committee on military affairs, yet leaves too much I think to the 'Fiend Discretion.' Some improvements upon the existing law will, I think, be greatly preferable to any of the sweeping undiscriminating changes which crush through society like a car of juggernaut, of which Congress seems fond, as in the case of the substitute bill. Supervision of the habeas corpus and Mr. Miles's exemption bill will make the executive absolute to every intent and purpose.

Jan. 28.   The quarrels between the President and the Senate are coming to a head. The military committee made a long ill-tempered report in the matter of the Quartermaster General, closing with two resolutions: 1st, that Myers is quartermaster general; 2nd, that Brigadier General Lawton has no right to exercise the duties of that office.

One of the points argued in the report was that Lawton had never been confirmed by the Senate and was not legally a brigadier general. They appended to their report in this connection a message of the President in 1862 asking advice of the Senate as to the necessity of a confirmation of officers already confirmed by the Provisional Congress. The report of the committee that it was necessary is stated to have been unanimously adopted. I understand Lawton's name was sent in today for confirmation.

The report which was written by General Sparrow [Edward, of La., chairman of the Senate committee on military affairs] is very petulant towards the Secretary of War and strongly illustrates what I said at the time the resolution was sent to the War Office—that it was unfair to put the thing on that officer when it was universally known to be the President's own quarrel.

There has been another tiff between the Senate and the President. He sent in some nominations for the Trans-Mississippi department with rank from a date prior to the end of the last session. They confirmed them but informed the President that nothing but a regard for the public necessity induced them to do so; that it was illegal; that they protested against it as in derogation of the rights of the Senate, etc. The President replied that he had not held these nominations back, that the delay was due to the difficulty of communicating with the Trans-Mississippi, etc. The Senate replied that they must not be lectured by the President. My information as to these things is not full, being by hear say only.

The law is clearly with the President. See opinions of Attorney General Cushing [Caleb, of Mass., U. S. attorney general under Buchanan]. But Mr. Benjamin in preparing the President's answer does not seem to have known it. I understand that these things have brought Mr. Benjamin a good deal under hack. They are doubtless aimed more at him than at Mr. Davis. He ought to resign.

The Postmaster General [John H. Reagan] has gotten up a quarrel with the Secretary of War about the failure of the latter to answer several communications respecting exemptions of mail contractors. He wrote yesterday that he should submit the whole correspondence to the President, and address no further communications to the Secretary of War. Mr. Seddon answered in a very conciliatory manner, apologizing for the seeming neglect, disclaiming all intended discourtesy, and promising to inform him of what had been done with his communications. This will prove a rash promise, for the most important one has been lying on his table since I submitted it in November last, leaving nothing to be said but that the crushing pressure of engagements caused it to be overlooked.

Jan. 31. The clamor against the nitre and mining bureau as a refuge for skulkers and exempts has caused Colonel St. John to resign. The crowning insult was the clause in the recently published military bill of the Senate, announcing cashiering against any quartermaster, commissary, or nitre officer who has in his employment a man liable to conscription. I doubt if the resignation will be accepted. [It was not.] Colonel St. John has developed the production of nitre from almost nothing to nearly a full supply. But for the loss of territory where the richest nitrous earths are found, he would have been wholly independent of importation. The loss of Tennessee has caused him to develop his works further in the interior, and in a few months his beds laid down near all the interior cities will be ripe. To his great energy, talent for organization, and skilful invention in supplementing defective resources, the country owes as much as to any man in the service, whatever his rank or fame. Others have made good use of what the country afforded in resources. He has *created* when resources there were none.

Hood has been made (or rather nominated) a lieutenant general and will be ordered, I expect, to Johnston. The latter has asked for Lovell but did not get him. The Secretary referred the application to the President with the remark that the assignment of General Lovell would not, he feared, tend to reassure that army.

I understand there is a very low state of feeling among members of Congress. Many of them do not expect any good results from the next campaign. Their legislation is of the wildest description, and as the London *Times* said of Governor Albert G. Brown's resolutions, [former governor from Miss., now C. S. Senator] sounds like the utterances of despair.

Feb. 4.   The proposal in the Senate is to scale the currency by reducing it to *one-third* of its nominal value. This is proposed under the name of a *tax*. The argument is that the remaining one-third will be as valuable as a medium of exchange as the whole now is, and that this is the fairest way in which a prompt reduction can be made.[6]

---

6 In order to reduce the currency, a complex measure was passed February 17, 1864, requiring the people to exchange their paper bills for long-term bonds bearing 4 per cent interest. By April 1, the currency was calculated to have been reduced by an amount ranging somewhere between 177 and 300 million dollars. The plan resulted in considerable contraction and a temporary sharp drop in price, but by the following March it gave way to an additional printing of paper money.

Feb. 10.   The President has succumbed in the matter of re-
nominations of officers confirmed by the Provisional Congress.
A direction has been given for all *general officers* so confirmed
to be renominated. The tender point is the case of the Commissary General. He is in the same situation; they have run him to
the wall. If he is nominated he will certainly be rejected—a deep
mortification to the President and himself; if he is not, the President will have put himself in a false position in order to save his
friend. The true solution is for Colonel Northrop to resign.

Colonel Myers reported a day or two ago for duty (having
received a leave of absence) and subscribed his letter as 'Quartermaster General, C. S. A.' It was referred by the Secretary of
War to the President with the suggestion that this assumption de-
served rebuke and [the proposal] to order him to the field. The
President returned the paper with the suggestion that the officer
should have resumed the duty he was upon when he received
the leave of absence. The Secretary ordered the Adjutant General to order Colonel Myers to resume duty in the office of the
Quartermaster General. I think this was wrong. It was a humiliation to Myers, which he might have been spared, to be put on
duty among those over whom he had so long been head, and that
too when he had remained there as a courtesy to assist Lawton
in getting hold of things. There was too much temper in it.

Feb. 26.   Judge Campbell tells me that in February 1861
Seward, in the Senate, announced in his speech in which he
argued the necessity to preserve the Union by every means, that
he considered the slavery question as settled by the admission of
California, which excluded slavery from the Pacific; that nature
kept it out of all the other territories; and that in the ten years
that New Mexico had been open to it but 24 slaves had gone
there. [Benjamin] Wade of Ohio went over to Fessenden [Will-

iam Pitt, of Maine] and said, 'Fessenden give the damned rascal hell.' Douglas [Stephen A., of Ill.] told Judge Campbell that but for Mr. Mason's reply [James M., of Va.] to Seward, there would have been an open rupture that day on the floor of the Senate between the radical Abolitionists and the moderate (?) Republicans. Not long before this at a dinner at Douglas's at which Seward, Crittenden, [John J., of Ky.] and Judge Campbell were present, after a long conversation in which Seward had expressed the same sentiments, he (Judge Campbell) asked Seward how he as an American statesman could stake the country on such a question as the admission of slavery into New Mexico where it was not by his own admission to go. Seward took a drink of brandy and remarked that his intelligence from Springfield [Illinois] that day was that Simon Cameron would *not* be secretary of the treasury, but that Salmon P. Chase would be, and that he was not at all sure that *he* would be in the cabinet. Douglas replied, 'I see, I see how you are situated,' and Crittenden also said, 'Yes, I see.' [7]

This and much more Judge Campbell told me on my asking him how Chase could be tolerated by Lincoln in his cabinet after the circular by Pomeroy [S. C., of Kansas, U. S. Senator and Radical Republican] in the [New York] *Herald* bringing out Chase for the presidency in opposition to Lincoln's administration. It was to illustrate the relations between the ultra radicals and the so-called moderate Republicans.

Judge Pearson of North Carolina has decided that the anti-

---

[7] The inference here is that Seward, not knowing what his place would be in the Lincoln administration, deemed it politically inexpedient to concede to Southern demands to keep the territories open to slavery. Lincoln himself was unwilling to make such a concession, which would repudiate a plank in the Republican platform of 1860.

substitute act of Congress is unconstitutional and will discharge all who are enrolled in North Carolina under it. Governor Bragg has advised that the enrollment cease.[8] I was present at a conversation on the subject between the Secretary and Assistant Secretary today. The Assistant Secretary said, 'Suppose he decides that the act of Congress suspending the writ does not apply and continues to discharge them.' 'Then,' said the Secretary, 'I will not hesitate a moment to arrest him.' 'That is the point to which it is coming,' said Judge Campbell. It is pitiful to see how closely the factionists of North Carolina and Georgia, in their resistance to the conscription by the abuse of the habeas corpus, are imitating the tactics with which the Abolitionists fought the fugitive slave law.

The assignment of Bragg as commanding general makes quite a buzz. The *Examiner* had yesterday, the 25th, one of the keenest pieces of irony on the subject that I ever read.[9]

The country takes the currency and tax bills with wonderful cheerfulness. The present effect of the former has been mainly to double prices in a week. The suffering is to come later. It is reported that Memminger is not disposed to execute these laws

---

[8] A measure had recently been passed abolishing substitution, the privilege previously accorded an individual to hire another person to take his place in the military services. Another measure, passed January 5, made those having substitutes liable for service. Congress promptly responded to Judge Pearson's obstructions by suspending the writ of habeas corpus in the case of persons trying to avoid military service. Thomas Bragg, former U. S. Senator, North Carolina governor, and Confederate attorney general, was one of Davis's most loyal supporters in North Carolina.

[9] Relieved from command of the Army of Tennessee, Bragg was called to Richmond to become the President's military adviser and general-in-chief of the Confederate armies.

with vigor, and apprehension is felt on that account lest results will be less beneficial than was at first hoped.

March 13.   Since my last note several matters of interest have come up which I had no opportunity to chronicle. The raid of Kilpatrick [was] a miserable failure, so confessed by the New York *Herald* of the 10th inst. which I saw today. The only point of secret history connected with this matter is that there was a strong disposition on the part of some of those in power to put the captured raiders to death. The Secretary of War wrote to General Lee for his opinion enclosing a copy of the Dahlgren papers. General Lee's answer put a quietus on the plan if such there was. It was a very calm, sober expression of the opinion that the criminal *intentions* of Dahlgren were not brought home either to his men or their Government; that he himself was killed; that crime was intent and act, and the latter was wanting; that it was reported to him that some of Gilmor's bad cavalry had done highway robbery on passengers on the Baltimore and Ohio railroad (which he was investigating), and the enemy might claim to treat them as felons; and that they had many better men of ours in their hands on whom they might retaliate. Bragg was said to favor the execution of the prisoners.[10]

---

[10] Near the end of February 1864, Judson Kilpatrick, Federal cavalry leader, raided Richmond, fruitlessly hoping to release Federal prisoners. Colonel Ulrich Dahlgren, young son of the Federal Rear Admiral, John A. D. Dahlgren, was slain, and on his body allegedly were found orders to kill President Davis and his cabinet. Kilpatrick's captured raiders, mostly Dahlgren's men, were not put to death owing in part to Lee's counsel of moderation. In 1863–4, Lieutenant Colonel Harry W. Gilmor, C. S. A., operating in the lower Shenandoah Valley, rivaled the exploits of John S. Mosby. Gilmor directed many of his raids against the Baltimore and Ohio railroad, overturning trains and procuring important military intelligence.

General Lawton has asked to be relieved as quartermaster general. His letter is a good one. The reason he assigns is that his usefulness is impaired by what the Senate said in the Myers controversy. He asks for field duty without expressing any preference as to where he may be assigned. This is pending before the President.

There is a row between Whiting [Major General W. H. C., C. S. A.] and Lynch [Captain W. F., C. S. N.] at Wilmington about certain steamers in whose freightage the War Department relinquished its right to the states of North Carolina and South Carolina. The Navy forthwith seized the space relinquished by the War Department. The states say it is bad faith in the Government. Lynch lays a gunboat alongside and tells them to move at their peril. Whiting came here yesterday about it. In Georgia, [Governor Joseph E.] Brown has denounced to the legislature the late military bill as unconstitutional, and [Vice-President Alexander H.] Stephens has made a speech in which he is reported by private letters to have denounced the tyranny of this Government (in the conscription) as not less worthy of resistance than the Yankees.

These people—Brown, Toombs [Robert, former Confederate secretary of state], Stephens and their set—are the most pestilent demagogues in the land, more injurious than the North Carolina buffaloes because more able and influential. Major Barton has told me that he heard General Howell Cobb denounce Brown before 20 persons at Atlanta last summer as a traitor.

Mr. Seddon has seemed out of spirits since the enemy [Dahlgren's raiders] burned his barns and stole his horses. Gold is reported in New York on the 10th at 170, nearly as high as it was after the battle of Fredericksburg. The greatest blow, which our cause has lately received of the occult kind, is I think the President's determination to put the cotton trade in the management of the treasury department. The regulations were drawn up with much care in the War Department and sent to the President's office. They came back so modified as to destroy the trade by their stringency; at least, Mr. Seixas [J. M., War Department blockade agent at Wilmington, N. C.] and Mr. Bayne [Major Thomas L., bureau head in the ordnance department and later director of the bureau of foreign supplies in the War Department] says so. These are earmarks which show Benjamin's hand, as is usually the case when mischief has been done at the granite building [former U. S. Customs House on Main street now housing presidential and cabinet offices].

A curious thing has occurred in the engineer bureau. Colonel [Alfred Landon] Rives, acting chief, inquired of the Secretary of War this morning where General Martin L. Smith, just assigned as chief in [Colonel Jeremy F.] Gilmer's absence, is, and when he would be here. It was the first that Mr. Seddon had ever heard of Smith's assignment. This thing must have been done by Cooper and Mr. Davis. It is of a piece with the wretched littleness of the spirit the small-minded West Point men about Richmond ever exhibit. The effort of Stevens [Colonel W. H., formerly on Beauregard's staff and now engineer of Richmond's defenses], Elzey, and Cooper to get Stevens into the position failed. The papers though addressed to the President never got beyond Mr. Seddon. I have a suspicion this one was taken to the Executive office by the Adjutant General, and Mr. Seddon ignored in the matter altogether. Smith is said to be a pleasant gentlemanly man, very lazy about papers.

March 15. I learn that an intrigue is on foot in the cabinet to turn out the Secretary of War. It is said that Benjamin, Memminger, and Mallory are parties to it, and Mr. Hunter thinks, so my informant tells me, that the President wants to get Benjamin back in the War Department. Memminger has tendered his resignation. The President has it in consideration.

Mr. Hunter was commissioned to recommend a successor to the treasury department. He conferred with Judge Campbell about it and he told me. Colonel Gorgas [Josiah, chief of ordnance] told me Mr. Davis proposed to Judge Campbell to take the treasury, but the Judge declined. Of this Judge Campbell said nothing to me.

April 3. The change in the currency has taken place without any further effect so far except a great increase in prices caused by the uncertainty of the old issue and the cutting down it was to suffer. Prices have reached the following: salt meats $7 per pound, flour $300 per barrel, eggs $7 per dozen, butter $12, osnaburg $7 per yard, etc.

The change in the treasury department has not taken place and seems to have blown over.

The President appears to be making very general use of the Commanding General [Braxton Bragg]. Orders of all kinds and appointments are made without consulting the Secretary of War at all—troops moved, officers assigned, etc. It is plain to me that there is to be a row between Bragg and Congress when they meet. General Bragg has already made two or three slaps at Congress over interfering into military matters. If he brings his former bitterness to wound what he calls 'politicians' here as he has done, he will be in no end of trouble. This with the exclusiveness of the adjutant general's office will ensure a row. An article in the *Enquirer* of April 2 (yesterday) is terribly severe on Bragg. I have not heard [the identity of] the author. It is extremely well written; the writer appears very familiar with the western campaigns and with matters about the headquarters of that army.

This article is in reply to one in Bragg's defense inserted some days ago.

The indications of failure in the United States treasury are less strong than they were some days ago. Gold has receded from 169 to 164 probably under the influence of Chase's operations under the gold bill of the Yankee Congress.

The foulness of the Yankee mind is strikingly exhibited by a letter from New York to the London *Times*, republished in the *Enquirer* of March 29, on 'miscegenation,' as the wretches call hybridity between whites and negroes. The pamphlet referred to in this letter advocates inter-marriages between whites and negroes as productive of a race greatly improved. It celebrates the amorous propensities of the negress as attractive to this end, declaring the she mulatto to be 'a ripe and complete woman; her complexion warm, dark, and golden; her lips full and luscious; her cheeks perfectly moulded; her hair curling and black as the raven's wing.' Should the South be beaten, what a Mussulman's paradise lewd Yankeedom will make among the negresses. 'Miscegenation' on the wrong side of the blanket will thrive exceedingly, and a cross of that *lues gentium* upon the 'Eboshin' will produce a 'type of mankind' which will add a missing link in the development theory by connecting the human and the baboon races.

Gold in New York $173\frac{1}{2}$ at last advices and tending upward. Many hopeful indications of a general breaking up in the United States, political as well as financial. The abolition proposition to 'postpone' the presidential election, military usurpation by Lincoln, the angry feeling between the Democrats and Abolitionists in their Congress, the intrigues for the Presidential succession, all promise well. Everything depends on the next battle in Virginia. The President and Bragg are very anxious to make Lee as strong as possible. Hence the circular 18 from the conscript bureau calling out the reserves on the 16th inst. These they wish to make garrisons, etc., of [in order] that all the veteran troops may go to Lee. Colonel Preston is opposed to the conscription of any more agriculturalists. He thinks the limit has been past already at which weakness rather than strength results. There is no doubt of this. In the last week, commissioners from the county courts of Appomattox, Fluvanna, Halifax, Spotsylvania, Caroline, and the town of Fredericksburg have been to see the Secretary to get bread for their poor, who are represented to be in danger of immediate starvation.

The invasions of the functions of the Secretary of War by the Commanding General continue more and more numerous, as are the remarks among the officers in the War Department. Nothing but a sense of duty can make a high spirited man like the present Secretary put up with it. All sorts of orders are published in the adjutant general's office, and a copy sent to the Secretary endorsed 'published by the order of General Bragg.'

The case of the military courts of the Southwest [Virginia] was particularly strong. The Secretary had made out his list for these courts. The papers were all sent by the President's direction to Bragg, who sent to the Adjutant General a different list altogether in his own handwriting for appointment, with only *four* out of *twelve* names the same as Mr. Seddon's list ([In margin:] See March 13 last.) The effect of the *manner* in which these things are done is to prejudice the position of the Head of the [War] Department in the eyes of his subordinates, and this effect has as a matter of fact been produced.

April 25.   Our arms have been recently illustrated by a handsome affair in the storming and capture of Plymouth, North Carolina, by General Hoke on last Monday the 18th. General

Beauregard has been assigned to the defense of the southern railroad through North Carolina. He will have 20,000 men movable and will look after any little expeditions by Burnside or Butler in that direction.

Hoke was made a major general immediately on the reception of the news from Plymouth, i.e. as soon as Colonel Wood, A. D. C. [John Taylor, a naval commando and Davis's aide and nephew by marriage] got to Richmond, who was with him. The *navy*, in the shape of an iron clad [the *Albemarle*] built in the Roanoke, participated in the affair. This expedition, embracing also the attempt to capture Washington and New Bern, was planned, as General Kemper [James L., later governor of Virginia] told me, by Pickett, and the command taken from him, i.e. he was anxious to conduct it in person.[11] Beauregard now has the whole force in hand. I have not heard whether any attempt will be made on New Bern. The extreme importance of getting possession of the Sounds and the rich country upon them makes it worth a sacrifice. The enemy have never introduced a monitor into those waters yet.

It is reported that the House of Lords has decided the *Alexandra* [a gunboat built in England for the Confederacy] case in our favor; yet gold in New York by last advices had receded to 164.

The concentration of troops under Lee goes on. A regiment passes every day or two from the South to his army.

Last week there was much debate about the removal of a large part of the clerical force in the Government departments to Montgomery. It was Bragg's plan I think. After two long cabinet meetings it was deferred, except in the case of the ladies who

---

[11] In late January 1864, Pickett, under orders from Lee, planned the attack on New Bern, which failed. Plans for the later surprise capture of Plymouth were devised by Bragg.

sign Memminger's notes who go to Columbia tomorrow. The alleged reason of this step, which would produce a total dislocation of the public business and make the transaction of affairs exceedingly dilatory besides the interruption of the move, was to diminish the number of consumers in Richmond. Another reason, which the Secretary of War communicated to us, was the hope thereby to stampede the citizens of Richmond and this was the *main point*. It was a shallow plan. The *poor* would not have gone because they could not subsist elsewhere. The rich would not leave their property. Those in moderate circumstances have at great cost and trouble accumulated some store of provisions which they could not transport, nor could they buy elsewhere if they sold what they have. Hence they would have held to what they have here. The scheme would have been, and will be whenever tried, a miserable failure. Besides, so large a population cannot be transferred to other points. They could not be subsisted elsewhere as easily as they can be here. The idea was worthy of the hero of Missionary Ridge!

April 28.   General Beauregard was put in command of the Southside and North Carolina a few days ago, headquarters at Weldon. He will have a movable column of 20,000 men to meet any attempt by Butler or Burnside against the North Carolina railroads or Richmond by way of the Southside. Should they advance from the Peninsula, he will doubtless come over to the north side of the James and cover Richmond.

The New Congress meets on Monday next. It has some rough material, some not particularly sound, and some better men. It will be amusing to watch the relations between them and Bragg. A row is nearly certain.

The French vessels which were at City Point to get their tobacco were ordered back down the river on Friday by Butler, having scarcely got any of the tobacco. The ground on which Butler put this was that they were licensed to come for a given number of days, and the time had elapsed. It is probable he had heard of the cordiality with which the French officers were receiving the hospitalities of General Pickett at Petersburg, and of other parties here in Richmond. Altogether it must have been a provoking disappointment to them. M. Paul, French consul here, was said [to] be greatly excited on the subject.

May 20.   Since the last entry the grand campaign has opened both in Virginia and Georgia, as well as in the Trans-Mississippi. 1. On the Rappahannock on the 5th (Wednesday) Grant crossed the Rapidan at Germanna and Ely's fords. On the 6th he attacked Lee on the plank road and turnpike and was repulsed. This day, on Saturday, he tried it again with the same result, some confusion occurring early in the morning when General Lee was relieving his front line with fresh troops. On the 8th and Tuesday the 10th, he had a scuffle with R. H. Anderson, commanding Longstreet's corps at Spotsylvania Court House and was handsomely beaten. On Thursday the 12th, he made a famous assault along the whole line and especially on a salient angle [Mule Shoe or Bloody Angle] in General Lee's line, which he carried capturing Edward ['Allegheny'] Johnson, George H. ['Maryland'] Steuart and 2000 men and pieces. Along the rest of the line he was repulsed with enormous slaughter. Since this, there has been no battle except an assault on Ewell (Lee's left) on the 18th, 2 miles from Spotsylvania Court House—'easily repulsed' as General Lee states.

Grant's general plan appears to be to try to overwhelm Lee in the first instance by mere dint of number. In this he was foiled and has sacrificed his men by thousands. Northern papers put his casualties at from 30 to 60,000, and say he has used up all his reserves. Failing in this he has drifted gradually by a movement to his left, along the high ground east of the waters of the Mattaponi towards Guiney's Station. Tonight General Lee telegraphs that the enemy continues slowly moving towards his right, that he had sent Ewell this morning across the Ni to find Grant's right. His main body was found to be between the road from Spotsylvania Court House to Fredericksburg and the Telegraph road. On the whole, prisoners are about equal; guns captured in the enemy's favor owing to the catastrophe to Ed Johnson's salient; killed and wounded enormously in our favor by General Lee's statements and the admission of Northern papers.

2. Contemporaneously, i.e. on Friday the 6th, Butler with a great fleet of iron clads and transports landed an army of 25 to 30,000 at Bermuda Hundred and advanced first towards Petersburg and the railroad. He dallied a week, effecting nothing but the burning of the bridge over Swift Creek and pulling up three miles of track near Chester. On Tuesday the 10th, [Robert] Ransom attacked him below Drewry's [Bluff] with a brigade and a half and got worsted. On Monday the 16th, Beauregard with 22,000 attacked upon a beautiful plan of battle. Ransom was to turn his flank on the James below Drewry's, [Brigadier General Montgomery D.] Corse to drive him from the railroad and turnpike about Chester, while Whiting from Petersburg was to push in behind his left. The first two parts of the plan were well executed, though with the loss incident to the attacking party. Whiting wholly failed to co-operate as ordered and spoiled what would else have been a brilliant and decisive action. A thousand prisoners, 5 guns and the clearing of the railroad were the results. Butler is now quite quiet.

3. On Tuesday the 10th, Stuart telegraphed that [Major General Philip] Sheridan with 9 brigades of cavalry and 20 pieces of artillery was on a raid by Beaver Dam towards Richmond. He

with Fitz Lee's division was after him. Great consternation was produced among the members of Congress at this, and some other persons were thought to be scared too. Troops were hastily moved from the south side to the lines around the city. Stuart headed them off at the Yellow Tavern on the Brook Road six miles from the city, and had a sharp action in which our cavalry were much worsted. Stuart and Brigadier General Gordon [James B.] were mortally wounded. Sheridan camped and entrenched on the tongue of land between the Chickahominy and the Run which crosses the Meadow Bridge road this side of Storr's house. Next morning there was skirmishing along the lines of the city works, some shelling, but that night and the next morning Sheridan moved off by Mechanicsville, recrossed the Chickahominy, and encamped near Malvern Hill where he remained quite quiet until today. He is now moving back through Hanover and is reported this evening at Old Church. Strong bodies of troops, both cavalry and infantry, are observing him and will defend the railroad bridges over the Annas. The results of the raid were only two days delay in running trains and the loss of two trains of commissary stores at Beaver Dam Station.

4. Averill [in Southwest Virginia] attempted to destroy the salt works and lead mines and break up the Virginia and Tennessee railroad. He captured Dublin Depot, worsted [John] McCausland and burned New River Bridge. When he advanced on Wytheville with part of his force he was met by General [John Hunt] Morgan and defeated. The main body going toward the salt works was met and repulsed by W. E. Jones.

5. In the Valley [Franz] Sigel with 8,000 advanced on Staunton, his object being to get possession of the Central railroad and the Lynchburg road, cutting off Lee's supplies from that quarter. Breckinridge by a forced march met him at New Market in Shenandoah County, and on Wednesday, the 11th, defeated

and evicted him. ([In margin, written later:] U. S. 8000, C. S. 2600.)

6. Butler sent out a raiding party to cut the Petersburg and Weldon railroad below Petersburg—under [Brigadier General August V.] Kautz. They burned a bridge, which was repaired in two days. He [Butler] then made a strike from Chester at the Danville railroad. This party burned the depot at Coalfield and went in to destroy the important bridge over the Appomattox, and they were met near Chula Station and handsomely beaten and foiled in their effort. Such have been the gigantic combinations by which the enemy have endeavoured to crush Lee's army, to occupy Richmond which he expected to find undefended, and to cut all the lines of communication and supply to this city and General Lee's army. Thanks be to God for His mercy, he has failed at all points in the main purposes of his movements and in most instances has been most severely punished.

Meanwhile about the 10th to the 12th, Sherman with a vast army [in Georgia] having failed to make or risk a direct attack on Johnston at Tunnel Hill and Dalton, made a flank march behind the mountains in the direction of Rome. We have no specific intelligence of the fighting which has occurred or the movements made except that Johnston fell back first to Resaca and then to Colburne to meet him, and that he was repulsed with loss in an attack on Rome. That campaign is not, so far as we know, yet developed. ([In margin, written Dec. 1864:] This throws light on the late inquiry arising in preparing the 'correspondence' of the Department with General Johnston, as to the *first* telegram announcing his retreat.)

In the Trans-Mississippi, Smith, Taylor, Price and [General John S.] Marmaduke have nearly destroyed [General Frederick] Steele's and Banks's armies. Steele escaped with a remnant to Little Rock, losing all his train and much of his force. Banks, defeated in two pitched battles and hemmed in at Alexandria [La.], has escaped to New Orleans, as it is reported, with but 5000 men. The rest of his 35000 fell in battle, straggled, or are prisoners; his equipment fell into Taylor's hands, and the flotilla which accompanied the [Red River] expedition was captured or destroyed. ([Insert, Jan. 1865:] This was a mistake. Most of the vessels escaped by building dams and running over the rapids—a very extraordinary achievement.)

In the midst of these great events one has no heart to chronicle the petty bickerings which tease Beauregard and take off the heads of brigadiers (as Barton).[12] Let that pass for another time.

May 22. Johnston has retreated still further, being when last heard from at Etowah. The Secretary is greatly dissatisfied. He told me this morning that General Johnston's theory of war seemed to be never to fight unless strong enough certainly to overwhelm your enemy, and under all circumstances merely to contrive to elude him. This is a very just criticism upon all of General Johnston's campaigns. Beauregard has crowded Butler still further back towards Bermuda Hundred and now holds a favorable line four miles long from Howlett's to Swift Creek, which he is fortifying. Pickett's division and Hoke's old brigade have been sent up to General Lee.

Grant continues his sidelong movement east of the Mattaponi. General Lee thinks he will make the Rappahannock at Port Royal his base and move by way of Bowling Green down the old Stage Road from Fredericksburg to Richmond. General Lee's

---

[12] Brigadier General Seth M. Barton's slowness had been in part responsible for the failure to capture New Bern, North Carolina, in late January 1864. General Pickett severely criticized Barton, and General Lee requested a court of inquiry which apparently was never held.

answering movement is by the Telegraph Road. He indicates that he does not expect to stop Grant till he gets to the Pamunkey. He does not say he will not try. Polecat Creek and the Mattaponi give an imperfect line because the river trends so much to the south that the position can be easily turned. When Grant reaches the Pamunkey he will be less well advanced than McClellan was at Seven Pines, or than he might have been by coming to the White House without fighting. His real difficulties will only have begun. Yet the actual nearing of Richmond will greatly excite the enthusiasm of Yankeedom, who will call it a retreat by Lee and pursuit by Grant. In making this movement if Grant exposes himself, General Lee will be sure to strike him. The Piedmont railroad is now running through, and by Wednesday the Petersburg road also will be. The supply of grain can then exceed army consumption nearly double and a stock be accumulated in case of further raids.

Sheridan's cavalry, or *mounted riflemen* more properly, are at Cold Harbor in New Kent in 12 miles of the city. They are greatly superior to our cavalry in number of arms and discipline and are the best fighters in the Yankee service. They will plague us infinitely. There seems to be a fatality about the concentration of our cavalry. It was begun in March and is not accomplished yet. That arm is doing next to nothing in this great campaign.[13] S. D. Lee was at Meridian three days ago. He and Forrest wield 12 to 15000 mounted men. They should be north of the Tennessee river before this time on Sherman's communications. The Secretary told me [S. D.] Lee was going there, but it is too late for the full effect.

---

[13] Confederate cavalry in the Army of Northern Virginia had been widely scattered by the necessity of finding forage.

May 30.   Our army fell back on Saturday, the 22nd, to Hanover Junction. Grant followed and crossed over [the North Anna river] part of his force at Butler's Mill and Ox Ford and Jericho [Ford] but he feared to attack. On Thursday he withdrew, then went down to King William, and on Friday crossed the Pamunkey at Hanover Tower. General Lee moved by Ashland, and the two armies are now in Hanover on each side of Totopotomoy Creek. General Lee's headquarters are at Atlee's Station. Both have been very quiet for two days. They are resting. Much dysentery prevails in our army. I hope the Yankees have the same. General Lee has been quite sick with it for some days.

Things are unquiet in Yankeeland. The suppression of the New York *World* and the *Journal of Commerce* is an act which will arouse to the intensest bitterness the hostility of Lincoln's enemies. A mass meeting in [Congressman Alexander] Long's district in Ohio has sustained him enthusiastically. The issues of the presidential canvass will probably make it necessary to Lincoln to force his own dictum in order to save it, and that will probably cause violent resistance. Major [Colonel John] Mulford of the Yankee exchange boat told Commissioner Ould yesterday that there was great depression there as to the campaign; also that 4700 and odd wounded were carried to Fort Monroe after the battle of Drewry's Bluff. Gold 186 on the 24th.

There is a stir in our cabinet. Memminger is said to have handed in his resignation. He told a member of Congress that they had as well let him alone, as he was going to go out as soon as they adjourned. Mr. Seddon is much disgusted with his position. In a conversation, a friend told me yesterday that he [Seddon] complained heavily that the President was the most difficult man to get along with he had ever seen. If the President cannot get on with a man as smooth and yielding as Mr. Seddon, nobody can please him. I doubt if he would stay except under the present circumstances of the country.

During the last dark moon, 17 vessels arrived in Wilmington, 3 in Charleston, and 2 in Mobile; 700,000 pounds of bacon came in them, besides other stores of every description.

Johnston has plucked up a spirit and made (or rather Cleburne has) a fight near Marietta, Georgia on the 18th in which the Yanks were worsted. The loss of material, manufactures, and skilled workmen by his [Johnston's] retrograde movements has been among our most serious disasters.

June 6.   Grant said to have moved from General Lee's front last night. W. E. Jones was defeated by Hunter at New Hope in Augusta yesterday morning and was killed. Enemy's force 10,000 infantry, 30 guns, and large cavalry. Staunton is at his [Hunter's] mercy—a great disaster. General Bragg coolly in a note to the Secretary of War shuffles off on General Lee in a single instance the responsibility and the work of repairing this disaster.

The Secretary of War and the President are at issue about appointments. The whole list of quartermasters and commissaries, amounting to some hundreds who have been on duty, many of them for months, sent to the President for transmission to the Senate for confirmation, he returned and refused positively to nominate. He is also angry about a law drawn by Gorgas, providing for additional ordnance officers with a proviso giving preference to those who have been *acting*. This was intended to do justice to the examiners of 1862 whom he excluded because so many were Virginians. He ranted and scolded Colonel Gorgas soundly, as he told me this morning, and claims that the law is an invasion of his *prerogative* in designating persons to be preferred, intimating that the whole list was a piece of favoritism to Virginians in [on the part of] the Secretary of War and the board of examiners in the first instance.

June 12.   I do not like the appearance things have taken on in the last week. While it is not a part of my plan to record military movements or events, the most important force themselves in. The defeat of W. E. Jones in Augusta on the 5th last Sunday, the subsequent occupation of Staunton and Lexington, and the cutting of the Orange [and Alexandria railroad] at Arrington's in Nelson county, indicate a progress there which will soon grow into a vast disaster. Sheridan set out on Wednesday with two divisions, went through King William, Caroline, and into Louisa. Hampton moved parallel on the west of the North Anna. There are rumors of a collision in Louisa, but no news. In Hanover, Grant has actually commenced approaches to Lee's lines on Turkey Hill, by regular steps. He evidently intends to take his time, burrow up to a key point, attempt to take it by assault, and meanwhile let his cavalry, aided by Hunter, Averill and [Brigadier General George] Crook, ravage all the state and cut the communications of Richmond with the West and South. Kautz made a bold dash at Petersburg on Thursday the 9th. The militia, 170 strong, fought him very well and really saved the city. He got inside the fortifications nearly a mile and almost to the suburbs.

All accounts agree that the deepest uneasiness pervades the army, officers and rank and file, at Bragg's being in Richmond. They think if anything should happen to Lee that Bragg would be assigned, which they regard with universal consent as the ruin of the army and the cause.

June 13.   We hear that Lincoln has been renominated at Baltimore and Andrew Johnson as vice-president. Gold 194 in New York.

General Bragg has written a letter to the President, dated June 12, urging that 6000 men be sent to reinforce Breckinridge. Early's corps marched up the Brook turnpike this morning [enroute to Lynchburg]. Those facts are in curious contrast with the pencil note to the Secretary of the 5th. See my memo of the 6th ante. The enemy are threatening Lynchburg in force from Amherst Court House. ([In margin, written later:] The main body went by Buchanan and the Peaks and approached Lynchburg from Liberty. The idea of a *force* in Amherst came from [Brigadier General John D.] Imboden whose performance was worse than ridiculous.)

This morning Grant disappeared from General Lee's front in Hanover. Some of his troops have appeared on the Charles City road in the neighborhood of Bigler's Ship, not far from Malvern Hill. There he has run nearly the course of McClellan. He will probably shift to the south side and operate against the Southern railroads; that is greatly the most dangerous part of our system of defense.[14]

It is said, and I believe truly, that the President has quarreled with General Sparrow, chairman of the military committee of the Senate. He seems to possess a most unenviable facility for converting friends into enemies. Many members of both houses who, when I came into the War Office, were his staunch supporters have become alienated and from one cause or another

---

[14] Here Kean was better at guessing Grant's intentions than General Lee, who was slow in realizing that Grant had crossed the James, despite Beauregard's urgent reports.

have, or deem themselves to have, received personal slights, which they resent by systematic opposition and attack. This administration could not go on a month in my opinion but for the war.

June 17.   People about the President speak in a tone of criticism of everything Beauregard does. I heard today of Bragg's having blamed Lee for the enemy's getting into the outer line between here and Petersburg—a satyr [Bragg] sneering at Hyperion [Lee].

[Brigadier General Raleigh E.] Colston was relieved by Bragg sometime ago because he stopped two Florida battalions ([Brigadier General Joseph] Finegan's, which were marching from Petersburg to this place along the turnpike) for four hours, when he was informed by General Beauregard that the enemy were advancing against the very point of the line where they were passing. He had no opportunity for explanation, and his act was approved and assured by Beauregard.[15]

June 18.   Lee recovered the line from Howlett's house to the Appomattox without much difficulty yesterday. There was heavy fighting yesterday at Petersburg and we lost some ground at one point, inflicting severe loss on the enemy. The force there was strengthened last night and heavy firing heard this morning. Early reached Lynchburg yesterday. Hunter and Company are at Forest Depot and New London, probably not aware that Breckinridge has been reinforced.

---

[15] Once before, following the battle of Chancellorsville, Colston had been relieved of command by General Lee, apparently for failure to carry out orders to attack. If Bragg removed Colston, as Kean here states, he was soon restored.

June 20.   Early, at last accounts, is running Hunter through Bedford at great speed. Major Paxton [James G., transportation inspector in Southwest Virginia] reports to the Quartermaster General that the retreat has degenerated into a rout, etc.

Beauregard's report of the battle of Drewry's Bluff on May 16 has come in. It discloses what nobody outside of the 'Headquarters A. C. S.' had any idea of, and what those 'Headquarters' would not *soon* hear the last of, if it was known: that Bragg had countermanded Beauregard's order of battle to Whiting and had ordered Whiting to join Beauregard on this side. This would have been equivalent to the evacuation of Petersburg and accounts for the failure of co-operation next day, *perhaps.* Beauregard instructed Whiting by a P. S. to execute the order of battle 'as above given' notwithstanding [Bragg's orders], which was not done.[16] Beauregard's report is pretty tight on Ransom too, and it appears he relieved Ransom a few days afterwards.

The greatest injustice of the many continually shown to Beauregard is the querulous and sneering way in which his moving his whole force to Petersburg on Tuesday (?) is spoken of by the President and those who *reflect* him, as B. N. H. [Burton N. Harrison, Davis's private secretary], J. C. S. [probably John B. Sale, Bragg's military secretary] and J. P. B. [Judah P. Benjamin] as giving his line of defenses to the enemy. It was really one of the finest movements of the war. Grant's whole strength was thrown on Petersburg. A choice was to be made

---

[16] Bragg's heading on his letters: Headquarters, Armies Confederate States. On the contrary, in his 'P. S.' Beauregard countermanded Bragg's orders. Bragg had ordered Whiting to join Beauregard at Drewry's Bluff. Subsequently, Beauregard ordered Whiting to Port Walthall Junction, south and in the rear of Federal lines. In the ensuing engagement, Whiting, seized with apparent mental paralysis, did not advance and attack in accordance with Beauregard's orders.

between that city and a line of earthworks which, when Petersburg was lost, was no longer of any value if not untenable by being turned. Then General Lee's army was moving by this very line and could regain it because the *force* of the enemy was at Petersburg. He [Beauregard] promptly took every man he had, flung them into Petersburg where the enemy were making great progress, and beyond doubt by this wise and vigorous movement saved that city from capture. Vital as this was to the defense of Richmond, it turned on the toss of a die, even after [General Bushrod R.] Johnson got there. It was a genuine case of military inspiration which is the mark of *genius* in war. Yet the President and his echoes *censure* this act as abandoning to the enemy the line of breastworks!

6

THE LAND IS FILLED WITH GLOOM

MOBILE BAY, ATLANTA, FRANKLIN, NASHVILLE, SAVANNAH

June 20, 1864. A curious secret society[1] has made its appearance in North Carolina, traitorous in its nature. Its principle is the 2nd and 6th chapters of Joshua, the bargain with Rahab; its object, peace. It has oaths, grips and signs. The essence of the thing is to betray your country in order to preserve yourself and your property. A similar thing has been discovered in Alabama. Both are said to exist in the enemy's army and in ours. It is a foul and contemptible conspiracy probably spawned by some miserable Yankee, which ignorant and deluded unionists in those unsound states have been induced to join in. I do not regard it as dangerous at all. See letter of Governor [Thomas] Bragg and General [Bushrod R.] Johnson received Friday the 17th and one from an inspector (name forgotten) from Alabama.

---

[1] The order of the Heroes of America, because of a red string worn in the lapel of the coat in allusion to the Bible story of Rahab, was commonly called the 'Red Strings' or the 'Red String Band.'

June 25. I have not been mistaken in the impression that matters were less smooth between the President and the Secretary of War than they were. There has been a fuss about appointments again, as in General Randolph's case. Mr. Seddon makes no appointments *at all*, referring them all through the Adjutant and Inspector General (!) to the President. Judge Campbell told me a few days ago that he had certain information that the President had said he desired a change in the War Department—a sentiment which he should never have expressed except to the incumbent. The fickle manner in which the President has dealt with the *honorable* men he has had in the War Office—Walker, Randolph and Seddon—and the acceptableness of Benjamin to him there and elsewhere, is the strongest fact against his good sense and capacity as a President I know; and this dealing with Mr. Seddon looks like a want of sincerity. There certainly was a want of that quality in the matter of General Randolph's resignation. With this feeling on the President's part, and the peevishness which results from it, added to the endless meddling of Bragg, I do not think a man of spirit, as I take Mr. Seddon to be, can stand it long.

Among matters of importance, it may be amusing to have recorded for future observations a petty intrigue by which Colonel Preston, chief of the bureau of conscription, got himself made a brigadier general. Before the meeting of Congress he had made a report swelling with big words, boasting how the harvest had been gathered in and there was now nothing but the gleanings of the field to collect, etc. Then he sought to magnify his services *past*. He has been hinting and suggesting a brigadiership for a long time. Making the organization of the bureau and the appointment of enrolling officers the pretext, he got up a bill 'organizing' what has been organized there two years, the bureau of conscription. This bill, reported by the military com-

mittee in the House, provided for a chief with the rank of brigadier general, etc. Garland of Arkansas attacked it, read from
the printed report as above, and *killed* the whole thing *dead*.
Why the use of all this paraphernalia of office for a work already
accomplished! Thereupon the Colonel, in his customary fashion
of talking at more or less length over a thing and then writing
the same thing in a letter, verbally and in a communication, asked
to be *relieved*. He was *relieved* accordingly, but it was by sending up his name to the Senate as one of the 20 supernumerary
brigadier generals. Nobody heard anything more of the impossi-
bility of discharging the duties without a 'staff' of 70 officers,
trained, etc., which Mr. Miles insisted was the indispensable
object of the bill to reorganize, etc. It's a funny world!

July 9.   Since my return from Cumberland county, the most
interesting affair not known to the public is the negotiation for
the succession to the Secretary of the Treasury. It was offered
to Mr. [T. Butler] King of Georgia. The severance of southern
communications caused great delay in hearing from him. The
offer was made as long ago as three weeks or nearly so. His
answer was a negative, received a few days since. Thereupon
the President urged Mr. Seddon to take it. Mr. Seddon does not
wish to leave the War Office. He does not know that the President wishes to get rid of him there, and wishes to put the
Assistant Secretary in. Judge Campbell consulted me on the subject. He had no direct communication from the President at all.
He knew Mr. Seddon's preference and that Mr. Seddon wished
him to take the treasury. They agreed that the Treasury and
War departments *must* be worked cordially together as one
systematic whole. Judge Campbell suggested that Mr. Seddon
take the treasury ad interim and let him manage the War Office

as assistant secretary. He stated to him too that he (Judge Campbell) did not wish to be in the cabinet; that he was willing to do what he could in the more subordinate positions; but he had not agreed with those who brought on the secession movement and had never forgiven them for it, and hence he preferred not being put in that prominent position among them.

The issue of the matter for the present is that R. R. Cuyler [banker] of Savannah has been invited to be secretary of the treasury. This leaves the President in the same difficulty which had existed all along as to the War Office, and Mr. Seddon without knowing it remains there against the President's wish. I have thought for some time that he would not remain long, and if Mr. Cuyler accepts, that will I expect be the result. Judge Campbell's delicacy on the subject is that he had been informed of the President's preference for himself and he did not wish to be in the place of a 'supplanter.' Ante June 25th [1864], I noted that Judge Campbell told me that he had certain information that the President desired a change in the War Department. He did not then tell me what he did today, that the President's preference was for himself. This incident has given an embarrassing turn to this whole affair.

July 11. The rapid rise of gold in New York in the last month is one of the most favorable indications of the time. It has oscillated since Mr. Chase's resignation between 225 and 280, the fluctuations in the same day's quotations often marking extremes 25 to 30 percent apart. The last quotation (on the 7th inst.) was 272, receding later and closing at 265.

Operations are active now everywhere except here where the principal armies are. Canby is about to attack Mobile. Smith is at La Grange [Tennessee] with 15000 to advance by way of

Ripley [Mississippi] into Alabama and then on to reinforce Sherman.[2] At Charleston they have been quite active, and Samuel Jones is in great tribulation.

An expedition planned (as was supposed) with the greatest secrecy to sail from Wilmington and rescue the prisoners at Point Lookout [Maryland] leaked out, from the navy as it is said, and our latest Northern news is that the prisoners have been removed to the interior of New York [Elmira]. The expedition has been in everybody's mouth for more than a week past.

Early's advance into Maryland seems to cause great fluttering among the Yankee officials. Attorney General Tucker [John Randolph, attorney general of Virginia] says Early assessed the town of York [Pennsylvania] a year ago with a tax of $40,000, which he was prevented by an armed force from collecting, and that he has gone now with a *paper* to enforce its payment. I greatly fear that the chief effect of his movement will be to kill off the peace party just beginning to show some head of strength and return the war party, i.e. the administration, to popularity.

A grievous drought lasting for six to eight weeks has afflicted the country. This evening there is at least a good promise of rain, though it has not yet come. The corn crop has already been materially shortened. There has been some advantage in the early maturity and dryness of the wheat, which has thereby been made available for the army much earlier than usual.

---

[2] General Edward R. S. Canby, in command at New Orleans of the Federal Trans-Mississippi department, did not attack Mobile at this time; nor did General Andrew J. Smith, threatened by Forrest in Tennessee, reinforce Sherman.

July 14. I do not recollect having made any note of the fact that a detective of the War Department about the end of June reported that the Treasurer [Edward C. Elmore of Alabama] had defaulted and gambled away a good deal of public money. That officer will as soon as his accounts are settled resign his office, and I suppose his sureties will have to pay up the deficit to the extent of his bond if it be so much. ([In margin, written later:] On investigation of the accounts it proved erroneous as to funds having been lost.)

The present excitements are (with the public) the doings of Early in Maryland; (with the Cabinet) the retreats of Johnston. Early has not been heard from except through Yankee papers, for ten days. We have their dates of the 12th. The rebel cavalry had destroyed the bridges over Gunpowder and Bush rivers, cutting them off from Pennsylvania and New York. They had burned the house of Governor Bradford [Augustus W., of Maryland], declaring it a retaliation for the burning of Governor Letcher's. They were in a few miles of Washington, at Silver Spring [Md.] which also was reported to be burned, and on other roads an attack in force at 3 o'clock the next morning was anticipated. Mr. Seddon told me he wished Early was safely back in Virginia with his army, though it would not surprise him if he took Washington. This is very doubtful. The 6th corps [from Grant's army] or a part of it is known to be there. They [the Federals] have a large force of convalescents, besides militia, etc., to man their forts. Still Early, Breckinridge, Rodes, [John B.] Gordon and [Stephen Dodson] Ramseur are men to dare and do almost anything.

A very gloomy view of affairs in Georgia prevails in the cabinet. Hon. B. H. Hill got here the day before yesterday on a special mission. Governor Joseph Brown had asked him to come and urge that something be done to save Georgia. He declined but said he would go and see General Johnston. He did so, had a full conference with him. General Johnston said that the enemy had given him no chance to fight a fair field; that his cavalry was superior to Sherman's but was necessary to the safety of his own army, and so could not operate on Sherman's communications; that he saw no way of resisting Sherman's advance except by Forrest falling on his communications. This was at Kennesaw Mountain. Mr. Hill understood him to intend to make several stands between there and the Chattahoochee, and that he would occupy a month or so before crossing it. But he went it at one leap. This was all stated at length in conversation. Mr. Seddon wrote to Mr. Hill this morning, embodying a statement of what he understood him to have represented as Johnston's aims, and requested him to reply whether that was correct. Mr. Hill said it was, except that it was not strong enough and he wrote it out himself. The subject now in hand with the President is the removal of Johnston. To this the *Examiner* is contributing not a little, as is apparent from the tone of cabinet officers and others intimate with the President, by representing that the responsibility of the failure of the campaign in Georgia is on the President for not sending Forrest against Sherman's communications. The real trouble is to find a successor. The only solution is to send Beauregard, but the President thinks as ill of him as of Johnston. The Secretary goes by special train at 5 in the morning to consult with General Lee.

Bragg went out some days ago to consult with Johnston, and telegraphed to the President advising his removal.[3] He also car-

---

[3] Bragg, conferring with Johnston before Atlanta, wired Davis that a change in leadership of the Army of Tennessee would be risky. If Johnston were removed nevertheless, Bragg advised that Hood would give 'unlimited satisfaction.'

ried out orders for General E. K. Smith to make a demonstration by crossing over a part of his force to this side [of the Mississippi]. This latter if done *now* might avail a great deal, but it will be 40 days before the inviolability of a departmental line can be removed. Thus again that dogma may cost us a campaign. Smith might easily keep Canby quiet at New Orleans and perhaps A. J. Smith in North Mississippi. That force [A. J. Smith's] is about coming into collision with Forrest. They were 8 miles apart three days ago between Okolona and Pontotoc [Miss.]

It would be a queer finale of the campaign in Virginia if while Grant is besieging Petersburg, Early was to capture Washington, and while the President is considering the removal of Johnston he was to deliver a solid blow before Atlanta, beat Sherman, and reinstate himself. Neither, I think, is very probable; the most so is the former, as far as I know the conditions.

July 16.   The trouble about Johnston may have come to a head. I have been confined to my house by indisposition today and have not heard. Yesterday morning the Secretary of War took a special train and went over to Petersburg to confer with General Lee at 5 o'clock. He got back at 11 and went to the President at once, remaining there all the morning.

The treasury has been offered to and declined by Mr. Seddon, Judge King, Mr. Cuyler, Mr. Trenholm [George A., of South Carolina], and indirectly Judge Campbell. Trenholm, who was the last, replied that the legislation of Congress had been so irreconcilably opposite to the ideas he has on the subject that he could not think of it; yet he was telegraphed to come on to Richmond. There remains not over $60,000,000 of the new issue to put out. It will last, say six weeks. At the end of that time there will be no resource. The sale of bonds seems as complete a failure as the certificates of indebtedness. Every day lost in getting a Secretary who expects to stay is a serious matter. I hear the President is anxious Mr. Memminger should remain. This would be a breach of faith after what passed this spring, is inconsistent with other statements I have had of his views, and I don't believe it.

General Johnston was removed by telegram today and Hood ordered to take command of the army.

Aug. 7.   From the 16th to the 21st ult. I was sick and on the 22nd left Richmond for a fortnight in Albemarle to recruit, returned on the 4th inst. Mr. G. A. Trenholm was appointed secretary of the treasury, when he came to Richmond as indicated in last entry, which was the end of that imbroglio. Bragg has been absent nearly a month in the South; hence no further trouble with him. Hood has held his own at Atlanta pretty well and has delivered some good blows.

On the 5th inst. the Yankee fleet passed the forts at the entrance of Mobile Bay, 14 ships and 3 ironclads getting in Fort Morgan; sank one [Federal] monitor. Our fleet was then destroyed, the *Tennessee* captured, the *Selma* sunk, the *Gaines* run aground. The *Morgan* alone escaped.

Yesterday a week ago Grant sprang his great mine at Petersburg [battle of the Crater] and Meade his grand assault, which was prognosticated with much flourishing of trumpets by the Yankee press. The disastrous defeat he met with in the assault has manifestly struck a chill to the Northern heart, as is indicated by their newspapers. The [N. Y.] *World* declaims his whole campaign a disastrous failure and declares the opinion that Richmond and Petersburg cannot be taken. The Democratic and anti-administration papers suggest that their army had better be moved to a position in which it will protect 'loyal' territory from invasion. The *Times* (N. Y.) argues at great length that the failure at Petersburg should not produce such excessive discouragement, that Sebastopol was ineffectually assaulted several times, etc. Recent Northern papers intimate that there is to be a change in the command of the army below Petersburg and indicated Hooker as Meade's successor. Meade being as near a gentleman as a Yankee comes, he's probably become distasteful to the Washington concern.

The war is taking on features of exaggerated harshness. Hunter when he re-entered the Valley caused a number of private residences of the finest character to be burned, e. g. Mr. Andrew Hunter's [a cousin of General David Hunter and a member of the Virginia Senate from Charlestown, now West Virginia], McCaig's, etc. Early has burned Chambersburg [Pa.] to enforce a refractory town into paying a requisition. The Yankees have had the unutterable meanness to make an expedition up the Rappahannock for the purpose of burning the house of Mrs. May Seddon, the widow of Major John Seddon, the brother of the Secretary. Her condition was perfectly well known to them, and the fact of her connection with the Secretary of War was avowed as the reason!! Somebody over the border will smoke for this outrage. I am satisfied that this thing which they have been doing now for three years in Florida (Jacksonville), Mississippi (Jackson), South Carolina on the Combahee, and all through Virginia on the northern border, can be stopped by deliberate and stern retaliation. They are in more of our territory but their people live so much more in towns that one expedition can burn more houses than they can destroy in a campaign. That they are amenable to the influences of retaliation is plain for the well known fact that when they have to deal with a man who they know will be as good as his word they are awed.

The whole Yankee army harks to [Ranger John S.] Jack Mosby. He caught a fellow who had burned a home near or in New Market, Shenandoah County, and shot him. The officer in command swore he would burn the village; Mosby sent him word if he did he would execute prisoners of whom he held a number. A party was sent to burn the village but receiving the message in time did nothing, and New Market is yet safe.

Captain [James V.] Brooke of Fauquier, delegate in the Virginia Legislature, told me (he has a son in Mosby's command) that one of Mosby's men, a captive, was murdered in Upperville by a Yankee. Mosby sent a citizen to investigate the facts, and sent the commanding officer word that unless the case was satisfactorily explained or the murderer punished he would take ample vengeance. The message produced great consternation, the case was inquired into, no explanation could be made—it was a brutal murder—and he promised that the offender should be punished. He failed to keep faith, which Mosby discovered, and he executed *ten*. Of the substantial truth of this I have no doubt.

It is a curious fact that precisely coincident with his [the enemy's] tendency to aggravation in the character of the war, a great development of a disposition towards peace is making in public sentiment in the North. With their conscription in September and their election in November, this sentiment may be fairly expected to increase to a head that will be influential, though it will probably not suffice to defeat Lincoln. It may get control of the next U. S. Congress. Gold 252.

Aug. 8.   General Lee has some scheme afoot. Lieutenant General R. H. Anderson, with Kershaw's division of infantry and Fitz Lee's division of cavalry, has gone up to Gordonsville, passing through yesterday.[4]

Aug. 20.   Some weeks ago Major Barton sought an interview with Lieutenant Colonel Ruffin, and told him that he (Barton) had it from the best authority that the President desired to get rid of Mr. Seddon in the War Department, that he thought Mr. Seddon ought to know it, that he did not feel intimate enough with him to converse with him on such a subject; but he believed he had sufficient credit with Mr. Seddon for the latter to credit the statement, and to give it weight as coming from him without the name of his author, which he did not feel at liberty to give. (It was General Cooper.) Ruffin told him he had already advised Mr. Seddon to resign for a different reason (viz., that his administration must be a failure with Cooper, Lawton, and Northrop for the heads of the most important bureaux), and he did not feel at liberty to press the matter further in consequence of the manner in which Mr. Seddon received the suggestion then, but that he would mention it to Mr. L. E. Harvie who might properly inform Mr. Seddon. He did so and was told by Mr. Harvie that it was a mistake; that Mr. Seddon had recently had a full explanation with the President, offering to resign in favor of Bragg or any other person the President might prefer to have there; that Mr. Davis had assured him (the Secretary) that there was *no one he preferred to him* in the War Office; that General Bragg had not the qualifications at all for that position. This explanation was last spring or summer, and was occasioned by some of the doings which trenched on Mr. Seddon's dignity and to

---

4 Lee was sending these divisions to support Early in the lower Shenandoah valley. Grant had been dispatching troops to the same area, which were being assembled under the command of Major General Philip Sheridan.

which allusion in general terms has been made in these memoranda. On comparing this statement derived from Colonel Ruffin with what I recorded ante July 9 [1864], I am at a loss how to reconcile the two. Averse as I am to suppose the President guilty of duplicity (which was the first impression), I prefer to trust that there is some possible explanation of his two opposite avowals, one *about* and the other *to* Mr. Seddon ([In margin, written later:] See post, Jan. 29, 1865.)

The President is in a bad humor with the adjutant general's office. A few days ago he walked into Melton rather unceremoniously and causelessly, and more recently into the concern generally, in connection with a letter of Messrs. Vest and Conrow [George C. Vest, Confederate House and Senate, and Aaron H. Conrow, House, both from Missouri] respecting Captain McMillen. In both cases the offense was the idea that information which had been given, or which he supposed had been, should have been withheld. In the latter case he was obviously and on the face of the paper mistaken in his suspicions, which were probably without a shadow of foundation.

Another evidence of Bragg's malignity of temper is shown in the case of Major A. B. Moore, a quartermaster in the Mississippi Valley, the same in connection with whom Melton got his rap. This inspection report, on which Bragg was depriving him of his position, was as soon as he had a chance to respond blown into atoms. Yet Bragg yesterday made to the President an endorsement in which he seeks the same used on two or three new and petty issues.

Aug. 28. I was pleased to see a few days ago that Beauregard had made Bragg eat dirt in reference to the letter of the latter charging the former with 'insubordination and disobedience of orders,' in the matter of Colonel [Lawrence S.] Baker's 1st North

Carolina regiment of cavalry reporting to Bragg in May last. Beauregard exploded Bragg statements, and then closed by demanding a court of inquiry, and sent his aid-de-camp here to await an answer. Bragg wrote asking to withdraw his letter.[5]

On Thursday last A. P. Hill struck Grant another hard blow at Ream's Station, taking 2000 prisoners and 9 guns and carrying his entire line of breastworks. This makes about 9000 prisoners captured upon the Weldon railroad since Grant sat down before Petersburg.

Just a year ago Rosecrans was maneuvering Bragg out of Chattanooga, Longstreet was on his way then to win the battle of Chickamauga, Myers had been turned out of the quartermaster general's office, Buckner had evacuated Knoxville, Lee was on the Rapidan resting his army after the disastrous campaign into Pennsylvania which culminated at Gettysburg.

Sept. 4.   Atlanta went up on the 1st. Sherman got on the railroad to Macon and West Point, and Hood tried but could not dislodge him. So on the night of the 1st he decamped. What loss of material, etc., we suffered I don't yet know. This is a triumph for Johnston and his friends. The 'authorities' look rather black today. General Lee is over here in consultation. To-morrow is the Yankee draft. If it is successful, it is hard to see how we are to raise men to meet their recruited armies.

Sept. 25.   In the last three weeks, while there has been no great blow struck, there has been a steady decadence of our affairs. Early twice defeated, at Winchester on the 19th and at

---

[5] In a letter to General Cooper, Bragg complained that Beauregard without authority detained the regiment which had been ordered to Richmond and thereby placed the capital in peril. Lee intervened in the squabble, Bragg withdrew his letter, and Beauregard withdrew his request for a court.

Fisher's Hill on the 22nd. He is now said to be in full retreat up
the Valley. At Petersburg there has been no change. Hampton
delivered a good blow about a week ago in the capture of 2500
good beef cattle just arrived from the North, giving Lee's army
a fresh meat ration for a month.

There is manifestly the deepest uneasiness among the military
authorities, from the weakness of our army and the recruiting of
the enemy's under the prospect of their draft. General Lee has
urged the pressing of the conscription through the general of
reserves [in the various states] which has been ordered. He has
also suggested calling out negroes to relieve the army from the
labor of entrenching, etc.; also the impressment of the 20,000
negroes under the act of Congress for that purpose, for teamsters, etc., both of which have been ordered. The conscription is
now being pressed mercilessly. It is agonizing to see and hear
the cases daily brought into the War Office, appeal after appeal
and *all* disallowed. Women come there and weep, wring their
hands, scold, entreat, beg, and almost drive me mad. The iron is
gone deep into the heart of society.

Yankee politics have simplified themselves very much. From
such indications as reach me Lincoln will walk over the course.
McClellan [General George B., Democratic nominee for the
presidency] stepped off his platform in his letter of accept-
ance, and is as strong a war man as Lincoln. He would be a
much more formidable one to us because he would constantly
offer peace and reconstruction on the basis of the Constitution,
which would rapidly develop a reconstruction party in the
South. Such a party is now beginning to form under the stress
of disaster. Men begin, too, to talk calmly about emancipation;
some as a cheap price for peace; others as good absolutely because we cannot afford to be under the ban of all the world,
though right in the abstract.

The President went south on Wednesday. About the time he started, Hood telegraphed that he had adopted a very bold purpose—nothing less than to turn Atlanta on the west, crossing the Chattahoochee, and falling on Sherman's communications. This is extremely hazardous. It is an imitation of Sherman's own maneuver, and exposes Hood as Sherman exposed himself. If it is successful, it will be a very great success as it will compel him to evacuate Atlanta or come out and fight on Hood's own ground.

Bragg gets worse and worse, more and more mischievous. He resembles a chimpanzee as much in character as he does in appearance. He is engaged now in persecuting quartermasters who have clerks liable to military duty, detailed by the Secretary of War for duty with them. One, Barksdale [Captain G. A., officer accounts, quartermaster department], he ordered under arrest for keeping his funds on deposit in the treasury where the law imperatively requires them to be kept.

One of his sneaking tricks is to find out something done or contemplated by the Secretary of War, and then write to the President making an *original* suggestion that it be done. This was conspicuously the case with reference to court martial records and the organization of the detailed men. His suggestions with respect to the former were [made] several months after their adoption and after his military secretary [Colonel J. B. Sale] had made particular inquiry as to what was done; on the latter, after the Secretary's order had been published in the newspapers for some weeks. Prying, indirection, vindictiveness, and insincerity are the repulsive traits which mark Bragg's character, and of which together or separately I see evidences almost daily.

Oct. 18.   On Thursday September 29 the enemy advanced on the north side, drove back our thin line from Signal Hill, and by assault carried Battery Harrison on Chaffin's farm, in the rear of the water battery at Chaffin's Bluff. They received a bloody repulse from Fort Gilmer, a stockade redoubt in the same line. At the same time they developed in considerable force on the New Market road and threw shells after [Brigadier General Martin W.] Gary's retreating cavalry, some of which burst within the intermediate line of the Darbytown road. General Pemberton [now a lieutenant colonel in the artillery corps] exhibited considerable excitement on the occasion, at the Secretary's office.

On the 8th the Secretary answered a long letter of Governor Joe Brown, a very sharp correspondence on both sides. The Secretary has the best of it because Brown is in the position of a factionist, if not a traitor. He has behaved in a manner which laid him open to grievous suspicion of treason, and the similarity of his proceedings to those of the governors of Massachusetts and Connecticut in the War of 1812 afforded Mr. Seddon an opportunity, the parallel of which he did not neglect to remind him.

The 'event' in the administration of the War Department of the past three or four weeks has been the revocation of all details, and the transfer of conscription from the bureau of conscription to the generals of reserves. These measures in Virginia have brought out a great many able bodied men, no reasons or excuses being listened to and the men taken to the army as fast as a medical examination could be given to them. Yesterday the President knocked Kemper [Major General James Lawson, general of reserves and later governor of Virginia] and the Secretary 'higher than a kite' by declaring that the generals of reserves have nothing to do with conscription, were not selected for that duty, and that the business should go back into the hands of the bureau. So there we are. The new system, general order No. 64 [73], was, as I understood, the President's scheme.

It dislocated established courses completely. The new one has just got to working, and it is now overthrown. Ruthless it certainly is, destructive of material and industrial resources it certainly will be, but it is marvellously efficient in putting men, and good ones too, into the army here in Virginia where every harsh measure is executed.

Oct. 20. On the 17th Bragg left Richmond bag and baggage to take command at Wilmington. Everybody fears that Wilmington will 'go up' with 'Josiah' there, but is notwithstanding delighted that this element of discord, acrimony, and confusion is withdrawn from here.

Nov. 20. Sunday. The Yankee election was evidently a damper on the spirits of many of our people, and is said to have depressed the army a good deal. Lincoln's triumph was more complete than most of us expected. Most judicious persons believed that he would be re-elected but nearly all, while thinking that his re-election would be better for us than McClellan's, hoped that it would be closely contested, possibly attended with violence.

In our Congress the suggestion of the employment of negroes as soldiers finds little favor except with that portion who represent imaginary constituencies. The representation of the planters are averse to it strongly, as were the native generals when Johnston laid Cleburne's memorial before a council of his major and lieutenant generals in May last.[6] See a letter of General Johnston

---

[6] At Dalton, Georgia, in May 1864 General Patrick Cleburne had circulated among the officers of Johnston's command a document advocating the recruiting of Negroes for the Confederate Army. A large majority of the officers voted against it, and Johnston persuaded Cleburne to suppress his memorial.

on this subject to the Secretary of War giving the result of the conference. This transaction is known to very few.

Johnston's report of operations in Georgia, down to the date of his being relieved in July last, is a very strong paper. It puts things in such a light that Mr. Seddon said to Judge Campbell that if they had been so understood, he would not have been removed. The results in Georgia since his removal have furnished powerful ground for his vindication. He thinks that Bragg was the cause of his removal. I thought differently at the time and supposed that Bragg was wholly innocent of it, but I now hear from Judge Campbell that Bragg had telegraphed from Atlanta to the President that Johnston ought to be removed and Hood put in command, and that Johnston had seen it. The present alarming condition of things in Georgia affords his friends a great triumph.

Sherman, after Hood had gone away off to Tuscumbia [Ala.], rapidly drew back five corps to Marietta and Atlanta, leaving Thomas with Rosecrans's force and two corps of his army to observe Hood, who has been weather bound on the Tennessee for three weeks. On the 15th he [Sherman] set out, after having destroyed the railroad and the bridge over the Chattahoochee, also many houses in Rome, Marietta, and Atlanta; started in three columns, one on each side of the Ogeechee on Macon, and one along the railroad towards Augusta. At our last advices they were 30 miles from Macon and at Social Circle. Hardee was ordered at once from Charleston and got to Macon yesterday. Beauregard [now in command of a military division stretching from Georgia to the Mississippi] also ordered Taylor there, and set out himself. Taylor is detained at Mobile by an accident on the railroad. Sherman will probably reach Macon today. [General Joseph] Wheeler with 13 brigades of cavalry seems not to have checked Sherman's march for a moment, and Cobb [Howell

Cobb, commander of Georgia reserves] made great time from Jonesboro to Macon. The reserves, militia, and Wheeler's cavalry will make some 12,000. Sherman's force estimated at 30,000 [actually 62,000], advancing on Macon.

Mr. Hunter is very much dissatisfied with Mr. Trenholm's scheme for benefitting the treasury [to stop issuing more currency, to sell more bonds, and to increase taxes]. The real difficulty I suspect is that he proposed very heavy taxation and to lay it fairly on the agricultural and planting interest. As this is the predominant interest in Congress, there is small chance for the adoption of the plan, and Trenholm will, like Memminger, have to administer a patched up plan without consistency.

Nov. 30.   Sherman's march through Georgia has been conducted with consummate skill. He has so directed it as to induce the collection of troops at points at which he seemed to be aiming and then he has passed them by, leaving the troops useless and unavailable. Two days ago he was at Millen. When Bragg was assigned to command down there [in Southeastern Georgia] I gave up all as lost, so far as opposing Sherman was concerned.

I have been preparing the correspondence with Johnston, to accompany copies of his report, which has been called for by both houses of Congress. The portion of it conducted with Bragg gave me a new light on the history of the early campaign in Georgia. It shows a mastery of the situation, a sagacity in anticipating the future, and a comprehensive view of the situation on Johnston's part, in strong contrast with Bragg's plans, which Johnston tears to tatters, and his speculations which events prove erroneous. One fact is very striking. Bragg writes the President one letter showing that Johnston was enormously overmatched, and evidently intended to get him (Bragg) 'right on the rears.' A few days later he writes another in which he represents that

Johnston's strength approaches more nearly to equality with the enemy to be opposed than General Lee's, and while he does not say so, implies that Johnston might do better if he would. The impression the whole thing makes on me is, that damaging as Johnston's report is, it would be better for the President to send it in as it is than to send the correspondence with it, better at least for Bragg and for the President.

Hood when last heard from (through Northern papers) was at Columbia, Tennessee, Thomas retiring before him on Nashville. If we regain Tennessee, we may get it in good time by losing Charleston and Savannah. *Sed guere.* The administration are manifestly much disheartened, and those behind the scenes look very gloomy. Congress has been debating the suspension of the habeas corpus for three weeks in connection with the secret society called H. O. A. [Heroes of America], which was first discovered in Alabama many months ago, then in North Carolina, and this fall in Southern Virginia. The difficulty they have in acting shows strong opposition to the measure.

Bishop Lay [Henry C., Episcopal missionary bishop for the Southwest] got here on Saturday 26th from the North through Grant's lines. He had gone to Huntsville [Alabama]. Sherman would not let him go through his lines as he was just setting out on his march and sent him around this way. Grant told him that Lincoln would be willing to make peace on much better terms than we supposed, and expressed a desire to have a conference with General Lee on the subject. Bishop Lay told this to Judge Campbell who told it to me and to Mr. Seddon. Mr. Seddon requested him not to relate it any more. Mr. Seddon also expressed to Judge Campbell the opinion that Grant and General Lee were the only men who could settle the matter and bring about a peace.

Dec. 25.   Since my last entry disasters have come thick and fast. Hood's battle at Franklin [Tenn.] involving fearful loss and no results: 13 general officers killed, wounded and captured, Cleburne among the killed [two major generals and ten brigadiers were lost]; then his total defeat by Thomas at Nashville, whence he is now fleeing with the shattered remains of that unfortunate army, which has never yet fought under a general nor gained a victory except the sorrowful one of Chickamauga; Sherman's triumphal march through Georgia and investment of Savannah, which has been (on the 21st) evacuated and surrendered; and the destruction of the Virginia and Tennessee railroad and saltworks, make up a tale of disaster which has filled the land with gloom.

This has been greatly heightened by the increased difficulty of feeding Lee's army. Ten days ago the last meat ration was issued and not a pound remained in Richmond. The President and Secretary were greatly alarmed. Fifteen thousand barrels were borrowed of the navy and some more of Governor Vance, which gave them another chance to get another start with beeves and hogs. A great pressure has been brought to bear, since Hood's overthrow, for the reassignment of Johnston. It would logically involve the retirement of Mr. Seddon whose administration seems totally broken down at all points. He is, I think, and has been for some time preparing his mind for going out. Congress is very sulky and very much alarmed. For the latter there is abundant reason. The truth is we are prostrated in all our energies and resources. The conscription has been pressed to its utmost limits, and beyond any reasonable ones, by the revocation of details. General order 77 [revocation of all details heretofore granted], which prostrated the industrial interests, private and public, went further to break the spirit of the people than any administrative act of the war.

At the instance of Mr. Hunter, the Secretary and others, Judge Campbell has written to Judge Samuel Nelson, of the Supreme Court of the United States, a letter proposing to visit him and confer with a view to ascertaining whether there is any way of putting an end to the war and suggesting conference if Judge Nelson thinks it may lead to any good result, to be held by Judge Campbell with Mr. Stanton or one or two other leading men. This letter Judge Campbell got me to copy, that he might have a witness; and he did me the honor to consult me respecting the manner of it, changing it from a first draft which seemed too cold, formal and diplomatic. The probability is that intercourse will be declined.

I had much conversation with Judge Campbell about this subject and our prospects. He thinks it will all end in reconstruction and that the only question now is *the manner of it*— whether the South shall be destroyed and subjugated or go back with honor and rights, though shorn of many advantages, of power, influence, and political supremacy. I told him that reconstruction, whether by subjugation or reconstruction, involved failure, and implied *defeat* and humiliation as well as emancipation. A state of society, in which the negroes had been suddenly freed and given political franchise as citizens, the whites over-awed by garrisons ruled by Yankee policy, and been bled by defeat and practical subjugation, was one in which I am unwilling my children shall grow up, and only the physical disability to accomplish it will prevent me from emigrating.

The negro enlistment has been revived by the late disaster. Deeper reflection has satisfied me that it is not a practical question at all. The difficulties by which it is surrounded prevent it from being feasible, except on the ground of universal emancipation. Men are beginning to say that when the question is between slavery and independence, slavery must go, and this is logical because when independence is lost slavery is at the same blow destroyed. The memoir I submitted in July 1863 now often recurs to me. [See above July 14 and 26, 1863.]

January 1, 1865.   Sunday morning, after several weeks of rainy damp weather, ending in a rain and snow storm on December 30 and 31, the new year opens with a bright winter sun. God grant that it may be an omen and that the affairs of this unhappy nation may from this day begin to improve. There is however little reason to found the hope upon, except the goodness and mercy of the All Wise. I now wish the hope that the great armada, which on the 24th and 25th assaulted Wilmington, or rather Fort Fisher, may have come to heavy grief in the rough and stormy seas of our coast. If they had not made a port at Beaufort or Port Royal, they doubtless suffered some loss, especially of iron clads. The small damage done to Burnside's expedition against Hatteras and Roanoke Island by the great storm of November 1861 has moderated my expectations from storms very much. There were no ironclads in the fleet however, and the fate of the first *Monitor* which foundered off Hatteras in 1863 affords ground for hope that this class of vessels, the most formidable, may have suffered severely.

It is quite obvious to an observant person that the public mind is rapidly familiarizing itself to the idea of general emancipation. With some, it is spoken of as a means of winning the good offices of European powers; with others, as a means of further utilizing the negro in the war; and others doubtless look to it as smoothing the way to reconstruction. That this last idea is making rapid strides, especially out of the army, is very certain, though not yet avowed. How emancipation is to aid in *carrying on the war* is to me incomprehensible. It would strike down at a blow the whole productive power of the country, introduce a thousand domestic questions of amazing intricacy and difficulty, and tear the vitals of society. As a step towards reconstruction it is very intelligible. The Yankees are arranging that matter on their side too by an amendment of the United States Constitution, and this agitation on this side looks like meeting them half way. Mr. [J. W.] Anderson has brought to my sickroom a rumor, which he says is general in town, that Congress has been engaged in secret session in discussing the gradual emancipation of slavery in connection with its effect upon foreign relations. This rumor gives me a great deal of concern. The thing is so perfectly impractical that no good can possibly come of it, and harm may.

Jan. 2.   Charles Blackford [of Lynchburg, who had entered the war with Kean in the 11th Va. regiment] tells me there is a better feeling abroad today, and that gold has gone back to 35, having been last week up to 60. (This was a mistake.) Gold is 50 and pretty steady at that figure.

Jan. 8.   I have just got out after a confinement to my home by sickness of ten days, and have been getting posted as to what is going on. Things are getting worse very rapidly and fast. The Assistant Secretary has prepared a letter to the Secretary of the Treasury, showing that the unpaid requisitions for the last year are $178 million, and arrearages not required for $180 million more. He also went to see Mr. Trenholm, to see what his resources were. There were taxes from which he expected $40 million this month. But Congress has passed a law that all the taxes of 1864 are payable in 4% except the soldiers' tax, which will make all these taxes 4% bonds instead of currency. Then he has bonds which he can't sell and certificates which the people won't take. The result of the exposé was that Mr. Trenholm said he would have to abandon his scheme and adopt a new one, which can't be anything but more treasury notes. The Secretary of the Treasury was astounded at the insolvency of the War Department, and said that Mr. Memminger had informed him that the arrearages were only $70 million, while he had paid $320 million since he came in. [Major W. L.] Bailey and [Captain John M.] Strother [financial agents of the commissary department] insist that they have informed him fully of the state of the respective departments.

Then, a joint committee has been raised in Congress, which is energetically looking into the state of the public service. It was raised first on the motion of Baldwin [John B.] of Virginia in the House to consider the state of subsistence supplies. The Senate enlarged it to embrace transportation, ordnance, quartermaster and foreign supplies, and the treasury. They are working very hard. No practical result that I can see can be reached except a vote to express the now almost universal 'want of confidence.' One solution which I have heard suggested is an entire change of the Executive by the resignation of the President and Vice-President. This would make Hunter, as president of the Senate, the president, would really make Lee commander-in-chief, and would go far to restore lost confidence.

The Secretary of War talks of resigning. He has lost his chance to do so with credit as he might have done last summer at any time. Now, under the Tennessee ruin, the march of Sherman, the break down of subsistence, the responsibility for which is largely thrown upon him, and the committee above mentioned, he would go out covered with odium, a large part of which belongs to others.

The visit of the Blairs [Francis P. Blair, Sr., famous Jacksonian and father of Lincoln's former postmaster general] probably had some connection with the letter to Judge Samuel Nelson mentioned in my entry of December 25, 1864. Old Blair wrote to the

President for a passport to come into our lines, alleging as the grounds for the application that he wished to inquire after certain papers taken from his house [at Silver Spring, Md.] at the time of Early's approach to Washington. He received a passport upon condition of his parole of honor that he should confine his intercourse to the object stated in his application. His going back is curious. The [N. Y.] *Tribune* had disclosed the nature of his embassage, which was closely accordant with the suggestion of Judge Campbell's letter. His return may be explained by the fierce assault on his expedition by the *Examiner*, coupled with the restricted character of his permits; or perhaps, since the letter of Judge Campbell referred to a conversation of Bishop Lay with General Grant, the latter may have made some new communication which may have changed Blair's views. Altogether it is curious. Some or all of these considerations may have brought him to the conclusion that to come in would be useless, and would tend to no good.

Mr. W. C. Rives's solution is a special embassage to the European powers to show our real condition and solicit intervention, coupling it with a proposition for prospective emancipation. Benjamin is quite confident that intervention is about to come of itself!! I am told that owners are selling their slaves very rapidly. Thus it appears that there is a general standing from under. The bad signs thicken.

Jan. 10.   I got down to the War Office yesterday, though not well enough. Saw General Wigfall, who as Judge Campbell says has come like Saul on his journey to Damascus 'breathing out threatenings and slaughter.' He represents the masses of the Gulf states as utterly discouraged.

The President was advised the other day to consult with leading men in Congress, as well his friends as his opponents, so as to draw the support and confidence of all parties back to the administration. He received the suggestion so coldly that the Secretary told Judge Campbell that he was satisfied no good would come of it for want of cordiality and confidence. The Assistant Secretary asked the Secretary what was the President's plan for meeting the emergency. The answer was that he had none, either for campaign or for the conditions and that he never *had had any*.

Jan. 13.   Old Blair came after all, on the 11th. He had interviews with the Secretary of War and especially with the President. The result of which, as far as I have heard, is that the President addressed a letter in which he stated that he would receive any minister, envoy, commissioner or agent who might be sent by the United States, or he would send one there. Blair expressed himself hopeful that something would be effected on this, and said he hoped to accomplish the sending or receiving of a commissioned agent to negotiate. I am told that he declared that all idea of confiscations and punishments would be laid aside. It is said that great pressure was brought to bear on the President in connection with Blair's visit. I also hear that the House of Representatives have been debating in secret on a proposition for the appointment of commissioners. Some represent that this is proposed to be done independently of the President; others deny this and say it is recommendatory to the President. Upon a vote it is said the proposition was lost by three votes and was then reconsidered, and will pass. A majority of Congress is represented to me to be in favor of treating for peace. Whether all these propositions imply independence as a *sine qua non* is not stated. The number is certainly increasing of those who do not insist on that, but would make peace with reconstruction on old grounds of property and right, and not a few would agree to gradual emancipation.

As the real condition of the treasury comes to be known—the hopeless bankruptcy in which it is plunged, the arrears of $320 million, and the proposition to tax 16% ad valorem as a means of meeting it—the Congress get more and more weak in the knees. I was told today that Mr. Trenholm had said if Congress did not adopt his scheme he would resign. This is consistent with what he said when he took the office, but is meant I suspect as an anchor to windward. They will not lay any such taxes, and he will go out creditably, in appearance at least. The truth is he had no idea of the condition of the treasury when he took it, or since till recently.

As an illustration of the condition of the treasury, the Commissary General wrote a day or two ago to state that a million of dollars had been put to his credit at the treasury to buy cotton with which to pay for meat. All his arrangements were made; holders would only sell for cash. He said he had cash, and gave drafts on the sum to his credit. They *could not* be paid, and though he had this million to his credit for *ten days*, not a dollar could he get!!!

I hear there has been a very sharp correspondence between the President and Vice President. The latter had said in a letter to Senator Semmes [Thomas J., of La.] that the influence of the administration had been thrown against McClellan [in the Federal presidential election of 1864]. Mr. Davis wrote to him desiring him to specify instances in which this had been done. Mr. Stephens answered in a long, sharp and able letter citing as instances the case of Kable [David F. Cable] and the President's Macon speech. This letter had been spoken of for sometime as a poser, and it was said the President *could not* answer it. Mr. Seddon told Mr. Hunter yesterday that Mr. Davis had made a triumphant answer, in which it is shown that Mr. Stephens had not been accurate in his facts.[7]

The Assistant Secretary has presented to the Secretary of War a memorandum of certain heads which require imperiously to be attended to, else we cannot carry on the war. Some of these are: 1. The supply departments to be put on a permanent footing and guaranteed against interference; 2. the army to be reorganized; 3. the finances to be restored; 4. absenteeism in the army to be corrected; 5. the production by the people to be guaranteed on a permanent footing; and other heads which I don't recall; he had eight. He has several times lately expressed to me the opinion that the Adjutant and Inspector General and his office were utterly, hopelessly inefficient, and with two or three exceptions among the subordinates, incompetency is the rule there.

Jan. 21. Saturday. Matters seem to be coming to a head between Congress and the President. The Virginia delegation adopted certain resolutions [calling for a complete change of the cabinet], in consequence of which the Secretary of War tendered his resignation on the 19th and the Assistant Secretary has *written* his also, putting it on the ground that the two are in fact

---

[7] Stephens had undertaken to procure a parole from the Andersonville prison for David F. Cable, a Federal prisoner of dubious identity who convinced Stephens that the two could devise a plan by which Southern aid would lead to a Northern Democratic victory in the presidential election of 1864. Before Cable's parole could be effected he died. Stephens thereupon bitterly assailed Davis and accused him of deliberately sabotaging Northern Democratic victory with McClellan the standard-bearer. It was an easy matter for Davis to point out the fallacies of the Vice President's ridiculous and reckless charges.

one office and that he is unwilling to serve except on the terms of known intimacy, confidence, and harmony with the Secretary. The fact, as I believe, is that he is glad of an opportunity to escape from the place. The passage in both houses of the measure for making General Lee general-in-chief by large majorities is very distasteful to the President. I am told he has approved it *totis vivibus*. Now it is a question whether he will have the hardihood to veto it.

Had Mr. Seddon resigned in the spring or early summer when Bragg so completely and offensively unseated him, making the issues with Bragg and the President that they must attend to their business and let him alone, he would have gone out with credit, and as far as the particular issue is concerned, with éclat, having the whole country with him. Now disaster has put his administration under a cloud. Submission to dictation has lost him much respect, and the unfortunate history of the Army of Tennessee and its commanders, as well as the breaking down of subsistence, finance and supply generally, and the wabbling about conscription and clamour about 'details,' have completely broken him down in Congress. Whether the President is willing to throw him over, I have not certainly heard. I heard it suggested yesterday that he was very anxious *not* to do so.

Jan. 23. Mr. Seddon's resignation has not yet been accepted. I am told that the President is disposed to resist the movement in Congress; that he will not reinstate Johnston; and that he does not intend to accept the resignations of the cabinet officers. Two courses are open to him—to hold out and refuse *any* compliance, or if the thing is pressed to a vote of want of confidence, either still to hold out or to resign himself. It probably tends to the last. I asked Judge Campbell, who told me this as having come from the Secretary, whether the parties in Congress who are pressing on this matter, look to reconstruction intentionally as a result, or are being drifted. His impression is that there is sufficient intention to control and direct. He thinks that result imminent. General Lee has declined to be general-in-chief. The President offered it with the greatest reluctance and disgust.

General Singleton has gone carrying a suggestion for intercourse by personal conversation between Grant and Lee.[8] Blair has come back. What he brings I have not yet heard. He got here yesterday. The Commissary General's head is to go off; this is settled. It is also said that the office has been offered to [Congressman] E. M. Bruce of Kentucky (!) and Major J. H. Claiborne, post commissary in this city. It is suggested that those who are pressing for a general change in the cabinet are for Mr. [William Cabell] Rives as secretary of state, being unwilling to trust to Benjamin any discussion of the terms of peace with the United States.

After the Virginia delegation communicated their resolution about a change of the cabinet, Mr. Bocock [Thomas S., speaker of the Confederate House from Va.], thinking their views had not been perhaps stated with sufficient distinctness, wrote to the President that their object was an *entire change in the cabinet*, and that if this was not done the result would certainly be the passage by the House of Representatives of a resolution of total want of confidence in the administration.

Jan. 24.   Tonight after I had come home, Colonel A. L. Rives came in and, as the parlor was full, told me he wished to see me

---

8 James W. Singleton, Virginia-born resident of Illinois, made so many visits to Richmond that it was suspected he was connected with peace missions. He was actually a war profiteer on a mission to trade in cotton and other produce, and apparently to escort Mrs. Lincoln's sister, Mrs. B. H. Helms, through the lines to Washington.

in private. I took him to my chamber and he opened his business. The President has sent for Hon. W. C. Rives and had a long, free and full talk with him. Said that he perceived that everything was jeopardized by the present state of the country; that despondency and distrust appeared universal; that we were on the eve of internal revolution; and that he is willing to take any course, make any appointment, which may be necessary. His conversation made a strong impression on Mr. Rives, who was impressed with his honesty of purpose and anxiety to do what is best. He further declared that he was ready to send commissioners to treat with Mr. Lincoln. Blair has brought a letter from Lincoln to the President, addressed to Hon. Jefferson Davis, in which he invites negotiation with a view to reconstruction, the states to return with all their rights including slavery. This is perhaps not expressed, but there is nothing said of emancipation. ([In margin, written later:] This was an entire mistake as to the tenor of Lincoln's letter.) The impression I derived was that the President thinks matters are quite desperate, and under all the circumstances of difficulty by which he is surrounded, is willing to waive all the issue of independence as unattainable and to treat, to spare the people the effects of subjugation.

At the same time Rives (A. L.) showed me a copy of a letter from General Lee to Mr. Andrew Hunter on the subject of negro enlistment, at the sentiments of which I was astonished. He favors emancipation *per se;* advocates large enlistments accompanied by the promise of prospective emancipation of the families of the negro soldier as a reward of good conduct; overlooks entirely all the difficulties, legal, constitutional and physical; and urges that the negroes be enlisted at once.

In view of all these matters, the question was *who* will be good selections of commissioners. That was the question on which Colonel Rives desired to confer. I advised that one should be from Virginia or North Carolina, one from the cotton states, and one from the Trans-Mississippi; all should be from states still in our possession. I suggested Mr. [William Cabell] Rives, Judge Campbell and A. H. Garland; or if Mr. Rives would not serve, General Lee or Governor Graham [Senator William A., of N. C.]. The especial point seemed to be as to Judge Campbell, whether or not eligible. I urged him as one of the ablest and best negotiators we could have, if it really be necessary to go into that subject.

Jan. 29. Sunday.   This morning Vice President Stephens, Mr. Hunter, president pro tem of the Senate, and Judge Campbell, assistant secretary of war, started to Washington as commissioners appointed and empowered by the President. This is the first [result] of Blair's missions. General Breckinridge was confirmed as secretary of conscription [war]. He will not take his seat for a week yet, having the affairs of his military department to arrange. I had a conversation with Mr. Seddon last night relative to his leaving the Department. He is deeply pained at the course of Lieutenant Colonel Ruffin and Colonel Northrop. His view is that when they reached the conclusion that they could not carry on the commissariat with him, they were bound themselves to resign instead of attacking their superiors, in the Congress.

Mr. Seddon has told me very kindly that the President has heard that I was hostile to him, and cautioned me to be careful in speaking; that there seem to be persons who carry such tales to him, and he from the opposition; and trouble he has had; is sore. I told him I was, and am, not hostile to the President or his administration, but the contrary; that it is true there have been particular acts of the administration that I dissented from, but when that was the case I had used great reserve in expressing any opinion except to a few persons with whom I had no conceal-ments, as Judge Campbell, and to a less extent Shepherd [V. E., clerk in War Office] and Wellford [Phillip A., captain in quartermaster department]. He said that was a matter of course; that for his part he tolerated the largest difference of opinions, but the President seemed to have persons about him who carry tales; that he had the fullest confidence in me and should express it to General Breckinridge. I told him I was quite free to resign, but he thought that unnecessary and advised against it; that he mentioned the subject merely to put me on my guard in the future.

I was glad to see a letter addressed by Mr. Seddon to the President March 24, 1865 [1864] on the subject of Bragg's encroachments, and insisting that the lines of demarcation should be drawn; that orders were published over his name for which he was responsible, of which he got only accidental knowledge; and that officers were actually assigned to duty in his bureaux in the same manner. On it was an endorsement that this subject had been satisfactorily disposed of in a personal interview which rendered sending the note unnecessary.

Feb. 5.   Last night at about 8 o'clock, Messrs. Stephens, Hunter and Campbell got back. After they were admitted into Grant's lines, they were carried down to City Point where they were taken in hand by Major [Thomas T.] Eckert, the censor of the telegraph [sent by Lincoln], who was the person to have charge of their going forward. Some notes passed on the subject of the character and objects of their mission, and delay was produced by which they were kept at City Point till Thursday morning from Monday night. Judge Campbell thinks this was in order to give time for the announcement of the vote in the Yankee House of Representatives on the emancipation amendment to the Constitution and the action of the Eastern states legislatures on it—all of which Seward, who was all the while at Old

Point [Comfort], was waiting for, and brought out in the conference. Finally on Thursday they were taken down on Grant's steamboat, getting into the [Hampton] Roads. Lincoln arrived from Washington that evening and sent them word that he was tired with travel, but would see them the next day. So next morning they were taken on board the steamer [*River Queen*] where Lincoln and Seward were, and had a conference of about three hours, in which a great deal was talked over.

Mr. Stephens reminded Lincoln of their intimacy in the time when they served on the secret committee together, which engineered the election of General [Zachary] Taylor. Lincoln remembered the acquaintance but appeared oblivious of the 'sleeping together' after the manner of [John Minor] Botts and [John] Tyler. Mr. Stephens then went into a long discussion of the 'Monroe Doctrine'[9] in its relations to this quarrel. After he had proceeded for some time (this cue having been taken from Blair) Lincoln appeared to have become impatient and interrupted with the remark that there was but one ground on which propositions could be made or received, and that was the restoration of the national authority over all places in the states. This diverted the discussion, but Mr. Seward said he desired to hear Mr. Stephens out; his view was one in which he was interested.

Mr. Stephens cited historical instances of nations at war laying aside their quarrel to take up other matters of mutual interest to both. Mr. Lincoln replied that he knew nothing about history, 'You must talk history to Seward.' It having become distinctly understood that no terms short of reconstruction were

---

[9] Stephens, like Blair, was proposing that the North and South cease fighting each other, join their forces together, and push the French out of Mexico.

to be considered, Judge Campbell took up the discussion and inquired searchingly into their ideas of the manner of it. It was brought out distinctly that submission was contemplated pure and simple, though they called our envoys to witness that they never used the word 'submission.' Their phrase was 'restoration of the national authority.' The terms of Lincoln's message in December last were all they had to offer.

On the subject of their penal legislation, Lincoln said that we must accept all the consequences of the application of the law, that he would be disposed to use liberally the power confided to him for the remission of pains and penalties. In this connection Judge Campbell remarked that he had never regarded his neck as in danger. Lincoln replied that there were a good many oak trees about the place where he lived, the limbs of which afforded many convenient points from which he might have dangled. This was said with temper, and was the only exhibition of it at all. They said there could be no convention on this subject with us either as a national government or as states, as to make such a convention would be a 'recognition.' Mr. Hunter replied that this did not follow; there were frequent instances of such conventions, as between Charles I and the parliament. Lincoln answered, 'And Charles I lost his head; that's all I know about that; you must talk history to Seward.' Judge Campbell stated the difference between the law of conquest and a pacification by convention. They left no opening for any convention. Everything was to be settled by the laws of Congress and the decisions of the courts.

The slavery question was mentioned. That, Lincoln said, would be decided by the courts. Some said his proclamations had no effect whatever; others, that they operated only in particular places; others, that they were of general operation. He supposed this would be tested by some one taking a negro, and the question of his freedom being brought before the courts.

([In margin, written later:]) In this connection and in reply to Mr. Hunter's suggestion as to negro women and children in exposed places, like Eastern Virginia where productive labor had all absconded, Lincoln told his *story* of the pigs.) [10]

In this connection Seward produced the vote in the House of Representatives on the [13th] amendment to the Constitution. He said this country was in a revolutionary condition, and as always was the case, the most extreme party succeeds. He cited Maryland. The first proposition was to get rid of slavery in 50 years. This would have been satisfactory, but a more extreme party arose for emancipation in seven years, then a more violent one for immediate emancipation, and this one succeeded. So in New York, the *Tribune* which a few years ago was the *only* abolition political paper supported by the country, was now the most conservative of the Northern press while the *Herald* leads the abolition party.

The conditions of a truce were also discussed, equally unsatisfactory. The only governments which could be recognized in states where there are two would be the bogus Yankee government. Judge Campbell also asked if Virginia went back whether it would be with her ancient limits. The reply was that it would be a question for the courts. West Virginia would be regarded as a state. The gentlemen [Confederate peace commissioners] prepared their answer to the President this morning, which I

[10] An Illinois farmer boasted that he had found an efficient method of harvesting a food crop for his pigs—grow potatoes and let the pigs harvest them at will. But what would happen when the ground was frozen, a neighbor asked? 'Let 'em root,' replied the farmer.

presume will be published. This ends this peace *fiasco* which must satisfy the most sceptical that we have nothing whatever to hope or expect short of the exaction of all the rights of conquest, whether we are overrun by force, or submit.[11]

---

[11] Under the date of February 7, Kean attached printed copies of the peace commissioners' report to the President (dated Feb. 5, 1865) and Davis's note (dated Feb. 6, 1865) transmitting the report to Congress.

7

AND THIS IN A TIME OF PROFOUND
PEACE!

APPOMATTOX AND AFTER

Feb. 7, 1865. Today Mr. Seddon took leave of us, and General [John B.] Breckinridge was sworn in [as secretary of war] by H. A. Claiborne, notary public, on the oath filed in the State Department. He and Judge Campbell had a long conference. When it ended—part of which resulted in my being ordered to send a circular to the chiefs of bureaux, to state for the Secretary's information what means and resources they have on hand, what are their necessities, what impediments, and what their ability for successful prosecution of their business—the Judge informed me he should stay a few weeks and then go. He told me in confidence and plainly that he regarded the cause as hopeless from our want of money and failing resources. Kemper is spoken of as our successor. He [Campbell] thinks the new Secretary is not a good appointment though this is only an impression from his appearing not to wish to grapple with the Department as a whole.

Feb. 10.   The new Secretary is evidently not a man of papers. It is hard to get him to take a pen in his hand or to read a letter. His work will be almost sure to get behindhand. On the 8th General Lee wrote that his troops beyond Petersburg had been in line of battle three days and nights in snow, hail and rain *without a mouthful* of meat; that they would be so weakened by exposure and privation as not to have the physical strength to march and fight. It gave the saddest picture of the sufferings of the soldiers I have ever seen. Colonel Northrop was present when General Breckinridge received it and he showed it to him. 'Yes,' the old stoic remarked, 'It is just what I predicted long ago.' And he went on to rehearse the record without a single suggestion of relief. General Breckinridge inquired, 'But Colonel, what shall we do?' 'Well, I don't know. If my plans had been carried out instead of thwarted etc., etc.'

The Secretary sent the letter up to the President, who presently returned it with a very sharp endorsement to the effect that this was the result either of gross incapacity or criminal neglect, and soon after, the President wrote the Secretary a note that meat and whiskey must be borrowed, or impressed, and should be sent over before the commissary officers slept that night. This too Colonel Northrop saw but laid coolly aside, remarking to Lawton *soto voce*, that it was 'sensational'; to the Secretary that he could not borrow because he had already borrowed more than could be returned, nor impress because by the law money had to be tendered; that it was partly General Lee's fault, and wholly Mr. Seddon's etc. And no suggestion of any means of relief was so much as offered by him. This probably hastens his fate which was sealed before.

Sherman is making steady progress in South Carolina. He has probably cut the railroad this side of Branchville. Before the end of this month he will have Charleston and Columbia. Beauregard is still at Augusta [Georgia] cut off from communication with Hardee. The end seems to be surely and swiftly approaching.

Feb. 18.   Columbia fell into Sherman's hands yesterday without a fight. Losses of public property very great including the gunstock machine and the machinery and plates for treasury printing.

Judge Campbell asked me what I thought of the state of things. I told him by the end of March I thought we would all be fugitives. 'What then?' [asked Campbell] 'There will come the 2nd stage of the War as some call it; the boldest will be bush whackers, etc.; the struggle will be outside of the laws of war.' [replied Kean] 'Do you think that is work for a patriot?' [asked Campbell] 'The enemy in your [Hampton Roads Peace] conference have left us nothing else. I don't think a patriot could consent to the carrying on the war a day after the struggle has become hopeless provided any door for terms is open.' The Judge agreed but said he thought that Lincoln and Seward were disappointed at the result of the conference. They expected terms to be mentioned, and this is confirmed by Lincoln's message. The Northern people too were dissatisfied until the speeches made here went North.[1]

He [Campbell] then told me that on the day they [the Peace

---

[1] Returning to Washington from the Hampton Roads Peace Conference, Lincoln submitted to his cabinet a proposal providing for compensated emancipation, pardons for all political offenses, and the return of all confiscated property, in case the South would cease all resistance to national authority by April 1. The cabinet rejected this proposal, and Lincoln next, upon request, submitted the Conference correspondence to the House. In Richmond, several Confederate leaders, including Davis, made speeches to arouse the Confederacy to a new fighting spirit.

Commissioners] got back, after they sent their letter[2] to the President, he sent for him. They had a conference in which he told the President all that had passed. Mr. Davis was not satisfied and said he wanted them to add that Lincoln and Seward insisted on abolition and submission. He replied that the letter stated the exact result of the conference and as written would speak for itself. The President wished to add the other to influence the people. In the evening, Mr. Hunter, Mr. Stephens and the Judge all called on the President; when he insisted on the addition, all declined it.

Judge Campbell says he has felt very much dissatisfied about the whole thing. It *ought not* to have been dropped when it was, but terms should have been distinctly offered. I told him the part of his account which most deeply impressed me was when he stated the distinction between the law of conquest and convention, and they refused to listen to any such thing as convention being admissable at all, taking this with the asperity of Lincoln's allusion to the oak trees. [See above, Feb. 5, 1865] He said this was true. As he said this, he shook his head and spoke in a low tone of despair.

March 23.   The interval since my last entry has been under the surface a very momentous one on which I regret I have not made continuous notes. A large part of the Congress was dissatisfied with the whole conduct of affairs and thought in their inner hearts that the cause was desperate, and they wished new

---

[2] The report of the Confederate Peace Commissioners to Davis indicated that Lincoln would not consider a truce, armistice, or peace terms until the Confederate government pledged complete restoration of national authority in the South and accepted the 13th amendment, at which time Lincoln promised he would use the pardoning power liberally to remit pains and penalties imposed on individual Confederates.

efforts to be made by the President to procure a settlement on terms. The President on the other hand fenced skillfully to avoid fresh overtures. He was willing to make them if *advised* by the Senate to do so. The Senate would not assume the responsibility so to advise, some not thinking the matter would be well handled in the hands of Mr. Davis and Benjamin. Judge Campbell, Mr. W. C. Rives, Senators Graham, Orr [James L., of S. C.], and Hunter concurred in the main in the view that some change in the treatment of the difficulty should be made. Some had hopes of a conference between Generals Lee and Grant, which was suggested by General Ord [Edward O. C., U. S. A.] to General Longstreet, but this issued in General Lee's writing a letter by authority to Grant proposing a conference looking to a settlement, to which Grant replied he had no authority to deal with any but military questions. The correspondence was immediately published here, to follow up the Hampton Roads business and make our people desperate.

Meanwhile Congress had resolved to adjourn. Judge Campbell had written a letter setting out fully the state of our affairs, to the Secretary of War, and closed with the suggestion that General Lee be called on to say whether the exposition was not correct, and to state his views of the situation explicitly. This was done; General Lee replied cautiously, admitting however that the crisis was extreme and suggesting that the heads of supply bureaux be called on for statements of what they were able to do. This was done. The President then sent in on March [13] a message to Congress requesting that they should not adjourn, but should take up certain measures, and reading them rather a lecture. At the same time another message was sent communicating the papers above mentioned. Congress in both Houses took the message in high dudgeon, and committees in each House made formal answer to the President's indictment. That of the

Senate, written by Semmes, was especially sharp. They remained in session however a week longer and passed some of the measures recommended, whence they adjourned full of wrath and most of them apparently with little hope for the country. The negro bill was passed by the votes of the Virginia Senators under instructions from the Legislature. Regular recruiting regulations are preparing, yet no appropriation was made for the expense of it!!

Through the effect of Sheridan's raid [in the Shenandoah Valley] Richmond is rapidly approaching a state of famine. Bacon is $20 a pound, flour $1200 a barrel, butter $25 a pound, beef and that the worst $10 to $12, wood $200 a cord, etc., and the supply exceedingly meager. The country, however, i.e. Virginia, is responding nobly to the appeal of General St. John, commissary general [replacing Northrop], and if the communications are kept up he has no doubt of feeding the army. Governor Vance was told by some of the North Carolina members of the President's communicating the real state of the country to Congress, and sent an aid-de-camp to ask for copies of the papers referred to above. He got an evasive answer, that they were communicated to Congress in secret session and hence as the injunction of secrecy had not been removed, they could not be furnished. Results may follow from this.

The negro enlistment regulations have been published and excite much criticism. This measure was passed by a panic in the Congress and the Virginia Legislature, under all the pressure the President indirectly, and General Lee directly, could bring to bear. My own judgment of the whole thing is that it is a colossal blunder, a dislocation of the foundations of society from which no practical results will be reaped by us. The enemy will probably get four recruits under it to our one. Wigfall says the whole thing was gotten up to divert attention from the movement to bring about a change in the Cabinet. Judge Campbell tells me that he understands he is regarded at headquarters as a sort of leader of opposition, and is in high disfavor, quite likely as the result of his endeavors to put backbone into Messrs. Hunter, Graham etc. A few days ago, the busy idleness of the State Department had a little matter of business. Earl Russell had written some sort of letter (I did not see it) protesting against the fitting out of war vessels in English ports, and expeditions in Canada [from Canada into the United States] which they had the insolence to send through Grant.

June 1 [April 2 to June 1]   Since the last entry the Southern Confederacy has been utterly overthrown and destroyed.

On the morning of Sunday, April 2, I went to the War Office about 8 A.M. as usual; found several persons, Colonel F. R. Lubbock [ex-governor of Texas and a member of Davis's staff], Postmaster General Reagan, etc., etc., sitting there. About 9:30 o'clock the messenger from the telegraph office brought in a telegram from General Lee that his lines were broken in three places and he doubted his ability to re-establish them; that preparations should be made to evacuate Richmond at once. Copies sent to President Davis and General Breckinridge at once, and I began to pack the papers and books of the War Office. About 11 a second telegram from General Lee that his efforts to re-establish his lines had failed and Richmond must be evacuated that night, that he had given the proper orders to General Ewell. I labored hard all day. Went up home about 3 to get something to eat and see how my family came on with their preparations to leave by the [James River and Kanawha] canal. At 6 P.M. got all the records to the Danville depot. The train (on which the President and Cabinet also went) did not start till 11 P.M. Reached Danville at 4 P.M. on April 3. Citizens hospitably took us in.

For a week we remained without news of Lee, which gave me great uneasiness as I feared Grant was pressing him back against the James River. I opened the War Office though the Secretary had not arrived, because I deemed it of great importance that the country should see that a government was in operation though Richmond was evacuated. On Monday, April 11 [10], we heard of Lee's surrender at Appomattox Court House, having had no communication with him. The President and Cabinet made hasty preparations to leave Danville that night for Greensboro, North Carolina, and did so without giving any orders to the bureau offices, which caused great confusion. I got my cases off on a troop train the next day, and reached Greensboro on Thursday night. Found the President still there; also Generals Beauregard and Johnston, and General Breckinridge. Johnston was retreating by Raleigh and Hillsboro, on Greensboro and Salisbury, Sherman actively pressing. On Saturday the Presidential party again took wing with as little observation as might be with a wagon train. Stoneman's cavalry destroyed the railroad bridge between Greensboro and Salisbury over Deep river, and much of the tracks at Salisbury.

I followed in wagons on Sunday, but camped three days at High Point, being ordered to wait and move with Johnston's army. The armistice having intervened the army did not move. On Thursday heard of the armistice and of the assassination of Lincoln; also of the agreement between Johnston and Sherman. Got to Charlotte, North Carolina, on Sunday, April 21, and expected to go forward. So instructed by Breckinridge on Wednesday. He had told me to wait the result of the effort to prepare the ferries on the Catawba. About noon on Wednesday April 25, he told me the U. S. authorities had rejected the Convention with Sherman; that I must store the records there and surrender them to the U. S. officer who occupied Charlotte, if they found them, preserving them from being destroyed if I could. I stayed there accordingly, and took a room at the Kerr House, the Presidential party getting ready for another flitting.

The Virgina officers had a meeting on Wednesday night, 52 in number, and appointed a committee to wait on the Secretary of War, and have a definite understanding as to what was expected of them under the circumstances. All believed the blow mortal. They were following along after a fugitive government which gave no orders, getting constantly farther from home, without means of any sort and many without transportation. The Secretary of War caused an order to be made by the Adjutant General, authorizing them to return home to Virginia and report to the Confederate officers in command or to the government. His reply to the committee of the meeting amounted to an implication that there was no way in which they could do any good by going farther, and that they were justified in returning to Virginia. Accordingly they nearly all set out the next day.

I heard this morning (April 26) from General Gorgas that Johnston would surrender his army at 12 noon. Accordingly, I determined to turn over the custody of my papers to Mr. [C. T.] Bruen, assistant secretary of the C. S. Senate, whose documents were stored in the same place with mine, and who designed remaining in Charlotte for a special private reason (He wished to secure the *Journals* of the Senate for future publication for private profit), and to join myself to a party of officers who were returning to Virginia. The Presidential party left soon after noon, and our party took the northern road in the afternoon, travelling till in the night, 19 miles. This was the final breaking up of the Confederate government. It was *sauve qui peut* from the rejection of the military convention between Johnston and Sherman. We kept well to the west of the debris of Lee's and Johnston's armies, and after a journey of 14 days I reached Albemarle.

June 1, 1865

Found Virginia quietly submitting to a military government by Generals Ord and Halleck, with small garrisons in all the country towns, the population generally taking the 'amnesty oath,' and all idea of further resistance entirely abandoned.

The *abolition of slavery* immediately, and by a military order, is the most marked feature of this conquest of the South. In Virginia where I am observing the effect of this overthrow of the labor system of a whole country without preparation or mitigation, the results of it are very striking as they unfold themselves. As there is great scarcity, and the crops were all immature, there was the utmost danger of a famine from a general cessation of labor. Great numbers of negroes quit work and flocked to Richmond and other garrisoned towns, where they had to be supported by the issue of rations. The Yankees perceiving the effect of their work, now gave stringent orders that the negroes should remain on the plantations and work. In some places where they broke out into excesses they dealt with them with great severity. I heard in Appomattox and Buckingham [counties] of several being shot, and some unmercifully whipped by them. The people of Albemarle waited patiently for the U. S. military authorities to take some order for reorganizing society and establishing a definite basis upon which such reorganization was to proceed, but none such was vouchsafed. Neighborhood meetings were held for conference on the subject, and then proceedings submitted to the U. S. [Military] Commissioners at Charlottesville, Palmyra, etc.

On some farms the negroes quit work in a body. The proprietors would acquiesce and give them a short time to clear out, old and young alike, and then hire unincumbered labor to their great profit. There is a general reduction of numbers on the farms. Some good laborers leave, and proprietors endeavor to get rid of the unproductive ones, retaining as far as possible the unincumbered and as few as possible of all classes. The result is a redundancy of labor, nearly everywhere. In particular neighborhoods, farmers will not hire the negroes who have left their owner's plantations. The object of this is to retain the present force as far as possible to mature growing crops. A loss of labor at this season would be very disastrous. No difficulty is experienced in hiring as many as are required. The price fixed in Fluvanna and Albemarle (this part) is $5.00 per month (specie) for a 1st class man, $3.00 for first class women, hands to be fed but not clothed, and those who remain on the plantations enjoy the privileges of gardens, fowls, etc., which they used to enjoy as slaves. The planters here (Edgehill) have fixed November 15 as the end of their year of labor, and contract till that time. The great scarcity of provisions throughout Virginia greatly facilitates the reorganization. The negroes must get prompt employment or starve. There is little to eat in the country and less currency. Hence wages are low and subsistence dear. Many however are idling about. They cannot by the harshest usage be kept from collecting at the garrisoned towns, whence (as in Richmond) they are arrested, put in barracks and hired out by the provost marshal without consulting their wishes as to employer or price.

On a large estate near Gordonsville (Colonel [John M.] Patton's) the negroes last week quit work and became insubordinate. Colonel Patton sent his overseer to Gordonsville to report the facts to the Commandant who sent an officer and several men back to the estate. The officer summoned the slaves and informed them that they were to work and behave themselves. The 'head man,' who acted as the spokesman, inquired what sort of freedom this was, and whether they were not to have land given them. The officer turned to the overseer and asked where the grave yard was; it was pointed out. Turning to the negro he said, 'The only land you will get, or any of you, will be 6 x 3 feet in that lot, and if you do not behave yourselves properly you will get your share very quickly.'

Manumission after this fashion will be regarded hereafter, when it has borne its fruits and the passions of the hour have passed away, as the greatest social crime ever committed on the earth. One-half of the negroes unable by age, sex, infirmity, or want of character to support and take care of themselves, are thrown on their own resources, or else on the charity of their former owners who are impoverished to the last degree and in many cases utterly unable to take care of them or materially to assist them. The community is wholly unable for the same reasons to take up the burden of a vast pauper system. The inevitable result will be destitution and suffering on a vast scale, and the number who will come to want will constantly increase as the old ties are broken by individuals and family after family by leaving their former owners voluntarily or by compulsion. Want, vice, crime, will follow disease, the jails. Punishments which in a state of slavery were domestic and light generally, will be inflicted by the public magistrate without mercy and at a cost to the community. Illicit intercourse, which heretofore did not involve want, and consequently did not bring the same measure of degradation because social relations were unchanged, will not probably be less common, but will generally lead to common prostitution as a means of subsistence. It reaches us from many quarters that the negroes are bitterly disappointed in the results of emancipation, and by the change in the tone of the Yankees to them *before* the overthrow of the South and *since*.

June 27. On the 10th I started to Lynchburg to see what the prospects were for business reviving, and remained there a fortnight.

The most perfect stagnation prevails from several causes: 1. The absolute want of money to conduct the simplest and most necessary business of daily supply. 2. General loss of capital and impoverishment of the whole community; insolvency of the banks and all the money corporations. 3. The cloud upon titles and the general feeling of insecurity produced by the 13th clause of Johnson's proclamation.[3] 4. A feeling of distrust of federal treasury currency. These operate in the order in which they are named. In Lynchburg as elsewhere in Virginia, the people yield implicit submission to the orders of the military authorities of the U. S. but socially ignore the presence of the Yankees. The latter are said to feel this.

In those parts of the country where the farmers promptly made regular and explicit contracts with the slaves for hire there has been comparatively little trouble, and the work has progressed pretty well. In the towns there is great confusion, and in the neighborhood of the towns the crops are left uncultivated by the flocking of the negroes into them. Lynchburg is crowded; so is Richmond. Many of them are fed by the military with regularly issued rations.

July 6. In Georgia a Yankee official [General Edward A. Wild] calling himself 'Superintendent of the Freedmen's Bureau' has made a general order to regulate the labor of a great state. The negroes are required to remain on the plantations. The owners are required to provide for all, productive and non-productive, as heretofore—food, clothing, medical attendance, fuel and quarters, and to pay $7 per month wages. The same folly has

---

[3] In Johnson's proclamation of pardon and amnesty of May 29, 1865, the 13th provision or exception left unpardoned those whose property was worth more than $20,000.

been wrought by Brigadier General [J. I.] Gregg at Lynchburg, commanding from Appomattox to Bristol, except as to price which he puts at $5. Thus the most intricate and variously conditioned of all social problems is dealt with off hand by petty officials, mere youths, without enlightenment or culture and profoundly ignorant of the subject over which they assume to legislate.

July 7. The Washington government has evidently resolved to hold the mind and wealth of the South in a condition of abject subjection. The Attorney General [James Speed] has addressed a circular letter to the so-called governments of the Southern states informing them that all applications for amnesty will be referred to them before being considered at Washington, the object being to prevent inconsiderate and uninformed action, and *to enable these governments to hold control over the parties during the period of reforming the states* and to secure proper treatment of the negroes! In the last day or two they have made it the duty of the district attorney to canvass the parties so applying.

The Pierpont Legislature (sic) composed of six Senators and eight Delegates met about June 20 and modified the oath in the Alexandria paper [Constitution of 1864] as to *voters*. Still there are no persons eligible as officers. The first legislature is to have conventional powers as to the subject of the test oath. It is suggested that persons proper to be elected in other respects be chosen, who shall meet as a convention, modify the oath, and then meet as a legislature and take the modified oath.[4]

---

4 In June 1861, Unionists of northwestern Virginia held a convention in Wheeling at which the 'Restored Government of Virginia' was established as a rival to the secessionist government at Richmond. Francis Harrison Pierpont was made governor of the 'Restored Government.' Subsequently the legislature of this government gave Virginia's consent to the creation of a new state, which by legal fiction was admitted into the Union as West Virginia late in 1862. The 'Restored Government' under

July 7, 1865

Mr. Francis Rives [son of William Cabell Rives] told me a few days ago that ex-Governor [William] Aiken of South Carolina told him that he estimated that 1,000,000 of the negroes had perished since 1860. A few days ago the N. Y. *Herald* had the same estimate. In the Southern towns they are densely crowded. A Macon paper speaks of 120 living in a single house there. A striking fact respecting the negroes in Virginia is their cat-like attachment to places. Nearly all who have gone off to the enemy during the War have this summer returned to their old neighborhood, and many of them are anxious to return to work for their former masters. The passion for change once gratified and themselves satisfied of the ability of the change in their condition by leaving their homes, they seem to desire to return at least to the neighborhood and their old associations.

THE CAUSES OF THE FAILURE OF SOUTHERN INDEPENDENCE

1st. A bankrupt treasury. This was the prolific source of other evils: (a) high prices of all supplies, and parties unwilling to furnish even for them (b) discontent of people and army for want of payment of dues and worthlessness of it when obtained; hence *desertion*, impressment (c) decay of railroad transportation due in part to this cause, the roads not having wherewith to keep themselves up. Causes [for bankrupt treasury:] (a)

Pierpont thereupon moved to Alexandria. From 1863 to the end of the war, this straw government, within the Union lines, was maintained as the government of Virginia. In 1864 the Pierpont government called a convention which drafted a new Constitution abolishing slavery and disfranchising Confederate civil and military officers. In May 1865 the Pierpont government moved to Richmond and immediately the legislature provided that the next elected legislature could act as a convention and repeal the disfranchising features of the Constitution of 1864.

belief of leaders in a short war (b) inability to deal with a very large subject; First Congress responsible as well as the President and Memminger.

2nd. Want of men; exhaustion of supply from which recruits of effective qualities to be drawn; severity of the conscription; desertion due to insufficient supply and worthlessness of money.

3rd. Shortness of subsistence, military operations fettered by; armies obliged to occupy certain fixed positions with reference to this as a main question. Due (a) to bad currency (b) to want of efficiency of transportation (c) to defective system. Behind all this the country not a food producing one.

4th. Incompetency of military men. Of the West Pointers; small, not capable of high command; promoted rapidly from grade of subalterns to command of divisions, corps and armies. Obstruction of way to command by men of capacity not bred to arms. Defective system of promotion fixed by law and President's construction of 'valor and skill.' Want of discernment in the selection of general officers; consequently want of discipline, especially in cavalry. Rapid destruction of best material in grade of regimental and company officers; difficult towards the last to find officers competent to command regiments and brigades. Bad selections made; losses resulting, e. g., Bragg, Pemberton, Holmes, Hindman, A. P. Hill, J. E. B. Stuart, Ewell, F. Lee, D. H. Hill. Bad system of cavalry and want of capacity to deal with the questions.

5th. Want of horses for transports and artillery; country stripped by impressment of horses, which straightway perished for want of forage; this want due to defective transportation by railroad and wagon, and limited supply in any given area of country.

6th. Difficulties of supply and recruiting aggravated by *faction*—Stephens, Toombs, J. E. Brown, Vance.

7th. Slavery an inherent weakness when deeply invaded, from desertion to the enemy and joining their army as recruits.

To these may be added one cause which in a certain sense may be said to include them all—the absence of a Representative Man, a *leader* in the *council* as well as in the field who should comprehend and express the movement. We had no one who approached it. The country by instinct, seeking such a reliance, gave its faith to Lee in vain.

July 11-12.　　One has taken the pains to look over the historical document known as the 'Constitution of the United States' to note the plain and palpable violations in letter and spirit, which have been made by the government of the U. S. in the last four years, and noted the following:

1. Art. I. sec. 2, cl. 3. 'Representatives and direct taxes shall be apportioned among the several States, etc., according to their respective numbers, etc.' *Violated* by frequent military fines and levies and confiscations, which might have been maintained (in some cases) by regarding the South as a foreign state, but, on the Yankee denial of this, were palpable breaches of the Constitution (Dec. '65) by the collection of the land tax for 1862[5] now going on.

2. Art. I. sec. 4, cl. 1. 'The times, places, and manner of holding elections for senators and representatives, shall be prescribed in each State by the legislature thereof, etc.' *Violated* by being regulated in eleven states by presidential proclamations and by

---

[5] Which provided for the collection of direct taxes assigned by the Federal government to all Confederate states in 1861. Collection of the tax led to seizures and forfeitures of land following the war. In 1891 Congress reimbursed the states for the amounts they had paid under this direct tax.

edicts of provisional governors appointed by the President of the U. S. in place of the legal constitutional governors and legislatures of the states.

3. Art. I. sec. 9, cl. 2. 'The privilege of the writ of *habeas corpus* shall not be suspended, unless when in cases of rebellion or invasion the public safety may require it.' At this present writing, July 11, 1865, the writ remains suspended over the whole U. S. territory, in which there walks not an armed man, save in the uniform and under the orders of the U. S. The writ was suspended in 1861 by Lincoln without authority of Congress, and Chief Justice [Roger B.] Taney's order defiantly set at naught by a lieutenant by the direction of the Secretary of War [the Merryman case].

4. Art. I. sec. 9, cl. 3. 'No bill of attainder or *ex post facto* law shall be passed.' *Violated* by the Confiscation Bill and all the penal war measure legislation.

5. Art. I. sec. 9, cl. 4. 'No capitation, or other direct tax, shall be laid unless in proportion to the census or enumeration herein before directed to be taken.' *Violated;* see No. 1; also by levies made by orders of military officers to support chargeable 'freedmen.'

6. Art. I. sec. 9, cl. 5. 'No tax or duty shall be laid on articles exported from any state.' *Violated* by export duties on *cotton* and *tobacco*, the object of which is to give to Yankee manufacturers and traders a *monopoly* and prevent direct trade by the South with foreign ports.

7. Art. 1. sec. 9, cl. 6. 'No preference shall be given by any regulation of commerce or revenue to the ports of one State over those of another; nor shall vessels bound to, or from, one state be obliged to enter, clear, or pay duties in another.' *Violated* in both branches by the proclamation and treasury regulations by which

the ports of North Carolina and Virginia were 'opened' in January 1865.

8. Art. III. sec. 2, cl. 3. 'The trial of all crimes, except in cases of impeachment, shall be *by jury*; and such trial shall be held in the State where the said crimes shall have been committed, etc.' *Violated* repeatedly, probably in many hundred cases, of civil persons (not spies) tried, executed, sentenced to every kind of corporal punishment and to ruinous fines, etc. by 'military commissions.' The most notable cases are Vallandigham's in 1863 and the trial of Payne, Mudd and Surratt, etc. at Washington. ([Later insert:] and Wirz)[6]

9. Art. III. sec. 3, cl. 2. 'The Congress shall have power to declare the punishment of treason, but no attainder of treason shall work corruption of blood or forfeiture except during the life of the person attainted.' *Violated* wholesale. By their several laws they have attainted a whole nation, and 'Judge' (!) Underwood[7] has decided that they have corrupted the blood and forfeited

---

[6] In the Lincoln assassination trials by a military court held from May to July 1865, Lewis Payne, Dr. Samuel A. Mudd, and Mrs. Mary Surratt were convicted. Payne, Seward's assailant, and Mrs. Surratt, allegedly an accomplice, were hanged. Dr. Mudd, who had given medical service to John Wilkes Booth after the assassination, was sentenced to prison for life. Henry Wirz, Swiss-American Confederate captain, at one time an official in the Confederate prison at Andersonville, was convicted by another military commission and hanged. Both commissions departed from traditional guaranties. The executions of Mrs. Surratt and Captain Wirz were miscarriages of justice.

[7] John C. Underwood, New York-born Virginian who married a cousin of Stonewall Jackson, was a Unionist of strong anti-slavery views. As a Federal circuit judge for the district of Richmond, he is alleged to have directed the libeling of much property for confiscation. As presiding officer of the Virginia Constitutional Convention of 1869, Underwood gave his name to this constitution which was adopted in 1870, technically ending Radical Reconstruction in Virginia.

the estates of all the people of the South *in fee*. He is said to have made large purchases of lands under his own decrees at prices not exceeding a year's rent.

10. Art. IV. sec. 1. 'Full faith and credit shall be given in each State to the public acts, records, and judicial proceedings of every other State, etc.' By proclamation in May last [May 9, 1865] President Johnson declared *all public* acts done by the officers of the State of Virginia for four years past *null and void*!!

11. Art. IV. sec. 2, cl. 3. (The fugitive slave clause). Systematically violated by the people, legislatures, governors and courts of *all* the Yankee states for 20 years—a crime which has found its crowning consummation in emancipation by presidential proclamation.

12. Art. IV. sec. 3, cl. 1. 'New states may be admitted by the Congress into this union; but no new state shall be formed or erected within the Jurisdiction of any other State; nor any State be formed by the junction of two or more States, or parts of States, without the consent of the legislatures of the States concerned as well as of the Congress.' *Violated* by the erection of a traitorous fragment of Virginia in the northwest corner of the State, into a new state [West Virginia] which was 'admitted' by the U. S. Congress. The force of considering Pierpont and his six Senators and eight Delegates as Virginia, makes this act not only revolutionary but fraudulent and contemptible, for the [United States] Senate refused to admit Senators [Joseph Segar and John C. Underwood] chosen by the legislature which gave the pretended assent. Even [Senator Charles] Sumner denounced it as equivalent to giving two Senators to the town council of Alexandria.

13. Art. IV. sec. 4. 'The U. S. shall guarantee to every State in this Union a Republican form of Government, etc.' *Violated* in every Southern state by the overthrow of their regular, legiti-

mate and constitutional governments, and the appointment by the President of the U. S. of government supported by garrisons in every town and county. In Virginia, especially flagrant by the setting up of a 'Pretender' [the Pierpont government] in the place of a government which has had regular succession since 1618.

14. Note: Before passing to the amendments, an omission of a violation of the original text is here supplied. Art. I, sec. 8, cls. 2 and 5. To borrow money, coin money. *Violated* by the Legal Tender treasury notes and by the National Banking Law.

The eleven additional articles were designed to secure the states and the people of the states against usurped powers. Behold how necessary! Of how little efficacy!!

15. Art. I. 'Congress shall make no law, etc., abridging the freedom of speech or of the press, etc.' Newspapers have been suppressed again and again by orders from Washington—N. Y. *World* and N. Y. *News*; Petersburg [Daily] *News*, A. M. Keiley's paper, June 1865; Richmond *Times* had warning, etc.; Mitchel lately arrested and thrown into prison; Vallandigham banished for a speech to his constituents, etc. ([Later insert:] *Commercial Bulletin* in Sept.)[8] [See below, Oct. 8, 1865]

---

[8] In May 1864 the New York *World* was suspended for three days for publishing a bogus proclamation, allegedly by Lincoln, calling for 400,000 men and a day of humiliation and prayer. The bogus story was designed to rig the stock market. The New York *News*, though critical of the war, was never suspended. Keiley's *Daily News* was suspended for his defense of the South and attack on the Radicals, and he was imprisoned for two days. John Mitchel, the Irish patriot, was editor of the Richmond *Enquirer*. The Richmond *Evening Commercial Bulletin* was established in May 1865 and supported the policies of Andrew Johnson. Suppression of the Richmond newspapers reflects the rising independence of the press under the moderate policies of Johnson and Pierpont, as well as the rising Radical power in Washington opposed to such policies.

220

July 11, 1865

16. Art. 2. 'A well regulated militia, *being necessary to the security of a free State*, the right of the people to keep and bear arms shall not be infringed.' The South are not only stripped of arms, but a gentleman going on a journey has to get a permit from a provost marshal to wear a pistol for his personal security against robbers (I have seen this done), and a general order of Major General Edward O. C. Ord, commanding Virginia, has prohibited the state button being worn.

17. Art. III. 'No soldier shall, in time of peace be quartered in any house, without the consent of the owner, nor in time of war, but in a manner to be prescribed by law.' In the absence of any 'law' a Yankee captain, commissary, has been in occupation of my house, furniture, and refusing me possession, and his refusal confirmed by General [John W.] Turner commanding in Richmond since April 11, 1865, and this is not uncommon. *Virginia has no courts of law*. They have been suppressed from the supreme court of appeals to the justice of the peace.

18. Art. IV. 'The right of the people to be secure in their persons, houses, papers, and effects, against unreasonable searches and seizures, shall not be violated, and no warrants shall issue but upon probable cause, supported by oath or affirmation and particularly describing the place to be searched, and the persons or things to be seized.' It was no idle boast Secretary Seward made to Dr. Russell [W. H., British newspaper reporter] that he touched a little bell on his right hand and caused an arrest to be made in New York; another on his left and caused another arrest in St. Louis. In the Yankee states, since May 1861 when the reckless triumph over liberty was uttered, no syllable of this article has been in force to this hour, nor in the South since it fell under their power. The instances are thousands.

19. Art. V. (a) 'No person shall be held to answer for a capital or otherwise infamous crime, unless on a presentment or indictment of a grand jury, except etc.; (b) nor shall any person, etc., be deprived of life, liberty, or property, without due process of law; (c) nor shall private property be taken for public use without just compensation.' (a) The U. S. fortresses built for defense of this people are crowded with persons—some of them illustrious for private virtues, great abilities, and public services—who have never been prosecuted or indicted, never informed of the charges against them, and not permitted even to hold correspondence with their families upon domestic business. Vallandigham's case and that of Payne, Mudd, Surratt illustrate (a) and (b); (c) has been illustrated everywhere. Systematic robbery has been the order of the day. See my own case noted under 17.

20. Art. VI. 'In all criminal prosecutions, the accused shall enjoy the right to a *speedy* and *public* trial by an *impartial jury* of the *state* and *district* wherein the crime shall have been committed, etc., and to be informed of the nature and cause of the accusation; to be confronted with the witnesses against him, etc.' Not a rag of this, which the men of old thought a bulwark of liberty, is left. As stated under 19, hundreds are bastiled for weeks and months, and to every inquiry as to the cause no answer is returned. (Hon. J. A. Campbell, J. A. Seddon, ex-Gov. Moore [Andrew B., of Ala.] Gov. Vance, etc.) The Washington Military Commission sat on the lives of many persons in secret conclave. Hundreds of citizens have been put to death or otherwise punished by military commissions. Impartiality has been guarded against as carefully as juries have been ignored. Instance, David Hunter, etc., and Vallandigham's case.

21. Art. VII. 'In suits at common law, where the value in controversy shall exceed twenty dollars, the right of trial by jury

shall be preserved, etc.' A 'Court of Conciliation,'[9] so-called, established by Halleck in Richmond by general order, consisting of three judges of law and fact.

22. Art. VIII. 'Excessive bail shall not be required, nor excessive fines imposed, nor cruel and unusual punishment inflicted.' Bail constantly taken by military officers; exhausting fines by provost marshals for trivial offenses, generally against the usurped power and dignity of the petty tyrants who exact them. Hard labor for life, imprisonment in a sea girt fortress, etc., and death are the cruel and hitherto unknown punishments inflicted on citizens of the U. S. by military commissions.

23. Art. IX. 'The enumeration in the Consititution of certain rights *shall not* be construed to deny or disparage others retained by the people.' Each of the preceding numbers furnishes a violation of this.

24. Art. X. 'The powers not delegated to the United States by the Constitution, nor prohibited by it to the States, are reserved to the States respectively, or to the people.' The violations of this furnish instances of enormity which universal history cannot match: (a) the overthrow and destruction of the social order and domestic institutions and private property of eleven hitherto sovereign states, in declaring freedom of their slaves. (b) the state murder of the same eleven states by the overthrow of their political frame, the subversion of their governments and laws, and the imposition of arbitrary military satrapies.

Thus *ten* out of the eleven additional articles inserted by the

---

[9] In the absence of courts in Richmond immediately following the end of the war, General H. W. Halleck, commander of the department of Virginia, established a court of arbitration and conciliation to act until the government was restored. The court had no jurisdiction in criminal cases or in cases involving the title of property.

patriots of 1789, and proposed chiefly by Virginia, to protect the people and the states against federal usurpation have been since necessarily, many wantonly, violated in the war made by Yankee power upon the Southern states. They claim that it was 'necessity'—the plea of tyrants, true in some of these cases because their cause was itself tyranny.

And then the whole of their action in their war against the Southern Confederacy has been a denial of the *Right of Self Government.*

August [to Oct. 8].   A new Military Commission with [General Lew] Wallace at the head of it has been organized to do to death Wirz, for a time commandant of the prison at Andersonville. See the N. Y. *News* of the 24th inst. In September, I was summoned as a witness before this and testified [See below, Oct. 23, 1865]. The real object of the proceeding is to make a case against Davis and Seddon, or at least blacken them.

The Satrap[10] in Alabama has recently (Oct. 8, 1865) suspended from all the clerical functions Bishop Wilmer and all the Episcopal clergy of that state because he in a pastoral letter directed the omission of the prayer for those in civil authority because there was no civil authority in Alabama, proposing to resume the use of the prayer when civil government should be restored to the people of the states.

It is now said that the courts will be required to hold all acts,

---

10 Major General George H. Thomas, commanding the military division of Tennessee, to which Alabama belonged, through Major General Charles R. Woods commanding at Mobile, temporarily suspended Bishop R. H. Wilmer's clerical functions. Both General Thomas and Bishop Wilmer were former Virginians.

executive, ministerial and judicial, of the state officers, since July 1861, to be void under some provision of the so-called constitution adopted at Wheeling in the latter year. This monstrous proposition can only be really set at rest by a convention, which is really required and should be held for that purpose alone, if there be nothing else.

Colonel Randolph [T. J., Kean's father-in-law] has just returned from Washington where he had an interview with President Johnson. Having procured his pardon, he held a conversation with Johnson in which he told him that the pacification of the country was absolute, but that there was no Union feeling among the people; that they looked to him as the person who had the power to protect them against the persecution of the Radicals, and if he exerted his power to that end he would win their grateful support. Their support of him would be support of the United States government, and thus they could be brought to the latter position; that in Boston several years after the War of 1812 he had seen strong evidences of hostility to the Union still remaining among the people whose descendants now clamor so loudly about their devotion to the Union; and that time must be allowed the Southern people to return to the habit of regarding the United States as *their* country. Johnson told him that the Southern States must send representatives to Congress and sustain him; that the pressure on him from the North was incalculably great; that the weight of 11 states in Congress would be a most material assistance in stemming the Northern torrent.

The result of the interview is that the Colonel, who previously was opposed to our having any representatives in Congress, is now strongly in favor of a delegation in support of the President.

I have recently heard that the reason why the granting of

pardons in Virginia by the President has been blocked,[11] is in this wise: Hughes [Robert W., a native Virginian and Republican] edits the *Republic* newspaper in Richmond. That paper has sought to produce the impression (as in the case of the Richmond charter elections) [12] that the people of Virginia have taken the oath of allegiance fraudulently and without the purpose to observe it. Hughes is in partnership with a Black Republican Congressman from Kansas named ———[13] as *pardon brokers*, and there is reason to believe that these parties have confederated to obstruct pardons to bring grist to their mill. The set in Richmond about the *Republic* paper assist in this infamous scheme.

A. [Alexander] Dudley of Richmond a few days ago got a pardon. Shortly after he got back to Richmond with it, he was arrested by the Commandant and required to surrender the document. The explanation is said to be that he had said on his return that he had been told by [Orville Hickman] Browning, one of President Johnson's aids or secretaries, [secretary of interior] that there was a hitch about his case, which required the lubrication of $500. He did not pay the money, however, and this alleged slander of the clerk is the cause of the anomalous pro-

[11] The apparent lull in the granting of pardons at this time corresponded with Carl Schurz's return from the South and his report that Johnson's plan of amnesty was not working. Johnson was disappointed with Schurz's report and sent General Grant on a second tour of the South. Grant's report was favorable to the South and Johnson's plan.

[12] In the Richmond municipal elections of July 25, 1865, ex-Confederate officers were elected mayor, commonwealth attorney, and superintendent of the almshouse, whereupon General John W. Turner declared the elections null and void.

[13] Sidney Clarke was the sole Congressman (Representative) from Kansas at this time. Jim Lane and Samuel C. Pomeroy were Kansas Senators.

ceeding of taking away by force the letters patent.[14] In law, whether a pardon once granted under the hand of the President and the seal of State, *can* be revoked for matter *ex post facto* or for any cause not made a condition on the face of the paper? I think not, unless perhaps it was procured by fraud, and then the revocation could not be by taking the paper away and cancelling it. But where could the question be tried fairly? Not before [Chief Justice Salmon P.] Chase or Underwood. President Johnson subsequently restored the paper to Mr. Dudley.

Oct. 8.   Terry [Major General Alfred H., in command of department of Virginia] Satrap of Virginia, has the attributes of a tyrant. The *Commercial Bulletin* newspaper in Richmond, successor of the *Sentinel*, was suppressed by him in September. The offense was quoting and commenting on a letter of Count Joannes to the N. Y. *News* upon the decline of manners in Washington brought in by Lincoln—the vulgarity of the reception in the East Room.

On Thursday the 5th inst. the Yank Commandant of this subdistrict, Voris [General Alvin C.] convened the negroes of the County of Albemarle in Charlottesville and addressed them. The agent of the meddling [Freedmen's] Bureau did the same. They were told that the impression they had that land would be divided out to them was unfounded; that they would get no land but what they could accumulate money to buy by industry, hard

14 Dudley later denied that any person 'in or about' the President's office demanded money for a pardon. On the other hand, he admitted that other persons applying for pardons repeatedly proposed the joint employment of a pardon broker. Although neither Johnson nor his immediate aids received money for pardons, pardon brokers flourished to a considerable degree from the demands for assistance of those seeking pardons.

work and thrift; that the United States had nothing further to
give them except protection in their freedom from their masters;
that they must not wander off to the free states and compete with
white labor there; that their best friends were the planters who
had owned them, etc. The effect on the negroes was evidently
that of a great disappointment. I talked with several very intelligent ones on the same and the next day. I was told by them
that the impression sought to be removed had been created by
the Yankees (soldiers and others) in their intercourse with the
negroes.

Oct. 23.   About September 18 last, I was summoned for the
prosecution before the Military Commission of which Wallace
is president and [Colonel N. P.] Chipman, judge advocate, in
the case of Captain Wirz. I reached Washington on Saturday at
day break. At 10 o'clock I went to the Court of Claims room in the
Capitol where the Commission sat; not in session, [J. W.] Geary
a member being absent. Chipman gave me what he called a 'preliminary examination' and a short hand writer to take it down.
After asking my official position, etc., he produced the *covers*
of Colonel Chandler's report[15] on inspection at Andersonville,
and inquired of hand writing of Judge Campbell, Wellford, and
my own; when report was received; whether Mr. Seddon saw
it; whether he read it; whether he talked of it; whether he took
any action on it; how long it was before him; whether the Presi-

---

15 In August 1864, Colonel D. T. Chandler was sent from Richmond to
inspect the Andersonville prison. With animus toward General John H.
Winder, formerly in charge of prisoners at Richmond and now in command at Andersonville, Chandler after a casual inspection submitted a
report wholly unfair to the prison administration under Winder. This
report is here being used to implicate Davis and Seddon in a conspiracy
to kill prisoners.

dent had seen it; what were the relations between General Winder and the President, by whose orders prisoners were transferred from Richmond to Andersonville; and much more of the same sort.

The examination before the Commission on Tuesday following was similar, omitting all to which answers had been unsatisfactory. The whole had no reference whatever to Wirz, but was obviously designed to inculpate Mr. Seddon and President Davis. ([Written in margin later:] While in Washington in attendance on the Commission, I told L. Q. Washington [a newspaper reporter from Va.] that from my observation of what was going on I deemed it very important that Mr. Seddon should have counsel to protect him; [that] while he was locked up in Fort Pulaski they were trying him. He wrote this to Richmond and Mrs. Seddon got P. W. [Phillip Wellford] to consult Mr. C. Robinson and other friends.)

Last week Mr. Phillip Wellford was in Lynchburg and I told him of all this. He informed me that he had been acting as a friend of Mr. Seddon in endeavouring to meet the insidious attacks of the Commission who were trying him in his absence. He had visited Washington and got information of what had been passing in the Commission. He then took steps to inform Mr. [O. H.] Baker, Wirz's counsel, that Colonel Robert Ould was a material witness in connection with Chandler's report, of which a great handle was made.

Mr. Ould was subpoenaed and went to Washington to prove as follows: 1. That as soon as Chandler's report was received, Mr. Seddon sent for him, informed him of the horrible condition of the prisoners, said he could not remove Winder without a hearing, but wished to take steps for relieving them at once, while the report was [being] referred to Winder that he might make defense. He instructed Mr. Ould to communicate to the Federal

Agent of Exchange [John Mulford] the condition of their prisoners, and to propose that they should send any number of surgeons, say 15, 20 or 30, on their mere parole to communicate nothing prejudicial to the Confederacy, who should relieve by attention, medicines, etc., their men; should freely receive and themselves distribute whatever should be sent by individuals or the United States for the prisoners; we to have same sort of agents at *their* prison depots.

2. That he [Ould] did immediately communicate as directed with Colonel Mulford (now brigadier general), and in a short time was informed that the proposal was *declined* by the Federal authorities. He reported this to Mr. Seddon about four weeks after the reception of Chandler's report. Mr. Seddon immediately instructed him to say to the U. S. Agent that in three days after we had notice that transportation for them was at Savannah, 10,000 to 15,000 of the Andersonville prisoners should be delivered then, *with* or *without* equivalents; that Mulford went in person immediately with this, to Mr. Secretary E. M. Stanton, and urged it; that the thing *was not done*, but dragged out till *December*, when something was finally done.

All this Brigadier General Mulford told Mr. Ould. He [Mulford] stood ready [at the trial] to confirm as far as related to what passed between them. Mr. Ould was waiting his time to be put on the stand, when one evening a young man in uniform presented himself and informed him he was authorized by Colonel Chipman to demand his subpoena. Mr. Ould declined to give it up, stating that it was his warrant for being in the District of Columbia, and the want of it might occasion him trouble. He feared an arrest after such a demand had been complied with. But he said he would be at the court room at 10 o'clock next morning and would see Colonel Chipman about it.

He went accordingly [and] finding General [Lorenzo]

Thomas, adjutant general of the United States, whom he knew, he consulted him. (General Thomas was a member of the Commission.) He said he did not understand such a proceeding and could not approve it, but advised Mr. Ould to send a note to Colonel Chipman who was in an adjoining room. This Ould did, enclosing the subpoena. Presently it was returned to him with an endorsement to the effect that '*this subpoena is revoked,* and Mr. Ould will return forthwith to Richmond.' Wirz's counsel protested in vain.

The Commission got the habit of *revoking* the subpoenas of witnesses for the defense, whose testimony they did not wish to hear. Thus was *suppressed* Mr. Seddon's defense, which would have put the sufferings at Andersonville where they belong, on the shoulders of E. M. Stanton. Had it come out, it would have appeared that that official preferred for thousands to perish miserably, in the effort to [have Federal prisoners] eat Confederate corn from the Confederate armies; that the perfidy by which the cartel was abrogated was a settled policy to starve the Confederacy, though thousands of their own men starved and rotted with scurvy; and [that] the object of the Wirz trial— to divert to the Confederate authorities the indignation which belonged on his [Stanton's] head—was saved from signal defeat.[16]

---

[16] On the charges of conspiring to kill prisoners and of violating the laws of war, Wirz was convicted and hanged, November 10, 1865, a victim of the postwar psychology. His execution was vigorously pressed by Stanton, Judge Advocate General Joseph Holt, and Judge Advocate of the Commission N. P. Chipman, by shocking irregularities and high-handed procedures. As co-conspirators, the Commission named Seddon, Davis, and several other Southerners, but Wirz was the only one to suffer. Seddon was pardoned by President Johnson in November 1867.

Memorandum made Dec. 1865. Inasmuch as I have never heard whether the papers and records of the surgeon general's office C. S., etc., were destroyed or are in existence, I have set down my recollection of a communication made to the Surgeon General by Dr. ———— ———————— of the medical staff of Hood's army about one year ago, probably in January 1865. It stated that after Hood's defeat at Nashville, the writer with other surgeons, of whom he was the ranking officer (and I think medical director of one of the corps) was left in charge of the wounded in that battle, and the battle of Franklin which occurred November 30, 1864. The wounded of Hood's army were collected at Nashville to the number of about 3,000, many of them very severely wounded, many having suffered amputation. The Federal surgeon under whose control they were acted with great humanity, furnished abundant supplies of everything necessary to their comfort and recovery, especially nourishing and delicate diet. A few days after Hood's retreat, General Meredith, the Yankee commissary general of prisoners, visited Nashville, and discovering the treatment used by the Federal surgeon (whose name I wish I could remember) he, Meredith, ordered that the Confederate wounded should receive *only* the prison ration, viz., ½ lb. salt pork and six hard crackers per day. The Federal surgeon protested against this wanton cruelty. The supplies were there, and the prisoners in very many cases suffering from wounds and amputation, suppurating extensively, and without nutritious food, must die. The order was reiterated. The Federal surgeon refused to obey it, and appealed to the War Department at Washington by telegraph. The response was a sharp rebuke and a threatening order to obey the instructions of Meredith. This act of wanton cruelty was incontestably vouched in the paper referred to, which if it ever came to the hands of Lieber[17] has probably been destroyed.

Today the papers announced that Terry, the Federal tyrant in Richmond, has just published an order prohibiting the execution by the civil officers of the state, of the act for the punishment of *vagrants* just passed by the Legislature!! which is now in session, assigning as a reason that it is designed to reduce the negroes to servitude. The act which I have not seen, I am told makes no discrimination between whites and negroes. What a mockery of government, when an ignorant half-educated, conceited army officer, assumes by his ipse dixit to forbid civil officers of a whole state to execute the laws!! And this in a time of profound peace!

---

[17] Francis Lieber, war publicist, author of rules of war, and at this time a Radical Republican, had been employed by Stanton as chief of a newly established bureau for the collection of Confederate archives. Stanton's immediate purpose was to find incriminating evidence for the prosecution of Jefferson Davis.

INDEX

Index

235

Davis, George, 106
Davis, Jefferson, xiii, xxiii, xxiv,
xxix, xxx, xxxi, xxxii, 28, 29, 30,
31, 32, 33, 34, 40, 40n, 43n, 45, 48,
50, 51, 53, 54, 67, 72, 75, 76, 77,
80, 83, 84, 85, 86, 87, 88, 89, 90,
92, 93, 94, 97, 98, 99, 100, 101, 102,
104, 106, 107, 109, 111, 115, 116,
117, 119, 121, 122, 124, 126, 127,
128, 132, 133, 134, 135, 136, 139n,
140, 141, 142, 143, 145, 153, 154-5,
156, 157, 158, 159, 161, 162, 163,
166, 167, 171, 172, 175, 176, 178,
179, 180, 181, 185, 186, 187, 188,
189, 190, 191, 192, 193, 194, 197,
198, 200, 201n, 202, 203, 204, 205,
206, 207, 214, 223, 227, 228, 232n
Davis, Mrs. Jefferson, 90
Disloyalty, xxviii, 17-18, 45, 55, 64,
73-4, 103, 104, 138, 140, 160, 160n,
176, 180, 212n, 213, 213n, 217n
Dranesville, Va., xxvii, 20
Drewry's Bluff, Va., 158, 158n
Dudley, Alexander, 225, 226
Duffy, George, 14

Early, Jubal A., 7, 54, 57, 156, 158,
164, 165, 167, 169, 171n, 173, 186
Eckert, Thomas T., 194
Edward's Depot, 66
Elmore, Edward C., 165
Elzey, Arnold, 56, 78, 104, 141
Emancipation, 174, 182, 183-4, 186,
188, 192, 194, 196-7, 201, 202, 208-
10, 211, 212, 226-7
England, 17, 23, 82, 89, 105, 112,
112n, 129, 145, 205
Evans, Nathan G., 12, 13, 34
Ewell, Richard S., xxi, xxii, 18, 21,
26, 64, 65, 73, 75, 79, 147, 148, 205,
214

Finance, xxviii, xxxiv, 32, 42, 43,
44-5, 52, 59-60, 98, 116, 117, 118,
119, 123-4, 129, 130, 135, 138, 140-41
142, 143, 167, 179, 184-5, 188, 189,
190, 199, 213, 214, 215, 216, 219

Finegan, Joseph, 157
Fisher's Hill, Va., 174
Floyd, John B., 25, 36, 37, 37n
Forrest, Nathan B., 59, 152, 166, 167
Fort Delaware, 86, 89
Fort Donelson, 25
Fort Fisher, 183
Fort Gilmer, 176
Fort Henry, 24
Fort Monroe, 101, 129n, 153
Fort Moultrie, 49
Fort Pemberton, 44n, 49n
Fort Sanders, 131n
Fort Sumter, xx, 49, 98, 99, 112, 113,
114n, 128
Fort Wagner, 79-80, 96, 96n
Fort Warren, 65
France, 32-3, 82, 87, 88, 89, 105, 110,
131, 146-7, 195n
Frankfort, Ky., convention, 42
Franklin, Tenn., 181, 231
Frazer, John W., 104n
Fredericksburg, Va., 33, 35, 57, 66
French, S. Bassett, 108, 111
Funsten, David, 6, 6n, 16, 17, 21, 26

Galleher, John N., 110
Gardner, Franklin, 74
Garland, A. H., 38, 162, 193
Garland, Samuel, 6, 6n, 16, 20, 22,
60
Garrott, Isham W., 67, 67n
Gettysburg, Pa., xxxi, 69, 78-9, 84,
91, 173
Gilmer, Jeremy F., xxiii, 141
Gilmor, Harry W., 139, 139n
Goldsboro, N. C., 34, 38n
Gordon, James B., 149
Gordon, John B., 165
Gorgas, Josiah, xxiii, 142, 154, 207
Gracie, Archibald, 74
Graham, William A., 193, 203, 205
Granbery, John C., 16
Grand Gulf, Miss., 54, 55, 67
Grant, U. S., 17, 44n, 49n, 52n, 55n,
62, 62n, 64, 67n, 68, 69, 74, 76, 82,
106, 119, 120, 123, 124, 147, 148,